The Essential Crock Pot Cookbook for Beginners

Unleash the Full Potential of Your Slow Cooker with 1800 Days of Easy, Flavorful and Healthy Recipes for Home Cooking and Heartwarming Meals

Andrew Comer

TABLE OF CONTENT

CHAPTER 11 SOUP AND STEW · 88

CHAPTER 12 APPETIZER AND SNACK · · · · · · · · · · · · · · · · · · · 101

CHAPTER 13 DESSERT · 108

CHAPTER 14 SAUCE AND DRESSING · · · · · · · · · · · · · · 119

INTRODUCTION

Let's talk about a familiar struggle - trying to master slow cooking on the stovetop. Believe me, I've been there, too, dealing with the frustration of un-even results and having to keep a hawk's eye on the pot. Who's got time for that constant monitoring? But guess what? I've got a secret weapon to share: the crockpot. Seriously, it's like having your own kitchen wizard. I remember my first encounter with it like it was yesterday - a day of cooking with ease and absolutely no stress. Toss in your ingredients, set the timer, and let it do its thing. No fuss, no muss.

I can't forget the time I dug into the most tender, flavorful pot roast that came out of my crockpot experiment. It was like a lightbulb moment - this was the answer to my cooking prayers, giving me deliciousness without the hassle. And now, brace yourselves because this cookbook is your ticket to crockpot nirvana. We've whipped up a bunch of crockpot recipes that span the culinary spectrum. From soul-warming soups to succulent roasts and even delectable desserts, we're covering all the bases. So whether you're all about classic comfort or craving bold new tastes, get ready to dive into a treasure trove of flavors.

Say goodbye to kitchen stress and hello to the crockpot revolution. Get ready to bask in the simplicity, revel in the reliability, and treat your taste buds to a medley of mouthwatering experiences. I can't wait for you to explore the world of easy, delightful crockpot cooking through this cookbook.

CHAPTER 1

WHAT TO KNOW ABOUT A CROCKPOT?

Let me break it down for you. A crockpot, also known as a slow cooker, is like your kitchen's magic helper. It's this nifty appliance that takes the stress out of cooking and makes your meals taste amazing. Here's the deal: A crockpot is kind of like a big pot with a lid that sits inside an electric heating unit. Inside the pot, there's this removable insert, usually made of ceramic or metal. You know, like the bowl, you'd use for mixing stuff, but this one's built for cooking.

So, here's what happens: You prep your ingredients, like meat, veggies, sauces, and spices. You throw everything into the crockpot, just like you'd toss things into a pot on the stove. But here's where the magic comes in - you set the temperature and the cooking time, usually low and slow. Then you put the lid on, and that's it. The crockpot takes over from there. The heating unit underneath starts to warm up, and the heat slowly transfers through the sides of the pot and into your food. This low and steady cooking lets all the flavors mix and mingle, and it makes tough cuts of meat super tender. Plus, it's like a hands-off process - you don't have to stand there stirring or checking every few minutes like you would on the stove.

Think of it as your culinary sidekick. You can leave it on while you're at work or taking care of other things, and when you come back, your home smells like a restaurant, and your dinner is ready to be devoured. It's seriously that easy!

How to Buy a Crockpot?

When you're on the hunt for a good crockpot, there are a few things you'll want to keep in mind. Let's break it down! First off, think about size. If you're cooking for a crowd, go for a bigger crockpot. But if it's just you or a couple of people, a smaller one will do the trick. Check out the settings. Most crockpots have low and high settings. That's your basic game. But if you're into versatility, look for ones with a "keep warm" setting or even programmable timers. That way, your food won't go from tasty to overcooked while you're out.

Lid fit is key. You want a snug lid that keeps all the moisture and flavor locked in. No one wants dried-out dinners, right? The removable insert is a game-changer. Go for a crockpot with a removable bowl. It makes cleaning up way easier, and you can even prep your ingredients ahead of time and keep them in the fridge. Make sure it's easy to clean. Trust me, you'll thank yourself later. Look for crockpots with dishwasher-safe parts or non-stick inserts.

And price? Well, you don't need to break the bank. There are awesome crockpots at different price points. Just pick one that fits your budget and your needs. Oh, and if you're all about tech, check out WiFi-enabled crockpots. You can control these bad boys with your phone. It's like having your own personal chef. So, to sum it up, size, settings, lid, removable parts, and cleaning ease are your must-checks. Remember, a good crockpot will make your life tastier and more convenient.

Perks of Crockpot'ting

Slow cooking in a crockpot is like a culinary wizard that transforms ordinary ingredients into extraordinary meals. From enhanced flavors and nutrient retention to the convenience of hands-free cooking, it's a technique that takes your kitchen skills to a whole new level.

1. Unbeatable Flavor Fusion

Slow cooking is like a symphony for your taste buds. When you cook ingredients over a long period at low heat, their flavors meld and mingle in ways that are hard to achieve with other methods. Your spices, herbs, and seasonings have ample time to infuse their magic into every bite. Plus, tough cuts of meat become incredibly tender, practically melting in your mouth.

2. Effortless Cooking

Picture this - you toss all your ingredients into the crockpot, set the timer, and walk away. No standing by the stove, no constant stirring. It's cooking that doesn't demand your constant attention. You're free to go about your day while the crockpot does all the work.

3. Time is on Your Side

Slow cooking is all about patience, and it's your culinary friend when you've got a busy day ahead. You can prep your ingredients in the morning or even the night before. When you come back later, your meal is ready and waiting, filling your home with mouthwatering aromas.

4. Nutrient Retention

Here's a secret - slow cooking retains more nutrients in your food compared to other cooking methods. Since the ingredients cook gently over a long time, they don't lose as many vitamins and minerals. It's like getting a healthy boost with every bite.

5. Budget-Friendly Magic

Tough cuts of meat that might not be your first choice can shine with slow cooking. They become tender and flavorful without breaking the bank. You're getting gourmet-level results with more economical ingredients.

6. No-Fail Cooking

Worried about burning or overcooking? Slow cooking in a crockpot eliminates that stress. The controlled, low temperature ensures your food won't turn into a disaster. It's like having a safety net for your culinary adventures.

7. Versatile Delights

Slow cooking isn't limited to just hearty stews and roasts (though they're amazing!). You can make soups, chili, curries, desserts, and even breakfast dishes like oatmeal. The possibilities are endless, making it perfect for experimenting with new recipes and flavors.

Working on a Crockpot

Before actually getting started, make sure that your crockpot is placed on a stable, flat surface in your kitchen, away from any potential hazards. Safety should always be a top priority, so make sure to inspect the plug and cord for any visible damage before proceeding. Once you've ensured a safe setup, take a moment to clean your crockpot. Thoroughly wash the removable insert, lid, and exterior to maintain the quality of your dishes and prevent any residual flavors from previous meals affecting your current creation.

To start your cooking process, gather all the necessary ingredients for your recipe. This includes prepping your ingredients, such as chopping vegetables and trimming meat, ensuring that everything is ready before you begin cooking. Depending on your recipe, layering might be required. Begin with the meat at the bottom, allowing its juices to infuse the other ingredients. For recipes that involve liquids like broth or sauces, add these next, keeping in mind that slow cooking retains more moisture than traditional methods. Season your dish with spices, herbs, and seasonings according to your taste preferences. Be mindful that flavors tend to intensify during slow cooking, so use restraint or consider adjusting seasonings towards the end of the process.

Select the appropriate temperature setting for your recipe. Most crockpots offer low and high settings. Generally, low is preferred for slow cooking, as it ensures gentle and thorough cooking over an extended period. Set the cooking time based on your recipe's guidelines. Slow cooking times usually range from 4 to 8 hours on low or 2 to 4 hours on high. Some models feature a "warm" setting that maintains your food at a safe temperature after cooking.

With the temperature and time set, carefully position the lid on the crockpot. This is crucial for maintaining the desired heat levels and creating an optimal cooking environment. The beauty of slow cooking lies in its hands-off nature. Once your crockpot is ready, you can go about your day without worrying about constant supervision. The extended cooking time allows you the freedom to run errands, work, or simply relax while your meal takes shape.

Towards the end of the cooking time, if your recipe calls for delicate ingredients like fresh herbs or dairy, incorporate them accordingly. Refer to your recipe for precise instructions on these finishing touches. As the cooking time comes to an end, carefully remove the lid and evaluate the doneness of your dish. Use a meat thermometer to ensure meat reaches a safe internal temperature, or test the tenderness of meat and vegetables through gentle pressing. With your slow-cooked masterpiece ready, serve your delicious creation and savor the flavors that the extended cooking process has artfully developed.

After your meal, be sure to turn off and unplug the crockpot. Allow it to cool before cleaning. While the removable insert is often dishwasher-safe, always consult the manufacturer's guidelines. Wipe down the exterior with a damp cloth for a polished finish.

Using the Accessories

There are several accessories that can enhance your crockpot cooking experience, offering versatility and convenience. Not all of them come with a crockpot, but you can use them inside your crockpot's insert. Let's check out different accessories that you can use and how they can elevate your cooking process.

- **Slow Cooker Liners:** These disposable liners are a time-saving accessory that makes cleanup a breeze. They prevent food from sticking to the crockpot's surface, reducing the need for soaking and scrubbing after cooking. Simply place the liner in the crockpot, add your ingredients, cook, and discard the liner when you're done.

- **Roasting Racks:** Roasting racks are designed to fit inside the crockpot and elevate your food, allowing heat to circulate evenly around it. This is particularly useful when cooking large cuts of meat or poultry, as it helps prevent them from sitting in their juices and promotes better browning.

- **Steaming Trays:** Steaming trays or inserts can transform your crockpot into a steamer. These accessories are ideal for cooking vegetables, fish, or even dumplings. They allow you to steam your ingredients while keeping them separate from any liquids in the crockpot.

- **Timer Attachments:** Some crockpots come with timer attachments that allow you to program the cooking time and temperature. This feature can be incredibly handy if you're away from home for extended periods and want to ensure your meal doesn't overcook.

- **Silicone Lids and Covers:** Silicone lids and covers are a versatile accessory that can replace the standard lid of your crockpot. They're great for preventing spills and splatters when transporting your crockpot or when serving food directly from it.

- **Temperature Probes:** These handy gadgets can monitor the internal temperature of your food while it's cooking. They're particularly useful for meats, ensuring that they're cooked to the desired level of doneness without the need to open the lid and release heat.

- **Glass Lids:** If your crockpot comes with a plastic lid, you might consider getting a glass lid as an accessory. Glass lids allow you to monitor the cooking progress without lifting the lid, helping to retain heat and moisture.

- **Divided Inserts:** Divided inserts are fantastic for cooking multiple items in one crockpot. They allow you to create separate compartments within the crockpot, making it possible to cook different dishes simultaneously without flavors mingling.

These tips are like secret ingredients that'll make your slow-cooking game in a crockpot even more impressive. From thoughtful layering to smart timing, these little details can turn a good dish into a great one.

Layer Wisely: If you're making a dish with meat and veggies, make sure to place the meat at the bottom. This way, it gets the most heat, ensuring it's properly cooked. Veggies on top will steam and cook with the meat's juices, adding extra flavor.

Don't Peek Too Much: It's tempting to lift the lid and check on your creation, but each time you do, you're letting out valuable heat and steam. This can affect the cooking time and overall result. Trust the process - just let it be!

Pre-Browning for Flavor: For some dishes, like roasts or stews, consider browning your meat before it goes into the crockpot. It adds a delicious layer of flavor and a nice color to your final dish.

Mind the Size: Cut your ingredients into similar sizes. This helps ensure even cooking, so you don't end up with some bits overcooked and others undercooked.

Use the Right Amount of Liquid: Slow cooking doesn't evaporate liquids like other methods do, so you'll need less liquid than you might think. Start with about half of what a traditional recipe calls for and adjust as needed. The ingredients' natural juices will create an additional liquid.

Timing is Everything: Different recipes require different cooking times. If you're adapting a traditional recipe for the crockpot, remember that flavors can intensify over long cooking times. So, consider reducing strong spices or acids.

Layer Herbs Carefully: Fresh herbs are awesome, but they can lose their flavor if cooked for hours. Add them toward the end of cooking, or opt for dried herbs at the start for a consistent taste.

Thicken it Up: If your dish ends up a bit too watery, you can thicken it by removing the lid for the last hour or so of cooking. The excess moisture will evaporate, leaving you with a richer consistency.

Dairy Delay: Dairy products like milk and cream can curdle if added too early. To avoid this, add them in the last 15-30 minutes of cooking.

Save Delicate Veggies: Veggies like peas, spinach, and zucchini cook quickly and can turn mushy in long cooking. Add them during the last 30 minutes to maintain their texture and color.

Noodles and Pasta: These guys can get soggy if overcooked. If your recipe calls for them, it's better to cook them separately and add them in the last 15 minutes.

Keep it Half Full: Ideally, your crockpot should be about half full for the best results. Too full, and your food might not cook evenly; too empty, and you might risk overcooking.

CHAPTER 2

BREAKFAST

Turkey Sausage and Mushroom Casserole

Prep Time: 15 minutes, Cook Time: 8 hours, Serves: 6

INGREDIENTS:

- Nonstick cooking spray
- 12 ounces (340 g) cooked turkey breakfast sausage
- 6 eggs
- 6 egg whites
- 2 red bell peppers, seeded and chopped
- 1 onion, chopped
- 8 ounces (227 g) fresh mushrooms, chopped
- ¼ cup low-fat grated Parmesan cheese
- ½ cup (120 ml) skim milk
- ¼ tsp. freshly ground black pepper

DIRECTIONS:

1. Spray the jar of your crock pot with nonstick cooking spray.
2. Mix the cooked sausage, onion, bell pepper, and mushrooms in a large bowl.
3. Whisk together the milk, eggs, egg whites, and pepper in a medium bowl.
4. Pour the eggs over the sausage mixture and mix well.
5. Add the cheese.
6. Put the mixture into the crock pot. Cook on low for 8 hours.
7. Cut into wedges to serve.

Nutrition Info per Serving:

Calories: 237, Total Fat: 14g, Saturated Fat: 4g, Carbohydrates: 7g, Protein: 23g, Cholesterol: 218mg, Fiber: 2g

Ginger Spiced Pear Oatmeal

Prep Time: 5 minutes, Cook Time: 8 hours, Serves: 1

INGREDIENTS:

- ¾ cup steel-cut oats
- 3 cups unsweetened almond milk or water
- 1 ripe pear, cored, peeled, and diced
- ⅛ tsp. ground ginger
- ⅛ tsp. ground cardamom
- ⅛ tsp. ground nutmeg
- ¼ tsp. cinnamon
- ⅛ tsp. sea salt

DIRECTIONS:

1. In the crock pot, add the ginger, cardamom, oats, nutmeg, cinnamon, and salt, and stir to combine. Add the almond milk and pear, stir well.
2. Cover the cooker and set on low, cook the oatmeal for 8 hours or overnight.

Breakfast Cherry Vanilla Quinoa Bowl

Prep Time: 5 minutes, Cook Time: 8 hours, Serves: 1

INGREDIENTS:

- 3 cups almond milk or water
- ¾ cup quinoa
- ½ cup dried cherries
- ⅛ tsp. sea salt
- 1 tsp. vanilla extract

DIRECTIONS:

1. In the crock pot, add the cherries, quinoa, and salt. Mix in the almond milk and vanilla, and stir all of the ingredients together.
2. Cover the cooker and set on low, cook for 8 hours or overnight.

Nutrition Info per Serving:

Calories: 426, Fat: 0 g, Carbohydrates: 78 g, Protein: 12 g, Fiber: 16 g, Sodium: 352 mg

Vanilla Cinnamon Pumpkin Pudding

Prep Time: 15 minutes, Cook Time: 6 to 7 hours on low. Serves: 8

INGREDIENTS:

- ¼ cup melted butter, divided
- 2 cups coconut milk
- 2½ cups canned pumpkin purée
- 4 eggs
- 1 tbsp. pure vanilla extract
- ½ cup granulated erythritol
- 1 cup almond flour
- 1 tsp. baking powder
- 2 ounces (57 g) protein powder
- ¼ tsp. ground nutmeg
- 1 tsp. ground cinnamon
- Pinch ground cloves

DIRECTIONS:

1. Use 1 tablespoon of the butter to lightly grease the insert of the crock pot.
2. Add the remaining butter, coconut milk, pumpkin, eggs and vanilla into a large bowl, whisk them together until well blended.
3. Add the erythritol, almond flour, baking powder, protein powder, nutmeg, cinnamon and cloves into a small bowl, stir them together.
4. Combine the dry ingredients with the wet ingredients.
5. Pour into the insert with the mixture.
6. Cover the cooker and cook on low for 6 to 7 hours.
7. Serve warm.

Nutrition Info per Serving:

Calories: 265, Total Fat: 22 g, Total Carbs: 8 g, Net Carbs: 5 g, Protein: 13 g, Fiber: 3 g

Baked Oatmeal with Berry

Prep Time: 15 minutes, Cook Time: 4 to 6 hours, Serves: 15

INGREDIENTS:

- 7 cups rolled oats
- 4 eggs
- 2 tbsps. melted coconut oil
- 1½ cups almond milk
- 1 tsp. ground cinnamon
- ¼ tsp. ground ginger
- ¼ tsp. salt
- ⅓ cup honey
- 1½ cups dried blueberries
- 1 cup dried cherries

DIRECTIONS:

1. Dip an appropriate amount of vegetable oil with a small brush and apply it to the inside of a 6-quart crock pot.
2. Pour the oatmeal into the crock pot.
3. Put eggs, almond milk, coconut oil, honey, salt, cinnamon and ginger in a medium bowl. Mix until fully mixed. Pour this mixture over the oats in the crock pot.
4. Sprinkle with dried blueberries and dried cherries. Close the lid.
5. Cook on low heat for 4 to 6 hours, until the oatmeal mixture is set and the edges start to turn yellow.

Nutrition Info per Serving:

Calories: 368, Fat: 7g, Protein: 9g, Carbohydrates: 68g, Sugar: 33g, Fiber: 6g, Sodium: 97mg

Cheesy Breakfast Veggie Omelet

Prep Time: 15 minutes, Cook Time: 4 to 5 hours on low, Serves: 8

INGREDIENTS:

- 1 tbsp. extra-virgin olive oil
- ½ cup heavy (whipping) cream
- 10 eggs
- 1 tsp. minced garlic
- ⅛ tsp. freshly ground black pepper
- ¼ tsp. salt
- 1 red bell pepper, chopped
- ½ cup chopped broccoli
- ½ cup chopped cauliflower
- 1 scallion, white and green parts, chopped
- 4 ounces (113 g) goat cheese, crumbled
- 2 tbsps. chopped parsley, for garnish

DIRECTIONS:

1. Use olive oil to lightly grease the insert of the crock pot.
2. Add the heavy cream, eggs, garlic, pepper and salt into a medium bowl, whisk them together. Then add the red bell pepper, broccoli, cauliflower and scallion, stir well. Pour the mixture into the crock pot. Sprinkle the goat cheese over the mixture.
3. Cover the cooker and cook on low for 4 to 5 hours.
4. Top with the parsley and serve.

Nutrition Info per Serving:

Calories: 200, Total Fat: 16 g, Total Carbs: 2 g, Net Carbs: 1 g, Protein: 11 g, Fiber: 1 g

Tasty Wheat Berry-Cranberry Pilaf

Prep Time: 20 minutes, Cook Time: 8-10 hours, Serves: 10

INGREDIENTS:

- 1½ cups dried cranberries
- 3 cups wheat berries, rinsed and drained
- 2 leeks, peeled, rinsed, and chopped
- 7 cups roasted vegetable broth
- ¼ tsp. salt
- 2 tbsps. lemon juice
- 1 tsp. dried thyme leaves
- 1½ cups shredded baby Swiss cheese
- 1 cup chopped pecans

DIRECTIONS:

1. Put wheat berries, leeks, vegetable broth, lemon juice, cranberries, thyme and salt in a 6-quart crock pot and mix and stir. Cover the lid and cook on low heat until the wheat berries are soft but still slightly chewy, about 8 to 10 hours.
2. Put the pecans and cheese in the crock pot. Let stand for 10 minutes and serve warm.

Nutrition Info per Serving:

Calories: 407, Fat: 14g, Protein: 13g, Carbohydrates: 59g, Sugar: 14g, Fiber: 10g, Sodium: 129mg

Spinach Cheese Casserole

Prep Time: 10 minutes, Cook Time: 5 to 6 hours on low, Serves: 4

INGREDIENTS:

- 1 tbsp. extra-virgin olive oil
- 1 cup sour cream
- 12 ounces (340 g) chopped spinach
- 8 ounces (227 g) cream cheese
- ½ cup Parmesan cheese
- ½ cup shredded Cheddar cheese
- ½ cup shredded mozzarella cheese
- ½ sweet onion, finely chopped
- 2 tsps. minced garlic

DIRECTIONS:

1. Use the olive oil to grease an 8-by-4-inch loaf pan.
2. Add the sour cream, Cheddar, cream cheese, Parmesan, mozzarella, garlic, onion and spinach to a large bowl, stir them together until well mixed.
3. Transfer the mixture to the loaf pan and place the pan in the insert of the crock pot.
4. Cover the cooker and cook on low for 5 to 6 hours.
5. After cooking, turn off the heat and serve warm.

Nutrition Info per Serving:

Calories: 245, Total Fat: 21 g, Total Carbs: 5 g, Net Carbs: 4 g, Protein: 9 g, Fiber: 1 g, Cholesterol: 57 mg

Cheese Hash Brown Bacon Casserole

Prep Time: 10 minutes, Cook Time: 1 Hour, Serves: 12

INGREDIENTS:

- 30 ounces (850 g) frozen shredded hash brown potatoes, thawed
- 1 can (10¾ ounces, 304 g) condensed cream of chicken soup, undiluted
- 1½ cups sour cream onion dip
- 2 cups cheddar cheese, shredded
- ½ cup cooked bacon, crumbled
- 1 envelope ranch salad dressing mix
- 1 tsp. onion powder
- 1 tsp. garlic powder
- ½ tsp. pepper

DIRECTIONS:

1. Preheat oven to 375ºF (190ºC)
2. In a large bowl, combine all ingredients except for potatoes, cheese and bacon.
3. Make sure the above ingredients are well coated and then stir in potatoes, cheese and bacon.
4. Transfer the mixture to a greased 13x9 inches baking dish.
5. Bake until golden brown, about 50-60 minutes. Serve warm.

Nutrition Info per Serving:

Calories: 273, Total Fat: 6 g, Total Carbs: 20 g, Protein: 14 g, Fiber: 2 g

Authentic Huevos Rancheros

Prep Time: 10 minutes, Cook Time: 3 hours on low, Serves: 8

INGREDIENTS:

- 1 tbsp. extra-virgin olive oil
- 1 cup heavy (whipping) cream
- 1 avocado, chopped, for garnish
- 10 eggs
- 1 cup shredded Monterey Jack Cheese, divided
- 1 cup prepared or homemade salsa
- 1 scallion, green and white parts, chopped
- 1 jalapeño pepper, chopped
- ½ tsp. chili powder
- ½ tsp. salt
- 1 tbsp. chopped cilantro, for garnish

DIRECTIONS:

1. Use the olive oil to lightly grease the insert of the crock pot.
2. Add the heavy cream, eggs, salsa, ½ cup of the cheese, jalapeño, scallion, chili powder and salt into a large bowl, whisk them together. Pour into the insert with the mixture and sprinkle the remaining ½ cup of cheese on the top.
3. Cover the cooker and cook for about 3 hours on low, until the eggs are firm.
4. Slightly cool the eggs, then cut into wedges and garnish with avocado and cilantro, and serve.

Nutrition Info per Serving:

Calories: 302, Total Fat: 26 g, Protein: 13 g, Total Carbs: 5 g, Fiber: 2 g, Net Carbs: 3 g

Cinnamon Steel-Cut Oatmeal with Almond Milk

Prep Time: 5 minutes, Cook Time: 8 hours, Serves: 1

INGREDIENTS:

- ¼ cup raisins
- ¾ cup steel-cut oats
- 1 tsp. ground cinnamon
- ⅛ tsp. sea salt
- 3 cups almond milk or water

DIRECTIONS:

1. In the crock pot, add the raisins, oats, cinnamon, and salt, and stir to combine. Add the almond milk and stir well.
2. Cover the cooker and set on low, cook the oatmeal for 8 hours or overnight.

Nutrition Info per Serving:

Calories: 293, Saturated Fat: 1 g, Trans Fat: 0 g, Carbohydrates: 56 g, Protein: 10 g, Fiber: 7 g, Sodium: 132 mg

Crock Pot Breakfast Casserole

Prep Time: 20 minutes, Cook Time: 8 hours, Serves: 1

INGREDIENTS:

- 1 tsp. butter, at room temperature, or extra-virgin olive oil
- 2 egg whites
- 2 eggs
- ½ cup canned fire-roasted diced tomatoes
- ½ cup canned black beans, drained and rinsed
- ½ cup shredded pepper Jack cheese
- 1 tsp. smoked paprika
- 1 tsp. ground cumin
- 1 tsp. minced garlic
- ⅛ tsp. sea salt
- Freshly ground black pepper
- 3 corn tortillas
- ¼ cup fresh cilantro, for garnish

DIRECTIONS:

1. Use the butter to grease the inside of the crock pot.
2. Add the egg whites, eggs, paprika, cumin, salt and a few grinds of the black pepper to a small bowl, whisk them together.
3. Add the tomatoes, black beans, cheese and garlic to another small bowl, combine them together.
4. In the crock pot, add one of the corn tortillas and top it with half of the cheese and bean mixture. Pour one-third of the egg mixture over the top of the cheese and beans. Place another tortilla on the top the egg mixture. Top that tortilla with the remaining cheese and bean mixture, followed by one-third of the egg mixture. On top of the egg mixture, add the last tortilla, and then pour the remaining egg mixture over the top of it.
5. Cover the cooker and cook on low for 8 hours or overnight. Garnish with the fresh cilantro and serve.

Nutrition Info per Serving:

Calories: 366, Saturated Fat: 9 g, Trans Fat: 0 g, Carbohydrates: 31 g, Protein: 24 g, Fiber: 8 g, Sodium: 640 mg

Buttery Pork Sauerkraut Casserole

Prep Time: 15 minutes, Cook Time: 9 to 10 hours on low, Serves: 6

INGREDIENTS:

- 3 tbsps. extra-virgin olive oil, divided
- 2 tbsps. butter
- 2 pounds (907 g) pork shoulder roast
- 1 cup chicken broth
- ½ sweet onion, thinly sliced
- 1 (28-ounce, 784 g) jar sauerkraut, drained
- ¼ cup granulated erythritol

DIRECTIONS:

1. Use 1 tablespoon of the olive oil to lightly grease the insert of the crock pot.
2. Heat the remaining 2 tablespoons of the olive oil and the butter in a large skillet over medium-high heat. Stir in the pork to the skillet and brown on all sides for about 10 minutes.
3. In the insert, add the pork and stir in the broth, onion, sauerkraut, and erythritol.
4. Cover the cooker and cook on low for 9 to 10 hours.
5. Turn off the heat and serve warm.

Nutrition Info per Serving:

Calories: 516, Total Fat: 42 g, Total Carbs: 7 g, Net Carbs: 3 g, Protein: 28 g, Fiber: 4 g

Cheesy Crustless Mixed Vegetable Quiche

Prep Time: 10 minutes, Cook Time: 8 hours, Serves: 1

INGREDIENTS:

- 1 tsp. butter, at room temperature, or extra-virgin olive oil
- 1 tsp. fresh thyme
- 4 eggs
- ⅛ tsp. sea salt
- Freshly ground black pepper
- ½ cup diced button mushrooms
- 2 slices whole-grain bread, crusts removed, cut into 1-inch cubes
- 1 cup shredded spinach
- 2 tbsps. minced onion
- ½ cup shredded Swiss cheese

DIRECTIONS:

1. Use the butter to grease the inside of the crock pot.
2. Add the thyme, eggs, salt and a few grinds of the black pepper into a small bowl, whisk them together.
3. In the crock pot, add the mushrooms, bread, spinach, onions, and cheese. Pour over the top with the egg mixture and stir gently to combine.
4. Cover the cooker and cook on low for 8 hours or overnight.

Nutrition Info per Serving:

Calories: 348, Saturated Fat: 9 g, Trans Fat: 0 g, Carbohydrates: 21 g, Protein: 24 g, Fiber: 6 g

Creamy Sausage and Potatoes with Cheese

Prep Time: 20 minutes, Cook Time: 4-10 hours, Serves: 8

INGREDIENTS:

- 2 lbs. (907 g) potatoes, sliced ¼-inch thick, divided
- 1 lb. (454 g) fully cooked smoked sausage link, sliced ½-inch thick, divided
- 2 medium-sized onions, chopped, divided
- 10¾-oz. (304 g) can condensed cheddar cheese soup, divided
- 10¾-oz. (304 g) can condensed cream of celery soup, divided
- 10-oz. (283 g) pkg. frozen peas, thawed, optional

DIRECTIONS:

1. Use nonstick cooking spray to spray the interior of the crock pot.
2. Layer one-third of the potatoes, one-third of the sausage, one-third of the onion, and one-third of the cheddar cheese soup into the cooker.
3. Repeat layers twice.
4. Pour in the cream of celery soup on the top.
5. Cover the cooker and cook on Low for 8 to 10 hours, or on High for 4 to 5 hours, or until the vegetables are tender.
6. Stir in the peas, if you wish. Cover and allow to stand for 5 minutes. (If you forgot to thaw the peas, stir them in but allow to stand for 10 minutes.)

Nutrition Info per Serving:

Calories: 273, Fat: 7 g, Carbohydrates: 30.59 g, Protein: 13.76 g

Cheesy Ham Broccoli and Rice Casserole

Prep Time: 20 minutes, Cook Time: 4-5 hours, Serves: 4

INGREDIENTS:

- 2-3 cups cubed, cooked ham
- 16-oz. (454 g) pkg. frozen broccoli cuts, thawed and drained
- 10¾-oz. (304 g) can cream of mushroom soup
- 4 oz. (113 g) of your favorite mild cheese, cubed
- 1 rib celery, chopped
- 1 small onion, chopped
- 1 cup instant rice, uncooked
- 1 cup milk

DIRECTIONS:

1. In a crock pot, add the ham and broccoli.
2. In a bowl, combine all of the remaining ingredients. Then stir into the ham-broccoli.
3. Cover the cooker and cook on Low for 4 to 5 hours.

Nutrition Info per Serving:

Calories: 310, Fat: 12.46 g, Carbohydrates: 35.36 g, Protein: 15.95 g

Bacon Quiche

INGREDIENTS:

- 3 large eggs
- ½ cup sharp cheddar cheese, divided
- ¾ cup (180 ml) unsweetened cashew milk or almond milk
- ¼ cup unflavored egg white protein powder
- 2 strips bacon, diced
- 1 tsp. baking powder
- 1 tsp. fine sea salt
- 2 tsps. diced fresh chives

DIRECTIONS:

1. Preheat the oven to 425°F (220ºC).
2. Place the diced bacon in a medium-sized cast-iron skillet. Set the pan over medium heat and cook about 5 minutes until the bacon is crisp. Leave the bacon drippings and ½ bacon in the pan, remove the other half of the bacon and set aside.
3. Combine the eggs, cashew milk, protein powder, baking powder, and salt in a blender. Blend for about 1 minute. Add ¼ cup of the cheese and the chives. Pour the mixture into the hot skillet over the bacon.
4. Transfer the skillet to the oven and bake for 10 minutes. Take it out of the oven and top with more cheese.
5. Bake for 10 more minutes until the Dutch baby crust is puffed and golden brown. Cut into wedges, serve garnished with the reserved bacon.

Nutrition Info per Serving:

Calories: 365, Carbs: 2g, Protein: 33g, Fat: 25g, Fiber: 0.2g

Feta Spinach Frittata

INGREDIENTS:

- 1 tbsp. extra-virgin olive oil
- 1 cup heavy (whipping) cream
- 12 eggs
- 2 cups chopped spinach
- 2 tsps. minced garlic
- ½ cup feta cheese
- Yogurt, for garnish (optional)
- Cherry tomatoes, halved, for garnish (optional)
- Parsley, for garnish (optional)

DIRECTIONS:

1. Use the olive oil to lightly grease the insert of the crock pot.
2. Add the heavy cream, eggs, spinach, garlic, and feta into a medium bowl, whisk them together. Pour into the crock pot with the mixture.
3. Cover the cooker and cook on low 5 to 6 hours.
4. Top the frittata with a dollop of yogurt, tomatoes, and parsley, if desired, and serve.

Nutrition Info per Serving:

Calories: 247, Total Fat: 22 g, Total Carbs: 2 g, Net Carbs: 2 g, Protein: 11 g, Fiber: 0 g

Creamy Mashed Potatoes

INGREDIENTS:

- 1 ½ cups 2% milk
- ½ cup butter, cubed
- 1 pkg. (8 oz., 227 g) cream cheese, softened
- ½ cup sour cream
- 3¾ cups boiling water
- 1 tsp. garlic salt
- 4 cups mashed potato flakes
- ¼ tsp. pepper
- Minced fresh parsley, optional

DIRECTIONS:

1. Add the milk, butter, cream cheese, sour cream and boiling water into a greased 4-qt. crock pot, whisk them together until smooth. Add the garlic salt, potato flakes, and pepper, stir well.
2. Cover the cooker and cook on low for 2 to 3 hours, until heated through. Sprinkle with parsley if desired.

Nutrition Info per Serving:

Calories: 299, Fat: 20 g, Carbohydrates: 25 g, Protein: 6 g, Sugar: 2 g, Fiber: 1 g, Sodium: 390 mg

Layered Vegetable Cheese and Egg Casserole

INGREDIENTS:

- 1 tbsp. extra-virgin olive oil
- 1 pound (454 g) breakfast sausage
- 12 eggs
- 12 ounces (340 g) shredded Cheddar Cheese
- 1 cup heavy (whipping) cream
- 1 zucchini, chopped
- ½ sweet onion, chopped
- 1 red bell pepper, finely chopped
- ½ tsp. salt
- ½ tsp. freshly ground black pepper

DIRECTIONS:

1. Use the olive oil to lightly grease the insert of the crock pot.
2. In the bottom of the insert, arrange half of the sausage. Place half of the zucchini, onion and pepper on top of the sausage. Then place half of the cheese over the vegetables. Repeat, creating another layer.
3. Add the heavy cream, eggs, salt and pepper into a medium bowl, whisk them together. Pour over the casserole with the egg mixture.
4. Cover the cooker and cook on low for 4 hours.
5. Serve warm.

Nutrition Info per Serving:

Calories: 338, Total Fat: 29 g, Total Carbs: 2 g, Net Carbs: 2 g, Protein: 18 g, Fiber: 0 g

Garlicky Bacon Egg Casserole

Prep Time: 15 minutes, Cook Time: 5 to 6 hours on low, Serves: 8

INGREDIENTS:

- 1 tbsp. bacon fat or extra-virgin olive oil
- 1 cup coconut milk
- 12 eggs
- 1 pound (454 g) bacon, chopped and cooked crisp
- 2 tsps. minced garlic
- ½ sweet onion, chopped
- ⅛ tsp. salt
- ¼ tsp. freshly ground black pepper
- Pinch red pepper flakes

DIRECTIONS:

1. Use the bacon fat or olive oil to lightly grease the insert of the crock pot.
2. Add the coconut milk, eggs, bacon, garlic, onion, salt, pepper and red pepper flakes into a medium bowl, whisk them together. Pour the mixture into the crock pot.
3. Cover the cooker and cook on low for 5 to 6 hours.
4. Serve warm.

Nutrition Info per Serving:

Calories: 526, Total Fat: 43 g, Total Carbs: 3 g, Net Carbs: 3 g, Protein: 32 g, Fiber: 0 g

Savory French Vegetable Omelet

Prep Time: 20 minutes, Cook Time: 3 to 4 hours, Serves: 6

INGREDIENTS:

- 12 eggs, beaten
- ½ tsp. dried thyme leaves
- ¼ tsp. salt
- ⅓ cup 2% milk
- 1 yellow bell pepper, stemmed, seeded, and chopped
- ½ tsp. dried tarragon leaves
- 2 shallots, peeled and minced
- 1 cup chopped fresh asparagus
- ½ cup grated Parmesan cheese
- 1 small zucchini, peeled and diced

DIRECTIONS:

1. Dip a brush with ordinary vegetable oil and apply it to the inside of a 6-quart crock pot.
2. Combine eggs, milk, thyme, tarragon, and salt in a large bowl, then use a whisk to mix well.
3. Combine asparagus, bell peppers, zucchini and green onions in a bowl. Pour the mixture into the crock pot and close the lid.
4. Put the pot on the stove and simmer for 3 to 4 hours until the eggs are set.
5. Sprinkle with Parmesan cheese at the end, continue to cook for 5 to 10 minutes, and serve as soon as the cheese starts to melt.

Nutrition Info per Serving:

Calories: 205, Fat: 12g, Saturated Fat: 5g, Protein: 17g, Carbohydrates: 7g, Sugar: 3g, Fiber: 1g, Sodium: 471mg

Cheesy Ham Breakfast Casserole

Prep Time: 10 minutes, Cook Time: 8 hours, Serves: 1

INGREDIENTS:

- 1 tsp. butter, at room temperature, or extra-virgin olive oil
- 2 egg whites
- 2 eggs
- 2 ounces (57 g) aged ham, diced
- 2 ounces (57 g) hard cheese, such as Parmesan, shredded
- 2 slices whole-grain bread, crusts removed, cut into 1-inch cubes
- Freshly ground black pepper

DIRECTIONS:

1. Use the butter to grease the inside of the crock pot.
2. Add the egg white, eggs and s few grinds of the black pepper to a small bowl, whisk them together.
3. In the crock pot, add the ham, bread, and cheese. Over the top pour with the egg mixture and stir gently to combine.
4. Cover the cooker and set on low, cook for 8 hours or overnight.

Nutrition Info per Serving:

Calories: 324, Saturated Fat: 8 g, Trans Fat: 0 g, Carbohydrates: 19 g, Protein: 27 g, Fiber: 5 g

Sausage Stuffed Peppers with Egg and Cheese

Prep Time: 15 minutes, Cook Time: 4 to 5 hours on low, Serves: 4

INGREDIENTS:

- 1 tbsp. extra-virgin olive oil
- 1 cup breakfast sausage, crumbled
- 4 bell peppers, tops cut off and seeds removed
- ½ cup coconut milk
- 1 cup shredded Cheddar Cheese
- 6 eggs
- ½ tsp. freshly ground black pepper
- 1 scallion, white and green parts, chopped

DIRECTIONS:

1. Line the foil into a crock pot insert and use olive oil to grease the foil.
2. Fill the sausage crumbles into four peppers evenly, and place them in the crock pot.
3. Add the coconut milk, eggs, pepper and scallion into a medium bowl, whisk them together. Pour into the four peppers with the egg mixture. Then, sprinkle the cheese to cover them.
4. Set on low and cook for 4 to 5 hours, until the eggs are set.

Nutrition Info per Serving:

Calories: 450, Total Fat: 36 g, Total Carbs: 8 g, Net Carbs: 5 g, Protein: 25 g, Fiber: 3 g

Herbed Breakfast Sausage

Prep Time: 10 minutes, Cook Time: 3 hours on low, Serves: 8

INGREDIENTS:

- 1 tbsp. extra-virgin olive oil
- 2 eggs
- 2 pounds (907 g) ground pork
- ½ cup almond flour
- 1 sweet onion, chopped
- 2 tsps. dried oregano
- 2 tsps. minced garlic
- 1 tsp. fennel seeds
- 1 tsp. dried thyme
- ½ tsp. salt
- 1 tsp. freshly ground black pepper

DIRECTIONS:

1. Use the olive oil to lightly grease the insert of the crock pot.
2. Add the eggs, pork, almond flour, onion, oregano, garlic, fennel seeds, thyme, salt and pepper into a large bowl, stir them together until well mixed.
3. In the insert of the crock pot, transfer the meat mixture and shape it into a loaf, leaving about ½ inch between the sides and meat.
4. Cover, and insert a temperature probe if you have.
5. Cook on low for about 3 hours, until the temperature probe reaches an internal temperature of 150°F(66°C).
6. Slice in the way you prefer and serve.

Nutrition Info per Serving:

Calories: 341, Total Fat: 27 g, Total Carbs: 1 g, Net Carbs: 1 g, Protein: 21 g, Fiber: 0 g

Vanilla Fruit and Quinoa Breakfast

Prep Time: 5 minutes, Cook Time: 8 hours, Serves: 1

INGREDIENTS:

- 2 cups fresh fruit
- ¾ cup quinoa
- 3 cups water
- 2 tbsps. toasted pecans, for garnish
- ⅛ tsp. sea salt
- 1 tsp. vanilla extract

DIRECTIONS:

1. In the crock pot, add the fruit, quinoa, and salt. Stir in the water and vanilla extract, and combine thoroughly.
2. Cover the cooker and set on low, cook for 8 hours or overnight.
3. Garnish with a sprinkle of the toasted pecans and serve.

Nutrition Info per Serving:

Calories: 323, Saturated Fat: 1 g, Trans Fat: 0 g, Carbohydrates: 53 g, Protein: 11 g, Fiber: 8 g

Crock Pot Vanilla Pumpkin and Pecan Oatmeal

Prep Time: 10 minutes, Cook Time: 8 hours on low, Serves: 4

INGREDIENTS:

- 1 tbsp. coconut oil
- 2 cups coconut milk
- 3 cups cubed pumpkin, cut into 1-inch chunks
- 1 ounce (28 g) plain protein powder
- ½ cup ground pecans
- 2 tbsps. granulated erythritol
- ½ tsp. ground nutmeg
- 1 tsp. maple extract
- ¼ tsp. ground cinnamon
- Pinch ground allspice

DIRECTIONS:

1. Use the coconut oil to lightly grease the insert of a slower cooker.
2. In the insert of the crock pot, add the coconut milk, pumpkin, protein powder, pecans, erythritol, nutmeg, maple extract, cinnamon, and allspice.
3. Cover the cooker and turn on low, cook for 8 hours.
4. Well stirred the mixture or create your preferred texture with a potato masher, and serve.

Nutrition Info per Serving:

Calories: 292, Total Fat: 26 g, Total Carbs: 9 g, Net Carbs: 7 g, Protein: 10 g, Fiber: 2 g

Chili Beans and Sausage Casserole

Prep Time: 20-25 minutes, Cook Time: 7 hours, Serves: 6

INGREDIENTS:

- 15½-oz. (439 g) can chili beans
- 14½-oz. (411 g) can diced tomatoes
- 1 lb. (454 g) bulk pork sausage, browned
- 2 cups water
- ¼ cup chopped onions
- ¾ cup brown rice
- 1 tsp. Worcestershire sauce
- 1 tsp. prepared mustard
- 1 tbsp. chili powder
- ¾ tsp. salt
- ⅛ tsp. garlic powder
- 1 cup shredded cheddar cheese

DIRECTIONS:

1. In the crock pot, add all of the ingredients except the cheese, mix well.
2. Cover the cooker and cook on Low for 7 hours.
3. Stir in the cheese during the last 10 minutes of cooking time.

Nutrition Info per Serving:

Calories: 285, Fat: 16.31 g, Carbohydrates: 21.51 g, Protein: 13.34 g

Crock Pot Verenike Casserole

INGREDIENTS:

- 2 cups cubed cooked ham
- 24 oz. (672 g) cottage cheese
- 3 eggs
- 2 cups evaporated milk
- 1 cup sour cream
- 1 tsp. salt
- ½ tsp. pepper
- 7-9 dry lasagna noodles

DIRECTIONS:

1. In a large bowl, combine all of the ingredients except the noodles.
2. In the bottom of the crock pot, add half of the creamy ham mixture. Then add the uncooked noodles. Cover with the remaining half of creamy ham mixture. Make sure that the noodles are fully submerged in the sauce.
3. Cover the cooker and cook on Low for 5 to 6 hours.
4. After cooking, serve with green salad, peas, and bread.

Nutrition Info per Serving:

Calories: 671, Fat: 29.49 g, Carbohydrates: 35.67 g, Protein: 63.97 g

Mediterranean Veggies Egg Breakfast

Prep Time: 10 minutes, Cook Time: 5 to 6 hours on low, Serves: 4

INGREDIENTS:

- ½ cup (120 ml) coconut milk
- 1 tbsp. extra-virgin olive oil
- 12 eggs
- 2 cups chopped spinach
- 1 tomato, chopped
- ½ cup crumbled goat cheese
- ¼ cup chopped sweet onion
- ¼ tsp. salt
- ½ tsp. dried oregano
- ½ tsp. freshly ground black pepper
- 1 tsp. minced garlic

DIRECTIONS:

1. Lightly grease the crock pot with the olive oil.
2. Whisk together the eggs, oregano, coconut milk, pepper, and salt in a large bowl, until well blended.
3. Add the spinach, shallot, tomato, and garlic, and stir to combine.
4. Pour the egg mixture into the crock pot and top with the crumbled goat cheese.
5. Cover and cook on low for 5 to 6 hours, until it is set like a quiche. Serve warm.

Nutrition Info per Serving:

Calories: 349, Total Carbs: 5g, Protein: 23g, Total Fat: 27g, Fiber: 1g, Net Carbs: 4g

Crock Pot Honey Strawberry Chia Jam

Prep Time: 15 minutes, Cook Time: 3 to 4 hours on low, Serves: 2½ cups

INGREDIENTS:

- 2 cups strawberries, fresh or frozen, stemmed and quartered
- 1 cup water
- 2 tbsps. chia seeds
- 2 tsps. freshly squeezed lemon juice
- 2 tbsps. raw honey, or to taste (optional)

DIRECTIONS:

1. Add the chia seeds, strawberries, lemon juice, water, and honey (if using) into the crock pot, combine them together.
2. Cover the cooker and cook for 3 to 4 hours on high.
3. Remove the lid and use a potato masher or fork to mash. Blend with an immersion blender after the jam cools if you prefer a smooth jam without any visible seeds.
4. Place in an airtight container and keep in the refrigerator.

Nutrition Info per Serving:

Calories: 14, Total Fat: 0 g, Total Carbs: 5 g, Sugar: 1 g, Fiber: 1 g, Protein: 0.5 g, Sodium: 0 mg

Cheesy Kale and Mushroom Quiche

Prep Time: 10 minutes, Cook Time: 5 to 6 hours on low, Serves: 8

INGREDIENTS:

- 1 tbsp. extra-virgin olive oil
- 12 eggs
- 1 cup heavy (whipping) cream
- 1 cup chopped kale
- 2 cups coarsely chopped wild mushrooms
- 1 cup shredded Swiss Cheese
- 1 tbsp. chopped fresh chives
- 1 tbsp. chopped fresh thyme
- ⅛ tsp. salt
- ¼ tsp. freshly ground black pepper

DIRECTIONS:

1. Use the olive oil to lightly grease the insert of the crock pot.
2. Add the heavy cream, eggs, chives, thyme, salt and pepper into a medium bowl, whisk them together. Add the kale and mushrooms, stir well. Pour the mixture into the crock pot, place the cheese on the top.
3. Cover the cooker and cook on low 5 to 6 hours.
4. Serve warm.

Nutrition Info per Serving:

Calories: 289, Total Fat: 24 g, Total Carbs: 5 g, Net Carbs: 4 g, Protein: 15 g, Fiber: 1 g

Healthy Zucchini and Carrot Loaf

Prep Time: 15 minutes, Cook Time: 3 hours on high or 5 hours on low, Serves: 8 slices

INGREDIENTS:

- 2 tsps. butter, for greasing pan
- 1½ cups finely grated zucchini
- ½ cup finely grated carrot
- 1 cup almond flour
- 1 cup granulated erythritol
- ½ cup coconut flour
- 4 eggs
- ½ cup (120 ml) butter, melted
- 1½ tsp. baking powder
- 1 tsp. ground cinnamon
- ½ tsp. ground nutmeg
- ½ tsp. baking soda
- ¼ tsp. salt
- 1 tbsp. pure vanilla extract

DIRECTIONS:

1. Lightly grease a 9 x 5-inch loaf pan with the butter and set aside.
2. Put a small rack in the bottom of your crock pot.
3. Stir together the cinnamon, almond flour, coconut flour, baking soda, erythritol, baking powder, nutmeg, and salt in a large bowl until well mixed.
4. In a medium bowl, whisk together the eggs, vanilla and melted butter until well blended.
5. Add the wet mixture to dry ingredients and stir to combine.
6. Mix in the zucchini and carrot.
7. Spoon the batter into the prepared loaf pan.
8. Put the loaf pan on the rack in the bottom of the crock pot, cover the lid, and cook on high for 3 hours.
9. Remove the loaf pan, let the bread cool down completely. Serve.

Nutrition Info per Serving:

Calories: 217, Total Carbs: 5g, Protein: 8g, Total Fat: 19g, Fiber: 3g, Net Carbs: 2g

CHAPTER 3

GRAIN AND RICE

Curried Lentils and Brown Rice

Prep Time: 10 minutes, Cook Time: 8 hours, Serves: 6

INGREDIENTS:

- 3 cups cooked brown rice
- 2½ cups dried lentils, soaked overnight and rinsed
- ½ cup (120 ml) canned light coconut milk
- 2 onions, chopped
- 4 cups (960 ml) vegetable broth
- 2 tbsps. curry powder
- 1 tsp. garlic powder
- 1 tbsp. grated fresh ginger
- 1 tsp. ground turmeric
- ¼ tsp. sea salt

DIRECTIONS:

1. Mix the lentils, broth, coconut milk, curry powder, onions, ginger, turmeric, garlic powder and salt in your crock pot.
2. Cover and cook on low for 8 hours.
3. Serve spooned over the cooked rice.

Nutrition Info per Serving:

Calories: 538, Total Fat: 7g, Saturated Fat: 5g, Carbohydrates: 94g, Protein: 26g, Fiber: 28g

Italian Sausage and Pepper with Rice

Prep Time: 10 minutes, Cook Time: 5-10 hours, Serves: 6

INGREDIENTS:

- 1½ lbs. (680 g) Italian sausage, cut in ¾-inch slices
- 28-oz. (784 g) can diced Italian-style tomatoes, with juice
- 2 chopped green peppers
- 2 cups minute rice, uncooked
- 2 tbsps. A-1 steak sauce
- ½ tsp. red pepper flakes, optional

DIRECTIONS:

1. In the crock pot, add all of the ingredients, except the rice.
2. Cover the cooker and cook on Low for 7½ to 9½ hours, or on High for 4½ hours.
3. Stir in the uncooked rice. Cover and cook on High or Low for another 20 minutes.

Nutrition Info per Serving:

Calories: 576, Fat: 44.14 g, Carbohydrates: 32.88 g, Protein: 23.76 g

Brown Rice and Dried Fruit Pudding

Prep Time: 10 minutes, Cook Time: 8 hours, Serves: 6

INGREDIENTS:

- 1 (13-ounce, 369 g) can light coconut milk
- ½ cup dried fruit of your choice, such as raisins, cranberries, apples, or a mixture
- 1½ cups (360 ml) skim milk
- ⅔ cup uncooked brown rice
- ¼ cup (60 ml) honey
- 1 tsp. ground cinnamon
- 1 tsp. pure vanilla extract
- ¼ tsp. ground nutmeg
- Pinch sea salt

DIRECTIONS:

1. Combine all the ingredients in your crock pot.
2. Cover and cook on low for 8 hours.

Nutrition Info per Serving:

Calories: 332, Total Fat: 15g, Saturated Fat: 13g, Carbohydrates: 46g, Protein: 6g, Fiber: 3g

Herbed Wild Rice and Bacon

Prep Time: 10 minutes, Cook Time: 8 hours, Serves: 1

INGREDIENTS:

- 1 tsp. extra-virgin olive oil
- 1 piece applewood-smoked bacon, cooked and crumbled
- ¾ cup wild rice
- ½ cup minced onion
- ¼ cup dried cherries
- 1 tsp. minced fresh rosemary
- 2 cups low-sodium chicken broth
- ⅛ tsp. sea salt

DIRECTIONS:

1. Use the olive oil to grease the inside of the crock pot.
2. In the crock pot, add all of the ingredients and stir them to thoroughly mix.
3. Cover the cooker and cook on low for 6 hours until the rice has absorbed all the water and is tender.

Nutrition Info per Serving:

Calories: 350, Saturated Fat: 1 g, Trans Fat: 0 g, Carbohydrates: 66 g, Protein: 13 g, Fiber: 10 g, Sodium: 268 mg

Wild Rice Egg Casserole

Prep Time: 20 minutes, Cook Time: 5-7 hours, Serves: 6

INGREDIENTS:

- 11 eggs
- 3 cups plain cooked wild rice
- 2 cups sliced mushrooms
- 1 red bell pepper, stemmed, seeded, and chopped
- 1 onion, minced
- 1½ cups shredded Swiss cheese
- 2 garlic cloves, minced
- ¼ tsp. salt
- 1 tsp. dried thyme leaves

DIRECTIONS:

1. Put wild rice, mushrooms, bell peppers, onions, and garlic in a 6-quart crock pot.
2. Beat the eggs into a large bowl, sprinkle with thyme and salt to taste. Pour the mixture into a crock pot. Then pour the cheese and close the lid.
3. Cook on low heat for 5 to 7 hours until the food thermometer shows 165°F and is soft. Serve immediately!

Nutrition Info per Serving:

Calories: 360, Fat: 17g, Saturated Fat: 8g, Protein: 24g, Carbohydrates: 25g, Sugar: 3g, Fiber: 3g, Sodium: 490mg

Wild Rice with Chili and Vegetable

Prep Time: 20 minutes, Cook Time: 6 to 7 hours, Serves: 8

INGREDIENTS:

- 1½ cups wild rice, rinsed and drained
- 2 (15-ounce, 425g) BPA-free cans no-salt-added black beans, drained and rinsed
- 2 cups sliced cremini mushrooms
- 2 red bell peppers, stemmed, seeded, and chopped
- 5 cups roasted vegetable broth
- 3 cups low-sodium tomato juice
- 1 tbsp. chili powder
- 2 onions, chopped
- 3 garlic cloves, minced
- ½ tsp. ground cumin

DIRECTIONS:

1. Combine all the ingredients in a 6-quart crock pot and cover. Transfer the pot to the stove, turn on a low heat, and cook for 6 to 7 hours. Cover the lid until the wild rice is soft.
2. Transfer the mixture from the pot to a small bowl and enjoy!

Nutrition Info per Serving:

Calories: 288, Fat: 5g, Saturated Fat: 0g, Protein: 13g, Carbohydrates: 58g, Sugar: 9g, Fiber: 10g, Sodium: 564mg

Slow Cooked Butternut Squash and Oatmeal

Prep Time: 15 minutes, Cook Time: 6 to 8 hours, Serves: 4

INGREDIENTS:

- 2 cups cubed (½-inch pieces) peeled butternut squash (freeze any leftovers after preparing a whole squash for future meals)
- 1 cup steel-cut oats
- 3 cups water
- 1 tbsp. chia seeds
- ¼ cup unsweetened nondairy milk
- 1½ tsps. ground ginger
- 2 tsps. yellow (mellow) miso paste
- 1 tbsp. sesame seeds, toasted
- 1 tbsp. chopped scallion, green parts only
- Shredded carrot, for serving (optional)

DIRECTIONS:

1. Add the butternut squash, oats and water into a crock pot.
2. Cover and cook on Low for 6 to 8 hours, or until the squash is fork-tender. Roughly mash the cooked butternut squash with a potato masher or heavy spoon. Stir to combine with the oats.
3. Add the chia seeds, milk, ginger and miso paste into a small bowl, whisk them together to combine. Stir the mixture into the oats.
4. Place the sesame seeds and scallion over your oatmeal bowl, and serve with shredded carrot (if using).

Nutrition Info per Serving:

Calories: 230, Fat: 5 g, Carbohydrates: 40 g, Protein: 7 g, Fiber: 9 g

Brown Rice in Stock

Prep Time: 5 minutes, Cook Time: 2 to 4 hours, Serves: 6 cups

INGREDIENTS:

- Nonstick cooking spray
- 2 cups brown rice
- 3⅓ cups (800 ml) vegetable broth, poultry broth, beef broth, or store bought
- 1 tbsp. olive oil

DIRECTIONS:

1. Spray the jar of your crock pot with nonstick cooking spray.
2. Add the broth, rice, and olive oil, stirring to combine.
3. Cover and set on high. Cook for 2 to 4 hours, stirring every hour or so, until the rice is fluffy.

Nutrition Info per Serving:

Calories: 126, Total Fat: 2g, Saturated Fat: 0g, Carbohydrates: 24g, Protein: 3g, Fiber: 1g

Simple Quinoa in Stock

Prep Time: 5 minutes, Cook Time: 6 hours, Serves: 6 cups

INGREDIENTS:

- Nonstick cooking spray
- 2 cups quinoa
- 4 cups (960 ml) vegetable broth, poultry broth, beef broth, or store bought
- 1 tbsp. olive oil

DIRECTIONS:

1. Spray the jar of your crock pot with nonstick cooking spray.
2. Add the broth, quinoa, and olive oil, stirring to mix.
3. Cover and set on low. Cook for about 6 hours. Fluff with a fork.

Nutrition Info per Serving:

Calories: 106, Total Fat: 2g, Saturated Fat: 0g, Carbohydrates: 18g, Protein: 4g, Fiber: 2g, Cholesterol: 0mg

Cheese Quinoa Stuffed Bell Peppers

Prep Time: 15 minutes, Cook Time: 8 hours, Serves: 6

INGREDIENTS:

- 1 (14-ounce, 397 g) can diced tomatoes and peppers, drained
- 6 bell peppers, tops cut off, seeds and ribs carefully removed
- 1 cup (240 ml) vegetable broth
- 4 ounces (113 g) shredded low-fat Cheddar cheese
- ¼ cup chopped fresh cilantro
- 1 cup uncooked quinoa
- 3 cups cooked black beans, rinsed
- 1 tsp. ground cumin
- 1 tsp. garlic powder
- ¼ tsp. sea salt

DIRECTIONS:

1. Rinse the quinoa in a fine-mesh colander under running water.
2. Combine the quinoa, black beans, cumin, garlic powder, tomatoes and peppers, cheese, and salt in a medium bowl.
3. Carefully stuff the bell peppers with the quinoa mixture.
4. Place the stuffed peppers in the crock pot, cut-side up and pour the broth around the peppers.
5. Cover and cook on low for 8 hours.
6. Serve with the chopped cilantro on top.

Nutrition Info per Serving:

Calories: 345, Total Fat: 10g, Saturated Fat: 4g, Carbohydrates: 47g, Protein: 18g, Cholesterol: 20mg, Fiber: 11g

Herb Barley Risotto with Lemon

Prep Time: 10 minutes, Cook Time: 6-8 hours, Serves: 1

INGREDIENTS:

- 1 tsp. extra-virgin olive oil
- 2 tbsps. minced preserved lemon
- ½ cup minced onion
- 2 cups low-sodium vegetable broth
- ¼ cup roughly chopped fresh parsley, divided
- ¾ cup pearl barley
- 1 tsp. fresh thyme leaves
- ⅛ tsp. sea salt
- Freshly ground black pepper
- ½ lemon cut, into wedges, for garnish

DIRECTIONS:

1. Use olive oil to grease the inside of the crock pot.
2. In the crock pot, add the preserved lemon, onion, thyme, 2 tablespoons of the parsley, vegetable broth and barley. Season with the salt and pepper, and stir thoroughly.
3. Cover the cooker and cook on low for 6 to 8 hours, until the barley is tender and all the liquid is absorbed.
4. Garnish with the remaining parsley and a lemon wedge and serve.

Nutrition Info per Serving:

Calories: 318, Saturated Fat: 1 g, Trans Fat: 0 g, Carbohydrates: 64 g, Protein: 10 g, Fiber: 13 g, Sodium: 200 mg

Healthy Quinoa with Brussels Sprouts

Prep Time: 20 minutes, Cook Time: 5-6 hours, Serves: 8

INGREDIENTS:

- 3 cups Brussels sprouts
- 2 cups quinoa, rinsed
- 2 avocados, peeled and sliced
- 1 cup broken walnuts
- 1 onion, finely chopped
- 4 cups roasted vegetable broth
- 2 tbsps. lemon juice
- 1 tsp. dried marjoram leaves
- 3 garlic cloves, minced
- ½ cup pomegranate seeds

DIRECTIONS:

1. Combine quinoa, onion, garlic, vegetable broth, Brussels sprouts, marjoram, and lemon juice in a 6-quart crock pot. Place the crock pot on the stove and simmer until the quinoa is soft, about 5 to 6 hours.
2. Put the avocado, pomegranate seeds and walnuts in a crock pot and serve immediately.

Nutrition Info per Serving:

Calories: 358, Fat: 17g, Saturated Fat: 1g, Protein: 10g, Carbohydrates: 42g, Sugar: 6g, Fiber: 8g, Sodium: 83mg

Oatmeal Crock Pot with Carrot

Prep Time: 20 minutes, Cook Time: 6 to 8 hours, Serves: 8

INGREDIENTS:

- 1 (8-ounce, 227g) BPA-free can unsweetened crushed pineapple in juice, undrained
- 4 cups water
- 3 cups steel-cut oats
- 2 cups finely grated carrot
- 2 cups almond milk
- ¼ cup honey
- 2 tsps. vanilla extract
- 2 tbsps. melted coconut oil
- 1 tsp. ground cinnamon
- ¼ tsp. salt

DIRECTIONS:

1. Coat the inside of a 6-quart crock pot with regular vegetable oil.
2. Add steel-cut oats, carrots and pineapple, and mix.
3. Put almond milk, water, coconut oil, honey, vanilla, salt and cinnamon in a medium bowl and stir to combine. Pour the mixture into the crock pot and close the lid.
4. Cook on low heat for 6 to 8 hours, until the oatmeal is soft. Serve immediately!

Nutrition Info per Serving:

Calories: 132, Fat: 8g, Saturated Fat: 4g, Protein: 8g, Carbohydrates: 58g, Sugar: 17g, Fiber: 7g, Sodium: 133mg

Black Bean and Brown Rice with Corn

Prep Time: Less than 5 minutes, Cook Time: 8 hours (low), 4 hours (high), plus 10 minutes, Serves: 6

INGREDIENTS:

- 1 cup uncooked brown rice
- ½ pound (227 g) dried black beans, rinsed
- 8 ounces (227 g) grated Cheddar cheese
- 3 cups fresh or frozen corn
- 1 cup chopped fresh cilantro
- 1 medium onion, chopped
- 2 jalapeños
- 4 cups vegetable stock
- 2 large tomatoes, diced
- Juice of 1 lime
- Sea salt

DIRECTIONS:

1. Add the rice, beans, jalapeños, onion and stock to the crock pot, combine them together.
2. Cover the cooker and cook on low for 8 hours or on high for 4 hours.
3. Place the tomatoes, lime juice, corn, cilantro, and cheese into the cooker. Stir gently and cook for 10 minutes on low. Taste and adjust with salt if needed.
4. Ladle into bowls with the beans and rice, and serve hot.

Mushroom Risotto with Brown Rice

Prep Time: 10 minutes, Cook Time: 8 hours, Serves: 6

INGREDIENTS:

- 1 pound (454 g) fresh mushrooms, chopped
- 4 cups (960 ml) vegetable broth
- 4 ounces (113 g) Neufchâtel cheese, cut into pieces
- ¼ cup (60 ml) dry white wine
- 2 ounces (57 g) dried porcini mushrooms
- 1 tsp. dried thyme
- 1½ cups uncooked brown rice
- 1 onion, minced
- ¼ tsp. sea salt
- ¼ tsp. freshly ground black pepper

DIRECTIONS:

1. The night before cooking, put the dried porcini mushrooms in a small bowl, cover with the broth, and soak overnight in the refrigerator.
2. The next day, remove the porcini mushrooms from the broth and roughly chop them. Add mushrooms with the broth to the crock pot.
3. Put in the rice, fresh mushrooms, white wine, onion, thyme, salt, and pepper.
4. Cover and cook on low for 8 hours.
5. Stir in the Neufchâtel cheese.

Nutrition Info per Serving:

Calories: 299, Total Fat: 6g, Saturated Fat: 3g, Carbohydrates: 49g, Protein: 11g, Fiber: 5g

Mexican Black Bean and Quinoa

Prep Time: 10 minutes, Cook Time: 8 hours, Serves: 6

INGREDIENTS:

- 1 (14-ounce, 397 g) can diced tomatoes and peppers, drained
- 2 cups uncooked quinoa
- 2 cups cooked black beans, rinsed
- 2 cups fresh or frozen corn
- 1 green bell pepper, seeded and chopped
- 1 red bell pepper, seeded and chopped
- 2 jalapeño peppers, seeded and chopped
- 4 cups (960 ml) vegetable broth
- 1 tsp. ground cumin
- ¼ cup chopped fresh cilantro

DIRECTIONS:

1. Rinse the quinoa in a fine-mesh colander under running water.
2. Mix the quinoa, black beans, tomatoes and peppers, broth, jalapeños, corn, bell peppers, and cumin in your crock pot.
3. Cover and cook on low for 8 hours.
4. Add cilantro just before serving.

Nutrition Info per Serving:

Calories: 361, Total Fat: 5g, Saturated Fat: 1g, Carbohydrates: 67g, Protein: 15g, Fiber: 11g

Classic Thai Peanut Rice

Prep Time: 10 minutes, Cook Time: 6-8 hours, Serves: 1

INGREDIENTS:

- 1 tsp. extra-virgin olive oil
- 4 collard leaves, ribs removed, chopped into thin ribbons
- 3 cups low-sodium vegetable broth, divided
- ½ cup minced red onion
- ½ cup brown rice
- ¼ cup unsalted creamy peanut butter
- 2 tbsps. tomato paste
- 1 tbsp. minced ginger
- ⅛ tsp. sea salt
- 1 tsp. Sriracha
- ¼ cup roughly chopped cilantro, for garnish
- Lime wedges, for garnish
- 2 tbsps. roasted peanuts, roughly chopped, for garnish

DIRECTIONS:

1. Use olive oil to grease the inside of the crock pot.
2. In the crock pot, add the collard greens, 2 cups of broth, rice, and onion.
3. Add the remaining 1 cup of broth, tomato paste, ginger, peanut butter, salt and Sriracha into a medium bowl, whisk them together. Transfer this mixture into the crock pot and stir well.
4. Cover the cooker and cook on low for 6 to 8 hours.
5. Garnish each serving with a lime wedge, fresh cilantro, and the peanuts, and serve.

Nutrition Info per Serving:

Calories: 554, Saturated Fat: 13 g, Trans Fat: 0 g, Carbohydrates: 59 g, Protein: 24 g, Fiber: 10 g, Sodium: 401 mg

Crock Pot Mushroom and Wild Rice

Prep Time: 15 minutes, Cook Time: 4 hours on low, Serves: 8

INGREDIENTS:

- 1 lb. (454 g) bulk pork sausage
- 1 can (10 ¾ oz., 304 g) condensed cream of chicken soup, undiluted
- 1 can (10 ¾ oz., 304 g) condensed cream of mushroom soup, undiluted
- 1 can (4 oz., 113 g) mushroom stems and pieces, drained
- 4 celery ribs, chopped
- 1 small onion, chopped
- 1 cup uncooked wild rice
- 3 cups chicken broth

DIRECTIONS:

1. Add the sausage into a large skillet, cook and crumble with onion and celery over medium heat for 6 to 8 minutes, until sausage is no longer pink and vegetables are tender, drain. Transfer this mixture into a 3-qt. crock pot. Then add rice, soups, and mushroom. Stir in chicken broth.
2. Cover and cook on low for 4 to 5 hours, until rice is tender.

Nutrition Info per Serving:

Calories: 236, Fat: 14 g, Carbohydrates: 19 g, Protein: 9 g, Sugar: 2 g, Fiber: 2 g, Sodium: 1059 mg

Simple Slow Cooked Pearl Barley

Prep Time: 10 minutes, Cook Time: 8 hours, Serves: 4 cups

INGREDIENTS:

- 2 cups pearl barley
- 5 cups (1200 ml) boiling water
- ½ tsp. salt

DIRECTIONS:

1. Mix all ingredients in your crock pot.
2. Cover and cook on low for 8 hours.

Nutrition Info per Serving:

Calories: 352, Total Fat: 1.2g, Saturated Fat: 0g, Carbohydrates: 78g, Protein: 10g, Cholesterol: 0mg, Fiber 16g

CHAPTER 4

POULTRY

Creamy Chicken with Bacon and Mushroom

Prep Time: 15 minutes, Cook Time: 7 to 8 hours on low, Serves: 8

INGREDIENTS:

- 3 tbsps. coconut oil, divided
- 2 pounds (907 g) chicken (breasts, thighs, drumsticks)
- ¼ pound (114 g) bacon, diced
- 1 sweet onion, diced
- 2 cups quartered button mushrooms
- 1 cup coconut cream
- ½ cup chicken broth
- 1 tbsp. minced garlic
- 2 tsps. chopped thyme

DIRECTIONS:

1. Use 1 tablespoon of the coconut oil to lightly grease the insert of the crock pot.
2. Heat the remaining 2 tablespoons of the coconut oil in a large skillet over medium-high heat.
3. Stir in the bacon and cook for 5 minutes, until it is crispy. Transfer the bacon to a plate with a slotted spoon, set aside.
4. Place the chicken into the skillet and brown for 5 minutes, turning once.
5. In the insert of the crock pot, add the chicken and bacon and stir in the garlic, onion, mushrooms, broth, and thyme.
6. Cover the cooker and cook on low for 7 to 8 hours.
7. Add the coconut cream, stir well and serve.

Nutrition Info per Serving:

Calories: 406, Total Fat: 34 g, Total Carbs: 5 g, Net Carbs: 3 g, Protein: 22 g, Fiber: 2 g

Lime and Jalapeño Chicken

Prep Time: 15 minutes, Cook Time: 8 hours, Serves: 4

INGREDIENTS:

- 4 bone-in, skinless chicken thighs
- ¼ cup (60 ml) honey
- ½ tsp. garlic powder
- ½ tsp. sea salt
- Juice of 2 limes
- Zest of 1 lime
- 1 jalapeño pepper, seeded and minced
- ¼ cup chopped fresh cilantro

DIRECTIONS:

1. Put the chicken thighs in the crock pot.
2. Whisk together the honey, lime juice, lime zest, jalapeño, garlic powder, and salt in a small bowl.
3. Pour the mixture over the chicken.
4. Cover and cook on low for 8 hours.
5. Serve garnish with the cilantro.

Nutrition Info per Serving:

Calories: 314, Total Fat: 16g, Saturated Fat: 5g, Carbohydrates: 18g, Protein: 26g, Fiber: 0g

Braised Chicken Thighs with Garlic and Onion

Prep Time: 15 minutes, Cook Time: 7 to 8 hours on low, Serves: 4

INGREDIENTS:

- ¼ cup extra-virgin olive oil, divided
- 1½ pounds (680 g) boneless chicken thighs
- 1 sweet onion, chopped
- ½ cup Greek yogurt
- ½ cup chicken broth
- Salt, for seasoning
- 4 garlic cloves, thinly sliced
- 1 tsp. paprika
- 2 tbsps. freshly squeezed lemon juice
- Freshly ground black pepper, for seasoning

DIRECTIONS:

1. Use 1 tablespoon of the olive oil to lightly grease the insert of the crock pot.
2. Use salt, paprika and pepper to season the thighs.
3. Heat the remaining olive oil in a large skillet over medium-high heat. Stir in the chicken and brown for 5 minutes, turning once.
4. In the insert, add the chicken and stir in the garlic, onion, broth, and lemon juice.
5. Cover the cooker and cook on low for 7 to 8 hours.
6. After cooking, add the yogurt, stir well and serve.

Nutrition Info per Serving:

Calories: 434, Total Fat: 36 g, Total Carbs: 5 g, Net Carbs: 4 g, Protein: 22 g, Fiber: 1 g

Maple Chicken Drumsticks

Prep Time: 10 minutes, Cook Time: 8 hours, Serves: 6

INGREDIENTS:

- 12 chicken drumsticks
- 4 scallions, sliced
- ½ cup (120 ml) pure maple syrup
- ¼ cup (60 ml) low-sodium soy sauce
- 1 tsp. sesame seeds
- 1 tsp. cornstarch
- ½ tsp. garlic powder
- 1 tsp. grated fresh ginger
- ¼ tsp. freshly ground black pepper

DIRECTIONS:

1. Put the drumsticks in your crock pot.
2. Whisk together the maple syrup, soy sauce, cornstarch, garlic powder, ginger and pepper in a small bowl.
3. Pour the sauce over the drumsticks and toss to coat.
4. Cover and cook on low for 8 hours.
5. Garnish with the scallions and sesame seeds, then serve.

Nutrition Info per Serving:

Calories: 237, Total Fat: 6g, Saturated Fat: 1g, Carbohydrates: 20g, Protein: 26g, Fiber: 0g

Classic Buffalo Wings

Prep Time: 10 minutes, Cook Time: 6 hours on low, Serves: 8

INGREDIENTS:

- ¾ cup melted grass-fed butter
- 1 (12-ounce, 340 g) bottle hot pepper sauce
- 2 tsps. garlic powder
- 1 tbsp. dried oregano
- 1 tsp. onion powder
- 3 pounds (1.4 kg) chicken wing sections

DIRECTIONS:

1. Add the butter, hot sauce, garlic powder, oregano and onion powder into a large bowl, whisk them together until blended.
2. Place the chicken wings into the bowl and toss to coat.
3. In the insert of a crock pot, add the mixture.
4. Cover and set on low, cook for 6 hours.
5. Serve hot.

Nutrition Info per Serving:

Calories: 529, Total Fat: 44 g, Total Carbs: 1 g, Net Carbs: 1 g, Protein: 31 g, Fiber: 0 g

Spinach Stuffed Chicken Breasts

Prep Time: 15 minutes, Cook Time: 8 hours, Serves: 4

INGREDIENTS:

- 2 boneless, skinless chicken breasts, cut in half horizontally to make 4 cutlets total
- 2 cups baby spinach, stems trimmed
- 2 cups cooked quinoa
- 1½ cups (360 ml) dry white wine
- ½ onion, finely chopped
- 4 ounces (113 g) fresh mushrooms, finely chopped
- 1 tsp. sea salt, divided
- ½ tsp. freshly ground black pepper, divided
- 2 tsps. dried tarragon or 1 tsp. minced fresh tarragon
- Zest of 1 lemon

DIRECTIONS:

1. Place each chicken breast cutlet between 2 pieces of plastic wrap and pound them flat.
2. Sprinkle the chicken cutlets with salt and pepper.
3. Arrange the spinach leaves in a layer on top of each seasoned cutlet.
4. Mix the quinoa, mushrooms, tarragon, onion, lemon zest, remaining salt and pepper in a small bowl.
5. Spread the stuffing on top of the spinach on each cutlet.
6. Roll each chicken cutlet around the filling, tying with kitchen twine to keep them rolled.
7. Place the stuffed chicken rolls in a single layer in the crock pot. Add the wine.
8. Cover and cook on low for 8 hours.
9. Remove the chicken rolls from the crock pot. Snip and remove the kitchen twine.
10. Transfer the wine and any accumulated juices to a small saucepan and simmer about 5 minutes until it reduces by half. Spoon over the chicken.

Nutrition Info per Serving:

Calories: 381, Total Fat: 8g, Saturated Fat: 2g, Carbohydrates: 33g, Protein: 28g, Fiber: 4g

Curried Coconut Chicken and Bok Choy

Prep Time: 15 minutes, Cook Time: 7 to 8 hours on low, Serves: 6

INGREDIENTS:

- 3 tbsps. extra-virgin olive oil, divided
- 1½ pounds (680 g) boneless chicken breasts
- 1 cup quartered baby bok choy
- ½ sweet onion, chopped
- 1 red bell pepper, diced
- 2 tbsps. almond butter
- 2 cups coconut milk
- 1 tbsp. coconut aminos
- 1 tbsp. red Thai curry paste
- 2 tsps. grated fresh ginger
- Pinch red pepper flakes
- 2 tbsps. chopped cilantro, for garnish
- ¼ cup chopped peanuts, for garnish

DIRECTIONS:

1. Use 1 tablespoon of the olive oil to lightly grease the insert of the crock pot.
2. Heat the remaining 2 tablespoons of the olive oil in a large skillet over medium-high heat. Stir in the chicken and brown for about 7 minutes.
3. Place the chicken into the crock pot and stir in the baby bok choy, onion and bell pepper.
4. Add the almond butter, coconut milk, coconut aminos, curry paste, ginger and red pepper flakes to a medium bowl, whisk them together until well blended.
5. Pour over the chicken and vegetables with the sauce, and stir to coat.
6. Cover the cooker and cook on low for 7 to 8 hours.
7. Top with the cilantro and peanuts, serve.

Nutrition Info per Serving:

Calories: 543, Total Fat: 42 g, Total Carbs: 10 g, Net Carbs: 5 g, Protein: 35 g, Fiber: 5 g

Curry Chicken and Sweet Potato

Prep Time: 15 minutes, Cook Time: 8 hours, Serves: 6

INGREDIENTS:

- 1 pound (454 g) boneless, skinless chicken thighs, cut into 1-inch pieces
- 2 sweet potatoes, peeled and cut into 1-inch cubes
- 2 red bell peppers, seeded and cut into large pieces
- 1 onion, chopped
- 1 cup (240 ml) canned light coconut milk
- 2 cups (480 ml) poultry broth, or store bought
- 2 tsps. curry powder
- 1 tsp. garlic powder
- ½ tsp. sea salt
- ¼ tsp. freshly ground black pepper

DIRECTIONS:

1. Mix all the ingredients in your crock pot.
2. Cover and cook on low for 8 hours.

Nutrition Info per Serving:

Calories: 323, Total Fat: 16g, Saturated Fat: 10g, Carbohydrates: 21g, Protein: 25g, Cholesterol: 67mg, Fiber: 4g

Delicious Chicken Provence with Olive

INGREDIENTS:

- 3 pounds (1.4kg) boneless, skinless chicken thighs
- 4 large tomatoes, seeded and chopped
- 2 red bell peppers, stemmed, seeded, and chopped
- 3 bulbs fennel, cored and sliced
- 2 onions, chopped
- ¼ cup sliced black Greek olives
- 4 sprigs fresh thyme
- 6 garlic cloves, minced
- 2 tbsps. lemon juice
- 1 bay leaf

DIRECTIONS:

1. In a 6-quart crock pot, mix all of the ingredients. Cover and cook on low for 7 to 9 hours, or until the chicken registers 165°F on a food thermometer.
2. Remove and discard the thyme stems and bay leaf and serve.

Nutrition Info per Serving:

Calories: 302, Fat: 14g, Saturated Fat: 4g, Protein: 34g, Carbohydrates: 13g, Sugar: 7g, Fiber: 4g, Sodium: 187mg

Quinoa and Carrot Stuffed Turkey Breast

Prep Time: 15 minutes, Cook Time: 8 hours, Serves: 6

INGREDIENTS:

- 1 (2-pound, 907 g) boneless, skin-on turkey breast
- 3 cups cooked quinoa
- 2 carrots, peeled and finely chopped
- 2 onions, finely chopped
- 2 celery stalks, finely chopped
- 1 egg, beaten
- ½ cup (120 ml) poultry broth
- 1 tsp. dried thyme
- 1 tsp. dried sage
- 1 tsp. sea salt, divided
- ½ tsp. freshly ground black pepper, divided

DIRECTIONS:

1. Mix the quinoa, carrots, celery, onions, egg, thyme, sage, ¼ teaspoon of black pepper and ½ teaspoon of sea salt in a medium bowl.
2. Put the turkey breast on a large cutting board, skin-side down, between two pieces of plastic wrap, and pound it slightly to flatten.
3. Spread the filling evenly over the flesh side of the breast.
4. Roll the breast around the filling, skin-side out. Sprinkle the skin side with the remaining salt and black pepper.
5. Put the stuffed turkey breast into your crock pot. Add the broth. Cover and cook for 8 hours on low.
6. Remove the turkey skin before slicing and serving.

Nutrition Info per Serving:

Calories: 361, Total Fat: 4g, Saturated Fat: 1g, Carbohydrates: 33g, Protein: 45g, Fiber: 5g

Healthy Artichoke Chicken

INGREDIENTS:

- 8 (6-ounce, 170g) boneless, skinless chicken breasts
- 2 leeks, chopped
- 1 cup chicken stock
- 2 tbsps. lemon juice
- 2 (14-ounce, 397g) BPA-free cans no-salt-added artichoke hearts, drained
- 1 tsp. dried basil leaves
- 3 garlic cloves, mince
- 2 red bell peppers, stemmed, seeded, and chopped
- ½ cup chopped flat-leaf parsley

DIRECTIONS:

1. Layer the leeks, garlic, artichoke hearts, bell peppers, chicken, stock, lemon juice, and basil in a 6-quart crock pot. Close the lid. Place the pot on the stove and simmer for 4 to 6 hours until the chicken shows 165°F on the food thermometer.
2. Put parsley at the end and enjoy.

Nutrition Info per Serving:

Calories: 200, Fat: 4g, Saturated Fat: 1g, Protein: 36g, Carbohydrates: 7g, Sugar: 2g, Fiber: 3g, Sodium: 372mg

Slow Cooked Chicken

Prep Time: 20 minutes, Cook Time: 5-7 hours, Serves: 8

INGREDIENTS:

- 8 (6-ounce, 170g) boneless, skinless chicken breasts
- 2 (8-ounce, 227g) BPA-free cans no-salt-added tomato sauce
- 2 onions, minced
- ⅓ cup mustard
- 8 garlic cloves, minced
- 3 tbsps. molasses
- 1 tbsp. chili powder
- 2 tbsps. lemon juice
- 2 tsps. paprika
- ¼ tsp. cayenne pepper

DIRECTIONS:

1. Combine tomato sauce, onion, garlic, mustard, lemon juice, molasses, paprika, paprika, and cayenne in a 6-quart crock pot.
2. Put the chicken in, use tongs to hold the chicken and move it in the sauce, so that the surface of the chicken is completely covered with the sauce. Cover the lid and cook on low heat for 5 to 7 hours until the chicken is cooked through and serve immediately!

Nutrition Info per Serving:

Calories: 231, Fat: 4g, Saturated Fat: 1g, Protein: 35g, Carbohydrates: 16g, Sugar: 10g, Fiber: 2g, Sodium: 490mg

Hungarian Chicken Paprikash

Prep Time: 10 minutes, Cook Time: 7 to 8 hours on low, Serves: 4

INGREDIENTS:

- 1 tbsp. extra-virgin olive oil
- 2 pounds (907 g) boneless chicken thighs
- 1 cup sour cream
- ½ cup chicken broth
- Juice and zest of 1 lemon
- 2 tsps. paprika
- 2 tsps. minced garlic
- ¼ tsp. salt
- 1 tbsp. chopped parsley, for garnish

DIRECTIONS:

1. Use the olive oil to lightly grease the insert of the crock pot.
2. In the insert, add the chicken thighs.
3. Add the lemon juice and zest, broth, paprika, garlic and salt to a small bowl, stir them together. Pour the broth mixture over the chicken.
4. Cover the cooker and set on low, cook for 7 to 8 hours.
5. After cooking, add the sour cream and stir well.
6. Top with the parsley and serve.

Nutrition Info per Serving:

Calories: 404, Total Fat: 32 g, Total Carbs: 4 g, Net Carbs: 4 g, Protein: 23 g, Fiber: 0 g

Chicken with Scallions

Prep Time: 20 minutes, Cook Time: 7-8 hours, Serves: 8

INGREDIENTS:

- 2 pounds (907g) skinless chicken drumsticks
- 2 pounds (907g) skinless chicken thighs
- 1 onion, chopped
- 2 cups chicken stock, divided
- 4 scallions, cut on the bias
- 3 garlic cloves, minced
- 2 tbsps. honey
- 2 tbsps. toasted sesame seeds
- 2 tbsps. grated fresh ginger root
- 2 tbsps. miso paste

DIRECTIONS:

1. Combine onion, garlic, and ginger root in a 6-quart crock pot. Place the chicken legs and thighs on top.
2. Combine ½ cup chicken broth with honey and miso paste in a medium bowl and stir well. Pour in the remaining chicken broth, stir well, then pour the mixture into the crock pot.
3. Cook on low heat for 7 to 8 hours until the chicken shows 165°F on the food thermometer.
4. Sprinkle sesame seeds and chopped green onions at the end, and serve immediately.

Nutrition Info per Serving:

Calories: 405, Fat: 19g, Saturated Fat: 4g, Protein: 48g, Carbohydrates: 10g, Sugar: 7g, Fiber: 1g, Sodium: 529mg

Italian Chicken and Mushroom Cacciatore

Prep Time: 10 minutes, Cook Time: 8 hours, Serves: 6

INGREDIENTS:

- 1 pound (454 g) boneless, skinless chicken thighs, cut into 1-inch pieces
- 1 (14-ounce, 397 g) can diced tomatoes, with their juice
- 1 pound (454 g) fresh mushrooms, halved
- 2 onions, sliced
- 2 green bell peppers, seeded and sliced
- 1½ tsp. garlic powder
- 1 tsp. dried Italian seasoning
- ¼ tsp. red pepper flakes
- ¼ tsp. sea salt
- ¼ tsp. freshly ground black pepper

DIRECTIONS:

1. Mix all the ingredients in the crock pot.
2. Cover and cook on low for 8 hours.
3. Serve the chicken with sauce spooned over the top.

Nutrition Info per Serving:

Calories: 204, Total Fat: 6g, Saturated Fat: 2g, Carbohydrates: 12g, Protein: 26g, Cholesterol: 68mg, Fiber: 3g

Roasted Chicken and Onion with Herbs

Prep Time: 15 minutes, Cook Time: 7 to 8 hours on low, Serves: 8

INGREDIENTS:

- ¼ cup extra-virgin olive oil, divided
- 1 (3-pound, 1.4 kg) whole chicken, washed and patted dry
- 1 sweet onion, quartered
- 1 lemon, quartered
- 4 garlic cloves, crushed
- 6 thyme sprigs
- 3 bay leaves
- Salt, for seasoning
- Freshly ground black pepper, for seasoning

DIRECTIONS:

1. Use 1 tablespoon of the olive oil to lightly grease the insert of the crock pot.
2. Use the remaining olive oil to rub all over the chicken, season with the salt and pepper. In the cavity of the chicken, stuff with the garlic, lemon quarters, thyme, and bay leaves.
3. Spread on the bottom of the crock pot with the onion quarters, then cover with the chicken, to make it does not touch the bottom of the insert.
4. Cover and set on low, cook for 7 to 8 hours, or until an instant-read thermometer reads 165°F(74°C) of the internal temperature.
5. Serve warm.

Nutrition Info per Serving:

Calories: 427, Total Fat: 34 g, Total Carbs: 2 g, Net Carbs: 2 g, Protein: 29 g, Fiber: 0 g

Crock Pot Chicken Mole

Prep Time: 15 minutes, Cook Time: 7 to 8 hours on low, Serves: 6

INGREDIENTS:

- 3 tbsps. extra-virgin olive oil or ghee, divided
- 2 pounds (907 g) boneless chicken thighs and breasts
- 1 (28-ounce, 784 g) can diced tomatoes
- 3 ounces (85 g) dark chocolate, chopped
- ½ cup coconut cream
- Freshly ground black pepper, for seasoning
- Salt, for seasoning
- 1 tbsp. minced garlic
- 1 sweet onion, chopped
- 4 dried chile peppers, soaked in water for 2 hours and chopped
- ¼ cup natural peanut butter
- ¾ tsp. ground cinnamon
- 1½ tsps. ground cumin
- ½ tsp. chili powder
- 2 tbsps. chopped cilantro, for garnish

DIRECTIONS:

1. Use 1 tablespoon of the olive oil to lightly grease the insert of the crock pot.
2. Heat the remaining 2 tablespoons of the olive oil in a large skillet over medium-high heat.
3. Season the chicken with pepper and salt lightly, place into the skillet, and brown for about 5 minutes, turning once.
4. Stir in the garlic and onion, sauté for another 3 minutes.
5. In the crock pot, place the chicken, garlic and onion, then add the tomatoes, chocolate, chiles, peanut butter, cinnamon, cumin, and chili powder, stir well.
6. Cover the cooker and set on low, cook for 7 to 8 hours.
7. Add the coconut cream, stir well, top with the cilantro, and serve hot.

Nutrition Info per Serving:

Calories: 386, Total Fat: 30 g, Total Carbs: 11 g, Net Carbs: 6 g, Protein: 19 g, Fiber: 5 g

Spicy Arroz con Pollo

Prep Time: 10 minutes, Cook Time: 8 hours, Serves: 6

INGREDIENTS:

- 6 bone-in, skin-on chicken thighs
- 1 (14-ounce, 397 g) can diced tomatoes and peppers, drained
- 1 cup uncooked brown rice
- 3 cups (720 ml) poultry broth
- 2 onions, chopped
- 1 tsp. garlic powder
- 1 tsp. ground cumin
- 1 tsp. dried oregano
- ¼ tsp. sea salt
- ⅛ tsp. cayenne pepper

DIRECTIONS:

1. Mix all the ingredients in your crock pot.
2. Cover and cook on low for 8 hours.
3. Remove the skin from the chicken, then serve.

Nutrition Info per Serving:

Calories: 409, Total Fat: 25g, Saturated Fat: 5g, Carbohydrates: 31g, Protein: 32g, Fiber: 3g

Peach-Bourbon Chicken Thighs

Prep Time: 15 minutes, Cook Time: 8 hours, Serves: 6

INGREDIENTS:

- 6 boneless, skinless chicken thighs
- 1 (14-ounce, 397 g) can tomato sauce
- 1½ cups peeled and chopped fresh peaches
- ½ cup (120 ml) bourbon
- ⅓ cup (80 ml) apple cider vinegar
- ¼ cup (60 ml) pure maple syrup
- ¾ tsp. liquid smoke
- 1 tsp. garlic powder
- ½ tsp. sea salt
- ¼ tsp. cayenne pepper

DIRECTIONS:

1. Put the chicken thighs in your crock pot.
2. Combine all the other ingredients in a small saucepan.
3. Simmer over medium-low heat, stirring frequently for about 5 minutes and mashing the peaches with a spoon, until the sauce thickens.
4. Cool the sauce for 5 minutes. Pour it over the chicken.
5. Cover and cook on low for 8 hours.

Nutrition Info per Serving:

Calories: 325, Total Fat: 9g, Saturated Fat: 2g, Carbohydrates: 16g, Protein: 34g, Cholesterol: 101mg, Fiber: 2g

Healthy Chicken Cacciatore

Prep Time: 15 minutes, Cook Time: 8 hours on low, Serves: 6

INGREDIENTS:

- 3 tbsps. extra-virgin olive oil, divided
- 2 pounds (907 g) boneless chicken thighs
- 1 (14-ounce, 397 g) can stewed tomatoes
- 1 cup quartered button mushrooms
- ½ sweet onion, chopped
- 2 cups chicken broth
- Freshly ground black pepper, for seasoning
- Salt, for seasoning
- 1 tbsp. minced garlic
- 1 tsp. dried basil
- 1 tbsp. dried oregano
- Pinch red pepper flakes

DIRECTIONS:

1. Use 1 tablespoon of the olive oil to lightly grease the insert of the crock pot.
2. Season the chicken thighs lightly with pepper and salt.
3. Heat the remaining 2 tablespoons of the olive oil in a large skillet over medium-high heat. Stir in the chicken thighs and brown for about 8 minutes, turning once.
4. Place the chicken into the insert and add the mushrooms, onion, tomatoes, garlic, broth, basil, oregano, and red pepper flakes.
5. Cover and cook on low for 8 hours.
6. After the cooking is finished, serve the cacciatore warm.

Nutrition Info per Serving:

Calories: 425, Total Fat: 32 g, Total Carbs: 8 g, Net Carbs: 7 g, Protein: 27 g, Fiber: 1 g

Thai Chicken with Kale

Prep Time: 20 minutes, Cook Time: 6 to 8 hours, Serves: 8

INGREDIENTS:

- 10 (4-ounce, 113g) boneless, skinless chicken thighs
- 2 (16-ounce, 454g) packages prepared collard greens
- 2 cups chopped kale
- 2 onions, chopped
- 1 cup canned coconut milk
- 1 cup chicken stock
- 2 red chili peppers, minced
- 6 garlic cloves, minced
- 1 lemongrass stalk
- 3 tbsps. freshly squeezed lime juice

DIRECTIONS:

1. Combine vegetables and kale in a 6-quart crock pot, then add onion, garlic, pepper, lemongrass, and chicken. Pour in chicken broth and coconut milk.
2. Cook on low heat for 6 to 8 hours, close the lid, until the chicken shows 165°F on the food thermometer and the vegetables are tender.
3. Take out the lemongrass. Serve with lime juice.

Nutrition Info per Serving:

Calories: 338, Fat: 17g, Saturated Fat: 9g, Protein: 33g, Carbohydrates: 15g, Sugar: 3g, Fiber: 7g, Sodium: 173mg

Slow Cooked Buffalo Chicken

Prep Time: 10 minutes, Cook Time: 6 hours on low, Serves: 4

INGREDIENTS:

- 3 tbsps. olive oil, divided
- 1 pound (454 g) boneless chicken breasts
- ½ sweet onion, finely chopped
- 1 cup hot sauce
- ⅓ cup coconut oil, melted
- ¼ cup water
- 1 tsp. minced garlic
- 2 tbsps. chopped fresh parsley, for garnish

DIRECTIONS:

1. Use 1 tablespoon of the olive oil to lightly grease the insert of the crock pot.
2. Heat the remaining 2 tablespoons of the olive oil in a large skillet over medium-high heat. Stir in the chicken and brown for 5 minutes, turning once.
3. Place the chicken into the insert and arrange in one layer on the bottom.
4. Add the coconut oil, onion, hot sauce, garlic and water to a small bowl, whisk them together. Pour the mixture over the chicken.
5. Cover the cooker and cook on low for 6 hours.
6. Top with the parsley and serve.

Nutrition Info per Serving:

Calories: 376, Total Fat: 31 g, Total Carbs: 2 g, Net Carbs: 1 g, Protein: 26 g, Fiber: 1 g

Slow Cooked Jambalaya

Prep Time: 15 minutes, Cook Time: 9 hours, Serves: 6

INGREDIENTS:

- 6 boneless, skinless chicken thighs, cut into 1-inch pieces
- 6 ounces (170 g) smoked turkey sausage, cut into 1-inch pieces
- 6 ounces (170 g) raw shrimp, peeled and deveined
- 3 cups cooked brown rice
- 2 cups chopped okra
- 2 green bell peppers, seeded and chopped
- 2 (14-ounce, 397 g) cans diced tomatoes and peppers, with their juice
- 1 onion, chopped
- 6 garlic cloves, chopped
- ½ tsp. sea salt
- ¼ tsp. cayenne pepper

DIRECTIONS:

1. Combine the chicken, turkey sausage, onion, garlic, okra, bell peppers, tomatoes and peppers (with their juice), salt, and cayenne in your crock pot.
2. Cover and cook on low for 8 hours.
3. Add shrimp. Cover and cook for 1 more hour.
4. Serve spooned over the cooked rice.

Nutrition Info per Serving:

Calories: 485, Total Fat: 11g, Saturated Fat: 3g, Carbohydrates: 49g, Protein: 46g, Fiber: 6g

Crock Pot Chicken, Carrot and Bacon Soup

Prep Time: 15 minutes, Cook Time: 8 hours on low, Serves: 8

INGREDIENTS:

- 1 tbsp. extra-virgin olive oil
- 3 cups cooked chicken, chopped
- 1½ cups heavy(whipping) cream
- 2 celery stalks, chopped
- 1 sweet onion, chopped
- 1 carrot, diced
- 1 cup cooked chopped bacon
- 1 cup cream cheese
- 6 cups chicken broth
- 2 tsps. minced garlic
- 1 tbsp. chopped fresh parsley, for garnish

DIRECTIONS:

1. Use the olive oil to lightly grease the insert of the crock pot.
2. Stir in the chicken, broth, celery, onion, carrot, and garlic.
3. Cover the cooker and turn on low, cook for 8 hours.
4. Add the bacon, cream cheese and heavy cream, stir well.
5. Top with the parsley and serve.

Nutrition Info per Serving:

Calories: 488, Total Fat: 37 g, Total Carbs: 11 g, Net Carbs: 10 g, Protein: 27 g, Fiber: 1 g

Buttery Herb Lemon Chicken

INGREDIENTS:

- 3 tbsps. extra-virgin olive oil
- 2 tbsps. butter
- 1½ pounds (680 g) boneless chicken thighs
- 2 tsps. minced garlic
- ½ sweet onion, diced
- 2 tsps. dried oregano
- ½ tsps. salt
- ⅛ tsp. pepper, depending on taste
- Juice and zest of 1 lemon
- 1½ cups chicken broth
- 1 tbsp. Dijon mustard
- 1 cup heavy (whipping) cream

DIRECTIONS:

1. Use 1 tablespoon of the olive oil to lightly grease the insert of the crock pot.
2. Heat the remaining 2 tablespoons of the olive oil and the butter in a large skillet over medium-high heat. Stir in the chicken and brown for 5 minutes, turning once.
3. Place the chicken into the insert and stir in the garlic, onion, oregano, salt, and pepper.
4. Add the lemon juice and zest, broth and mustard to a small bowl, whisk them together. Pour over the chicken with the mixture.
5. Cover the cooker and cook on low for 7 to 8 hours.
6. After cooking, add the heavy cream and stir well, serve.

Nutrition Info per Serving:

Calories: 400, Total Fat: 34 g, Total Carbs: 2 g, Net Carbs: 2 g, Protein: 22 g, Fiber: 0 g

Turkey Legs with Parsley

INGREDIENTS:

- 3 tbsps. extra-virgin olive oil, divided
- 2 pounds (907 g) boneless turkey legs
- ½ cup chicken broth
- 2 tsps. poultry seasoning
- 1 tbsp. dried thyme
- Salt, for seasoning
- Freshly ground black pepper, for seasoning
- 2 tbsps. chopped fresh parsley, for garnish

DIRECTIONS:

1. Use 1 tablespoon of the olive oil to lightly grease the insert of the crock pot.
2. Heat the remaining 2 tablespoons of the olive oil in a large skillet over medium-high heat.
3. Season the turkey with salt and pepper generously. Sprinkle poultry seasoning and thyme over. In the skillet, add the turkey and brown for about 7 minutes, turning once.
4. Place the turkey into the crock pot, pour in the broth.
5. Cover and set on low, cook for 7 to 8 hours.
6. Top with the parsley and serve.

Nutrition Info per Serving:

Calories: 363, Total Fat: 29 g, Total Carbs: 1 g, Net Carbs: 1 g, Protein: 28 g, Fiber: 0 g

Turkey Meatballs with Marinara Sauce

INGREDIENTS:

- 3 tbsps. extra-virgin olive oil
- 1 pound (454 g) ground turkey
- 1 pound (454 g) breakfast sausage, crumbled
- 2 cups simple marinara sauce
- 1 cup shredded
- Mozzarella Cheese
- 1 egg
- ½ cup almond flour
- 1 tbsp. chopped basil
- 2 tsps. chopped oregano
- ½ tsp. salt
- ¼ tsp. freshly ground black pepper

DIRECTIONS:

1. Use 1 tablespoon of the olive oil to lightly grease the insert of the crock pot.
2. Add the egg, turkey, almond flour, sausage, basil, oregano, salt and pepper into a large bowl, mix them together. Form the mixture into golf ball-sized meatballs.
3. Heat the remaining 2 tablespoons of the olive oil in a large skillet over medium-high heat, place the meatballs in the skillet and brown for 7 minutes, turning several times.
4. In the insert of the crock pot, add the meatballs and marinara sauce.
5. Cover the cooker and set on low, cook for 6 hours.
6. Top with the mozzarella cheese and serve.

Nutrition Info per Serving:

Calories: 514, Total Fat: 41 g, Total Carbs: 4 g, Net Carbs: 3 g, Protein: 35 g, Fiber: 1 g

Slow Cooked Tom Kha Gai

INGREDIENTS:

- Juice of 1 lime
- 1 pound (454 g) boneless, skinless chicken thighs, cut into 1-inch pieces
- 1 pound (454 g) fresh shiitake mushrooms, halved
- 3 cups (720 ml) poultry broth, or store bought
- 3 cups (720 ml) canned light coconut milk
- 2 tbsps. chopped fresh cilantro
- 1 tbsp. Asian fish sauce
- 2 tbsps. grated fresh ginger
- 1 tsp. garlic powder
- ¼ tsp. freshly ground black pepper

DIRECTIONS:

1. In your crock pot, combine the chicken thighs, mushrooms, broth, fish sauce, ginger, coconut milk, garlic powder, and pepper.
2. Cover and cook on low for 8 hours.
3. Add the lime juice and cilantro just before serving.

Nutrition Info per Serving:

Calories: 481, Total Fat: 35g, Saturated Fat: 27g, Carbohydrates: 19g, Protein: 28g, Fiber: 5g

Hearty Spiced Garlic Pumpkin Chicken Soup

Prep Time: 15 minutes, Cook Time: 6 hours on low, Serves: 6

INGREDIENTS:

- 1 tbsp. extra-virgin olive oil
- 2 cups coconut milk
- 4 cups chicken broth
- ½ sweet onion, chopped
- 1 pound (454 g) pumpkin, diced
- 1 cup heavy (whipping) cream
- 2 cups chopped
- cooked chicken
- ½ tsp. ground cinnamon
- 1 tbsp. grated fresh ginger
- 2 tsps. minced garlic
- ¼ tsp. freshly ground black pepper
- ¼ tsp. ground nutmeg
- ¼ tsp. salt
- Pinch ground allspice

DIRECTIONS:

1. Use the olive oil to lightly grease the insert of the crock pot.
2. In the insert of the crock pot, add the coconut milk, broth, onion, pumpkin, cinnamon, ginger, garlic, pepper, nutmeg, salt, and allspice.
3. Cover the cooker and cook on low for 6 hours.
4. After cooking, purée the soup with an immersion blender or regular blender.
5. Return the soup to the pot if you blend with a regular blender, and stir in the cream and chicken.
6. Cook the soup on low for 15 minutes to heat the chicken through, and then serve warm.

Nutrition Info per Serving:

Calories: 389, Total Fat: 32 g, Total Carbs: 10 g, Net Carbs: 5 g, Protein: 16 g, Fiber: 5 g

Tomato Chicken Breasts

Prep Time: 15 minutes, Cook Time: 3-8 hours, Serves: 6

INGREDIENTS:

- 6 bone-in chicken breast halves
- 2 14½-oz. cans diced tomatoes, undrained
- 1 small can jalapeños, sliced, drained
- ¼ cup reduced-fat, creamy peanut butter
- 2 tbsps. fresh cilantro, chopped

DIRECTIONS:

1. Fetch skin from chicken and leave bone in.
2. In medium-sized bowl, combine all ingredients except chicken.
3. Pour one-third of sauce into bottom of crock pot sprayed with non-fat cooking spray, arrange the chicken on top.
4. Pour remaining sauce over chicken.
5. Cover and cook for 3-4 hours.
6. Fetch from crock pot gently, chicken will be tender and will fall off the bones.

Nutrition Info per Serving:

Calories: 230, Total fat: 7g, Sodium: 650mg, Total carbohydrate: 11g, Protein: 31g

Savory Butter Chicken

Prep Time: 20 minutes, Cook Time: 7½ to 9½ hours, Serves: 8

INGREDIENTS:

- 10 (4-ounce, 113g) boneless, skinless chicken thighs
- 4 large tomatoes, seeded and chopped
- 2 onions, chopped
- ⅓ cup lemon juice
- ½ cup plain Greek
- yogurt
- ⅔ cup canned coconut milk
- 8 garlic cloves, sliced
- 5 tsps curry powder
- 2 tbsps. grated fresh ginger root
- 3 tbsps. cornstarch

DIRECTIONS:

1. Mix yogurt, lemon juice, curry powder and ginger root in a medium bowl. Add chicken and stir well, set aside and let stand for 15 minutes.
2. Combine tomatoes, onions, and garlic in a 6-quart crock pot.
3. Pour the chicken yogurt mixture into the crock pot. Cover the lid and cook on low heat for 7 to 9 hours, until the chicken is cooked through.
4. Mix the coconut milk and cornstarch in a small bowl. Then pour into the crock pot.
5. Cook on low heat for 15 to 20 minutes, until the sauce thickens. Serve immediately!

Nutrition Info per Serving:

Calories: 295, Fat: 15g, Saturated Fat: 7g, Protein: 30g, Carbohydrates: 12g, Sugar: 5g, Fiber: 2g, Sodium: 124mg

Spicy Jerk Chicken

Prep Time: 15 minutes, Cook Time: 7 to 8 hours on low, Serves: 6

INGREDIENTS:

- ½ cup extra-virgin olive oil, divided
- 2 pounds (907 g) boneless chicken (breast and thighs)
- 1 sweet onion, quartered
- 2 habanero chiles, stemmed and seeded
- 4 garlic cloves
- 2 scallions, white and green parts, coarsely
- chopped
- 2 tbsps. granulated erythritol
- 1 tbsp. grated fresh ginger
- 1 tsp. dried thyme
- 2 tsps. allspice
- ½ tsp. cardamom
- ½ tsp. salt
- 2 tbsps. chopped cilantro, for garnish

DIRECTIONS:

1. Use 1 tablespoon of the olive oil to lightly grease the insert of the crock pot.
2. In the bottom of the insert, arrange with the chicken pieces.
3. Add the remaining olive oil, garlic, onion, chiles, scallions, ginger, erythritol, thyme, allspice, cardamom and salt in a blender, pulse them until a thick, uniform sauce forms.
4. Over the chicken, add this sauce, toss to coat the pieces.
5. Cover the cooker and set on low, cook for 7 to 8 hours.
6. Top with the cilantro and serve.

Nutrition Info per Serving:

Calories: 485, Total Fat: 40 g, Total Carbs: 5 g, Net Carbs: 4 g, Protein: 27 g, Fiber: 1 g

Garlicky Whole Chicken

Prep Time: 15 minutes, Cook Time: 3 to 4 hours, Serves: 3 or 4

INGREDIENTS:

- 1 tbsp. extra-virgin olive oil
- 1 whole chicken (3 to 3½ pounds, 1.4 to 1.6 kg)
- Onion powder
- Garlic powder
- Black pepper
- Salt

DIRECTIONS:

1. Use olive oil to rub all over the skin of the chicken. In a bowl, combine the pepper, salt, onion powder and garlic powder, then use the mixture to season the chicken all over, including in the cavity.
2. Tear four or five sheets of aluminum foil and roll them into balls. In the bottom of a 5- to 6-quart crock pot, place the foil balls. On top of the foil balls, set with the chicken, adjusting them as necessary to support the chicken and keep it above the cooking juices that will accumulate in the bottom of the crock pot as the chicken cooks.
3. Cover the cooker and cook on high for 3 to 4 hours or until the juices run clear and insert into the thickest part of a thigh with an instant-read meat thermometer registers 180°F(82°C).
4. Remove the chicken from the cooker and transfer onto a large plate or platter. Allow it to cool completely. Remove the meat from the bones and shred it with two forks.

Turkey, Cranberries and Wild Rice

Prep Time: 10 minutes, Cook Time: 8 hours, Serves: 6

INGREDIENTS:

- 1 pound (454 g) boneless, skinless turkey thighs, cut into 1-inch chunks
- 1 cup uncooked wild rice
- 1 cup fresh or frozen cranberries
- 1 onion, chopped
- 3 cups (720 ml) poultry broth
- Zest and juice of 1 orange
- 1 tsp. garlic powder
- 1 tsp. dried thyme
- ½ tsp. sea salt
- ¼ tsp. freshly ground black pepper

DIRECTIONS:

1. Mix the turkey, wild rice, cranberries, broth, onion, garlic powder, orange zest (reserve the juice), thyme, salt, and pepper in your crock pot.
2. Cover and cook on low for 8 hours.
3. Stir in the fresh orange juice and serve.

Nutrition Info per Serving:

Calories: 202, Total Fat: 2g, Saturated Fat: 1g, Carbohydrates: 25g, Protein: 21g, Cholesterol: 63mg, Fiber: 3g

Sweet and Sour Meatballs

Prep Time: 15 minutes, Cook Time: 8 hours, Serves: 6

INGREDIENTS:

- 1 pound (454 g) ground turkey breast
- 1 onion, grated
- 1 egg, beaten
- 2 tbsps. honey
- 1 tbsp. cornstarch
- 1 tsp. sea salt, divided
- ¼ tsp. freshly ground black pepper
- 1 (8-ounce, 227 g) can pineapple chunks (no sugar added), with its juice
- ¼ cup (60 ml) apple cider vinegar
- ½ cup whole-wheat bread crumbs

DIRECTIONS:

1. Mix the ground turkey, onion, egg, bread crumbs, salt, and the pepper in a medium bowl.
2. Form the mixture into meatballs with small scoop. Put the meatballs in your crock pot.
3. Whisk together the juice from the canned pineapple (reserve the pineapple chunks), honey, vinegar, cornstarch, and remaining salt in a small bowl.
4. Add the mixture to the crock pot, then add the pineapple chunks.
5. Cover and cook on low for 8 hours.

Nutrition Info per Serving:

Calories: 217, Total Fat: 7g, Saturated Fat: 2g, Carbohydrates: 16g, Protein: 23g, Fiber: 1g

Roasted Chicken with Squash and Mushroom

Prep Time: 20 minutes, Cook Time: 6 to 8 hours, Serves: 8

INGREDIENTS:

- 8 (6-ounce, 170g) bone-in, skinless chicken breasts
- 1 (3-pound, 1.4kg) butternut squash, peeled, seeded, and cut into 1-inch pieces
- 2 (1-pound, 454g) acorn squash, peeled, seeded, and cut into 1-inch pieces
- 1 (8-ounce, 227g) package cremini mushrooms, sliced
- 2 fennel bulbs, cored and sliced
- 1 cup chicken stock
- ½ cup canned coconut milk
- 3 sprigs fresh thyme
- 1 bay leaf
- 2 tbsps. lemon juice

DIRECTIONS:

1. Combine butternut squash, acorn squash, fennel, mushrooms, chicken, thyme, bay leaf, chicken broth, and coconut milk in a 6-quart crock pot. Cover the lid and cook on low heat for 6 to 8 hours until the chicken turns white.
2. Take out thyme sprigs and bay leaves. Finally, top with lemon juice and serve immediately!

Nutrition Info per Serving:

Calories: 330, Fat: 8g, Saturated Fat: 3g, Protein: 43g, Carbohydrates: 21g, Sugar: 3g, Fiber: 4g, Sodium: 67mg

Turkey Breast with Avocado Salsa

Prep Time: 25 minutes, Cook Time: 7 to 8 hours on low, Serves: 6

INGREDIENTS:

- 3 tbsps. extra-virgin olive oil, divided
- 1½ pounds (680 g) turkey breasts
- 1 cup coconut milk
- 1 tomato, diced
- 1 avocado, peeled, pitted, and chopped
- ½ jalapeño pepper, diced
- Salt, for seasoning
- freshly ground black pepper, for seasoning
- 2 tsps. minced garlic
- 1 tsp. dried oregano
- 2 tsps. dried thyme
- 1 tbsp. chopped cilantro

DIRECTIONS:

1. Use 1 tablespoon of the olive oil to lightly grease the insert of the crock pot.
2. Heat the remaining 2 tablespoons of the olive oil in a large skillet over medium-high heat.
3. Season the turkey with salt and pepper lightly. Place the turkey into the skillet and brown for about 7 minutes, turning once.
4. In the insert of the crock pot, add the turkey, garlic, coconut milk, oregano and thyme.
5. Cover and set on low, cook for 7 to 8 hours.
6. Add the tomato, avocado, cilantro and jalapeño pepper into a small bowl, stir them together.
7. Pour the avocado salsa over the turkey and serve.

Nutrition Info per Serving:

Calories: 347, Total Fat: 27 g, Total Carbs: 5 g, Net Carbs: 2 g, Protein: 25 g, Fiber: 3 g

Chicken Corn Chowder

Prep Time: 10 minutes, Cook Time: 8 hours, Serves: 6

INGREDIENTS:

- 1 pound (454 g) boneless, skinless chicken thighs, cut into 1-inch pieces
- 2 onions, chopped
- 1½ cups fresh or frozen corn
- 3 jalapeño peppers, seeded and minced
- 2 red bell peppers, seeded and chopped
- 6 cups (1440 ml) poultry broth, or store bought
- 1 cup (240 ml) skim milk
- 1 tsp. garlic powder
- ½ tsp. sea salt
- ¼ tsp. freshly ground black pepper

DIRECTIONS:

1. In your crock pot, combine the chicken, onions, corn, broth, jalapeños, red bell peppers, garlic powder, salt, and pepper.
2. Cover and cook on low for 8 hours.
3. Put in the skim milk just before serving.

Nutrition Info per Serving:

Calories: 236, Total Fat: 6g, Saturated Fat: 2g, Carbohydrates: 17g, Protein: 27g, Cholesterol: 68mg, Fiber: 3g

Crock Pot Whole Duck

Prep Time: 15 minutes, Cook Time: 7 to 8 hours on low, Serves: 8

INGREDIENTS:

- 3 tbsps. extra-virgin olive oil, divided
- 1 (2½-pound, 1.1 kg) whole duck, giblets removed
- 1 sweet onion, coarsely chopped
- ¼ cup chicken broth
- 6 thyme sprigs, chopped
- 4 garlic cloves, crushed
- Freshly ground black pepper, for seasoning
- Salt, for seasoning
- 1 cinnamon stick, broken into several pieces

DIRECTIONS:

1. Use 1 tablespoon of the olive oil to lightly grease the insert of the crock pot.
2. Use the remaining 2 tablespoons of the olive oil to rub all over of the duck, season with pepper and salt. Stuff into the cavity of the duck with the thyme, garlic, and cinnamon.
3. Spread the onion onto the bottom of the crock pot and over it place with the duck and make it does not touch the bottom of the insert, and add the broth.
4. Cover and set on low, cook for 7 to 8 hours, or until an instant-read thermometer reads 180°F(82°C) of the internal temperature.
5. Serve warm.

Nutrition Info per Serving:

Calories: 364, Total Fat: 28 g, Total Carbs: 2 g, Net Carbs: 1 g, Protein: 29 g, Fiber: 1 g

CHAPTER 5

BEANS AND LEGUMES

Mixed Beans Chili

Prep Time: Less than 5 minutes, Cook Time: 8 hours (low), 4 hours (high), Serves: 8

INGREDIENTS:

- 2 (14.5-ounce, 411 g) cans diced tomatoes with chiles
- 2 (15-ounce, 425 g) cans chili beans (don't drain)
- 2 (15-ounce, 425 g) cans kidney beans, drained and rinsed
- 1 (15-ounce, 425 g) can black beans, drained and rinsed
- 1 (15-ounce, 425 g) can pinto beans, drained and rinsed
- 2 zucchini, chopped
- 2 medium onions, chopped
- 1 green bell pepper, seeded and chopped
- 3 cups grated Colby cheese
- ¼ cup tomato paste
- 1 dried chipotle
- 4 garlic cloves, minced
- 1 tbsp. chili powder
- 1 tsp. ground cumin
- tortilla chips for serving

DIRECTIONS:

1. Add all of the ingredients except the cheese into the crock pot, combine well.
2. Cover the cooker and cook on low for 8 hours or on high for 4 hours.
3. Take the chipotle out, add the cheese, and stir until it melts.
4. Serve with tortilla chips.

Lentils in Stock

Prep Time: 5 minutes, Cook Time: 7 to 8 hours, Serves: 6 cups

INGREDIENTS:

- 6 cups (1440 ml) vegetable broth, poultry broth, beef broth, or store bought
- 3 cups dried lentils, soaked overnight and rinsed

DIRECTIONS:

1. In your crock pot, mix the lentils and broth.
2. Cover and set on low. Cook for 7 to 8 hours until the lentils are soft.

Nutrition Info per Serving:

Calories: 172, Total Fat: 1g, Saturated Fat: 0g, Carbohydrates: 29g, Protein: 13g, Fiber: 15g

Garlic Black Beans with Sausage

Prep Time: 15 minutes, Cook Time: 8 hours, Serves: 6 to 8

INGREDIENTS:

- 3 (15-oz. 425 g) cans black beans, drained
- ¾ lb. lean smoked sausage, sliced in ¼-inch pieces and browned
- 8-oz. (227 g) can tomato sauce
- 1½ cups chopped green bell peppers
- 1½ cups chopped onions
- 1½ cups chopped celery
- 1 cup water
- 4 garlic cloves, minced
- 1½ tsps. black pepper
- 1 chicken bouillon cube
- 2 tsps. dried thyme
- 1½ tsp. dried oregano
- 3 bay leaves

DIRECTIONS:

1. Put all the ingredients into a crock pot.
2. Heat on High for 4 hours.
3. Discard bay leaves before serving.

Nutrition Info per Serving:

Calories: 250, Protein: 13 g, Fat: 9g, Carbohydrates: 34 g, Fiber: 11 g, Sodium: 1080 mg

Hearty Mixed Beans

Prep Time: 10 minutes, Cook Time: 4-5 hours, Serves: 8

INGREDIENTS:

- 16-oz. (454 g) can red kidney beans, drained
- 15½-oz. (439 g)can black beans, rinsed and drained
- 15-oz. (425 g) can butter beans, drained
- 15-oz. (425 g) can Great Northern beans, drained
- 1 lb. smoked sausage, cooked and cut into ½-inch slices
- 1½ cups ketchup
- ½ cup chopped onions
- 1 green pepper, chopped
- ¼ cup brown sugar
- 2 garlic cloves, minced
- 1 tsp. Worcestershire sauce
- ½ tsp. Tabasco sauce
- ½ tsp. dry mustard

DIRECTIONS:

1. Put all the ingredients into a crock pot. Stir well.
2. Cover the crock pot and heat on High for 4-5 hours.
3. Serve hot.

Quinoa and Beans Soup

Prep Time: 20 minutes, Cook Time: 3 to 8 hours, Serves: 6

INGREDIENTS:

- 1 (15-ounce, 425 g) can red kidney beans, drained and rinsed
- 1 (15-ounce, 425 g) black beans, drained and rinsed
- 1 (14-ounce, 397 g) can diced tomatoes
- 1 (14-ounce, 397 g) can whole-kernel corn, drained
- 6 cups no-sodium vegetable broth, plus more as needed
- 1 cup dried quinoa
- 2 celery stalks, cut into slices
- 2 carrots, cut into coins
- 1 zucchini, cut into coins and quartered
- ¼ cup tomato paste
- 2 garlic cloves, minced
- ½ large yellow onion, diced
- 1 tbsp. water, plus more as needed
- 1 tsp. ground cumin
- 2 tsps. chili powder

DIRECTIONS:

1. In a fine-mesh sieve, add the quinoa and rinse under cold water for 2 to 3 minutes, or until the cloudy water becomes clear.
2. Heat a 5-quart or larger crock pot on High for 5 to 10 minutes.
3. Combine the garlic, onion, celery, carrots, and 1 tablespoon of water in the preheated crock pot. Cook for 2 to 3 minutes. Stir in the tomato paste to combine.
4. Add all of the remaining ingredients to the cooker. Stir well. The tomato paste will fully incorporate as the soup cooks.
5. Switch the heat to low. Cover and cook on Low for 6 to 8 hours or cook on High for 3 to 4 hours. Add more broth or water, ½ cup at a time, if the soup seems too thick.

Nutrition Info per Serving:

Per Serving Calories: 334, Fat: 4 g, Carbohydrates: 62 g, Protein: 16 g, Fiber: 14 g

Chickpea and Potato Curry

Prep Time: 10 minutes, Cook Time: 9 hours, Serves: 6

INGREDIENTS:

- 1 pound (454 g) dried chickpeas, soaked overnight and rinsed
- 2 medium sweet potatoes, peeled and chopped
- 1 (14-ounce, 397 g) can crushed tomatoes
- 8 scallions, chopped
- 7 cups (1680 ml) vegetable broth
- ¼ cup chopped fresh cilantro
- 2 tbsps. curry powder
- 1 tsp. garlic powder
- ½ tsp. sea salt
- ¼ tsp. freshly ground black pepper

DIRECTIONS:

1. Mix the chickpeas, sweet potatoes, scallions, broth, tomatoes, salt, pepper, curry powder, garlic powder in your crock pot.
2. Cover and cook for 9 hours.
3. Add the cilantro just before serving.

Nutrition Info per Serving:

Calories: 394, Total Fat: 5g, Saturated Fat: 1g, Carbohydrates: 73g, Protein: 18g, Fiber: 19g

Five Beans and Bacon with Brown Sugar

Prep Time: 30minutes, Cook Time: 3-4hours, Serves: 15 to 20

INGREDIENTS:

- 28-oz. (794 g) can baked beans
- 16-oz. (454 g) can kidney beans, rinsed and drained
- 15½-oz. (439 g) can pinto beans, rinsed and drained
- 15½-oz. (439 g) can black-eyed peas, rinsed and drained
- 15-oz. (425 g) can lima beans, rinsed and drained
- 8 bacon strips, diced
- 2 onions, thinly sliced
- 1 cup packed brown sugar
- ½ cup cider vinegar
- 1 tsp. ground mustard
- ½ tsp. garlic powder
- 1 tsp. salt

DIRECTIONS:

1. In skillet, cook the bacon until crisp.
2. Remove it to paper towels. Drain, reserving 2 tbsps. drippings.
3. Sauté the onion until tender.
4. Add brown sugar, vinegar, salt, mustard and garlic powder to skillet and bring to a boil.
5. Add the beans, peas, onion mixture and bacon in a crock pot. Stir well.
6. Cover lid and heat at High for 3-4 hours.

Italian Lentils and Spaghetti

Prep Time: 10 minutes, Cook Time: 8 hours, Serves: 6

INGREDIENTS:

- 1 pound (454 g) dry lentils, soaked overnight and rinsed
- 2 (14-ounce, 397 g) cans diced tomatoes, drained
- 5 cups (1200 ml) vegetable broth
- 3 cups cooked whole-wheat spaghetti
- 2 carrots, peeled and finely chopped
- 1 onion, chopped
- 1 fennel bulb, finely chopped
- 2 tsps. garlic powder
- 2 tsps. dried Italian seasoning
- ½ tsp. sea salt

DIRECTIONS:

1. Mix the lentils, tomatoes, broth, garlic powder, onion, carrots, fennel, Italian seasoning, and salt in your crock pot.
2. Cover and cook on low for 8 hours.
3. Serve spooned over the whole-wheat spaghetti.

Nutrition Info per Serving:

Calories: 426, Total Fat: 2g, Saturated Fat: 0g, Carbohydrates: 80g, Protein: 26g, Fiber: 30g

Hearty White Bean and Chickpea Stew

Prep Time: 10 minutes, Cook Time: 6-8 hours, Serves: 1

INGREDIENTS:

- ½ cup lentils, rinsed and sorted
- ½ cup diced red bell pepper
- ½ cup diced carrots
- ½ cup white rice
- ½ cup canned chickpeas, drained and rinsed
- ½ cup canned white beans, drained and rinsed
- 2 cups low-sodium vegetable broth
- 1 ounce (28 g) pancetta, diced
- ¼ cup parsley
- ⅛ tsp. sea salt

DIRECTIONS:

1. In the crock pot, add all of the ingredients and stir to mix thoroughly.
2. Cover the cooker and set on low, cook for 6 to 8 hours.

Nutrition Info per Serving:

Calories: 599, Saturated Fat: 3 g, Trans Fat: 0 g, Carbohydrates: 91 g, Protein: 35 g, Fiber: 22 g

Spicy Quinoa and Black Beans with Pepper

Prep Time: 5 minutes, Cook Time: 10 hours (low), 5 hours (high), Serves: 6

INGREDIENTS:

- 1 pound (454 g) dried black beans, rinsed
- 2 large tomatoes, diced, or 1 (28-ounce, 784 g) can fire-roasted diced tomatoes
- ¾ cup uncooked quinoa, rinsed
- 1 medium onion, diced
- 2 jalapeños, halved and seeded, optional
- 2 medium bell peppers (any color), seeded and diced
- 3 cups vegetable stock
- 4 cups water
- 2 dried chipotles
- ¼ cup chopped fresh cilantro
- 1 garlic clove, minced
- 1 tsp. ground cumin
- 2 tsps. chili powder
- Sea salt
- Chopped avocado and lime wedges, for garnish

DIRECTIONS:

1. Add the black beans, chipotles, tomatoes, quinoa, onion, garlic, jalapeños, bell peppers, stock and water into the crock pot, combine them together.
2. Cover the cooker and cook on low for 10 hours or on high for 5 hours.
3. After cooking, add the cumin, chili powder, and cilantro, stir well. Taste and adjust with salt as needed.
4. Remove the chipotles, and place the chopped avocado and a squeeze of lime over the quinoa and beans before serving.

Slow Cooked Black Beans and Ham

Prep Time: 20 minutes, Cook Time: 10-12 hours, Serves: 8 to 10

INGREDIENTS:

- 4 cups dry black beans
- 1-2 cups diced ham
- 1 quart diced tomatoes
- 1 tsp. cumin
- ½-1 cup minced onion
- 2 garlic cloves, minced
- 1 tsp. salt, optional
- 1 tbsp. brown sugar
- 3 bay leaves

DIRECTIONS:

1. Place the black beans in a bowl and fill in the water to cover, allow to soak for 8 hours, or over night. Drain and pour beans into a crock pot.
2. Place all of the remaining ingredients in the cooker and stir well. Pour in the water to cover.
3. Cover the cooker and cook on Low for 10 to 12 hours.
4. After cooking, serve this black bean mixture over the rice.

Nutrition Info per Serving:

Calories: 275, Fat: 1.21 g, Carbohydrates: 50.6 g, Protein: 17.07 g

Curried Seitan and Chickpeas

Prep Time: 10 minutes, Cook Time: 6-8 hours, Serves: 1

INGREDIENTS:

- 1 tsp. extra-virgin olive oil
- 1 (15-ounce, 425 g) can chickpeas, drained and rinsed
- 8 ounces (227 g) seitan, cut into bite-size pieces
- 1 cup light coconut milk
- ½ cup minced onion
- 2 tbsps. tomato paste
- 1 tsp. curry powder
- 1 tsp. minced garlic
- 1 tsp. minced fresh ginger
- ½ tsp. garam masala
- ½ tsp. sea salt
- Pinch red pepper flakes

DIRECTIONS:

1. Use the olive oil to grease the inside of the crock pot.
2. In the crock pot, add all of the ingredients and stir to mix thoroughly.
3. Cover the cooker and set on low, cook for 6 to 8 hours.

Nutrition Info per Serving:

Calories: 302, Saturated Fat: 12 g, Trans Fat: 0 g, Carbohydrates: 17 g, Protein: 4 g, Fiber: 4 g, Sodium: 995 mg

Beans with Peppers and Onions

Prep Time: 15-20 minutes, Cook Time: 5-7 hours, Serves: 14 to 16

INGREDIENTS:

- 16-oz. can kidney beans, rinsed and drained
- 15½-oz. can Great Northern beans, rinsed and drained
- 15½-oz. can black-eyed peas, rinsed and drained
- 15-oz. can lima beans, rinsed and drained
- 15-oz. can black beans, rinsed and drained
- 1 onion, chopped
- 1 sweet red pepper, chopped
- 1 green pepper, chopped
- ⅛ tsp. pepper
- 1½ cups ketchup
- ½ cup packed brown sugar
- ½ cup water
- 2 bay leaves
- 2-3 tsps. cider vinegar
- 1 tsp. ground mustard
- grilled hamburgers, tossed salad for serving

DIRECTIONS:

1. Put the first 10 ingredients in a crock pot. Mix well.
2. Add remaining ingredients to the cooker.
3. Cover lid and heat on Low for 5-7 hours.
4. Discard bay leaves before serving.
5. Serve with grilled hamburgers, tossed salad.

Brown Sugar and Beef Calico Beans

Prep Time: 20 minutes, Cook Time: 2-6 hours, Serves: 10

INGREDIENTS:

- 1 lb. ground beef
- ¼-½ lb. bacon
- 1 medium onion, chopped
- 2-lb. can pork and beans
- 14½-oz. (411 g) can French-style green beans, drained
- 1-lb. can Great Northern beans, drained
- ½ cup brown sugar
- 2 tbsps. cider vinegar
- ½ cup ketchup
- 1 tbsp. prepared mustard
- ½ tsp. salt

DIRECTIONS:

1. In a skillet, cook ground beef, bacon, and onion until soft. Drain.
2. Put all the ingredients in the crock pot.
3. Cover the cooker and heat on High for 2-3 hours.
4. Serve warm.

Nutrition Info per Serving:

Calories: 400, Protein: 25.9 g, Fat: 11.22 g, Carbohydrates: 51.62 g

Sausage and Beans with Rice

Prep Time: 25 minutes, Cook Time: 4-6 hours, Serves: 8

INGREDIENTS:

- ½ lb. (227 g) or more fully cooked smoked turkey sausage or kielbasa, cut into ¼-inch slices
- 2 (16-oz. 454 g) cans kidney beans, drained
- 1 onion, chopped
- 4 cups rice, cooked
- 3 celery ribs, chopped
- 1¾ cups tomato juice
- 2 garlic cloves, minced
- ¾ tsp. dried thyme
- ¾ tsp. dried oregano
- ¼ tsp. pepper
- ¼ tsp. red pepper flakes
- shredded cheese, optional

DIRECTIONS:

1. In the crock pot, add all of the ingredients except the rice and shredded cheese, mix together well.
2. Cover the cooker and cook on Low for 4 to 6 hours.
3. Garnish with the shredded cheese, if you wish, and serve over the rice.

Nutrition Info per Serving:

Calories: 148, Fat: 7.7 g, Carbohydrates: 9.62 g, Protein: 10.38 g

Red Beans and Pepper Brown Rice

Prep Time: 10 minutes, Cook Time: 8 hours, Serves: 6

INGREDIENTS:

- 1 tbsp. smoked paprika
- 1 pound (454 g) dried red beans, soaked overnight and rinsed
- 8 cups (1920 ml) vegetable broth
- 3 cups cooked brown rice
- 2 green bell peppers, seeded and chopped
- 2 jalapeño peppers, seeded and chopped
- 1 tbsp. Creole seasoning
- 2 tsps. garlic powder
- 1 tsp. dried thyme
- ½ tsp. sea salt

DIRECTIONS:

1. Mix the beans, bell peppers, broth, thyme, paprika, jalapeños, Creole seasoning, garlic powder, and salt in your crock pot.
2. Cover and cook on low for 8 hours.
3. Stir in the rice.

Nutrition Info per Serving:

Calories: 467, Total Fat: 2g, Saturated Fat: 0g, Carbohydrates: 93g, Protein: 22g, Fiber: 15g

Crock Pot Mixed Beans with Sausage

Prep Time: 30 minutes, Cook Time: 7-9 hours, Serves: 6

INGREDIENTS:

- 1 tbsp. oil
- 28-oz. (794 g) can stewed or whole tomatoes
- 16-oz. (454 g) can kidney beans, drained
- 16-oz. (454 g) can pinto beans, drained
- ¾ lb. bulk Italian sausage
- 2¼-oz. (85 g) can ripe olives sliced, drained
- 1 green pepper, chopped
- 1 medium onion, chopped
- 1 garlic clove, minced
- 1 tsp. dried oregano
- 1 tsp. dried basil
- Parmesan cheese
- 1 tsp. salt

DIRECTIONS:

1. Place tomatoes, beans and olives in a crock pot, mix well.
2. Place sausage in skillet and brown on all sides. Transfer sausage to crock pot.
3. Add green peppers and stir-fry for 1 minute. Add onions and continue to stir until onions start to become translucent. Add garlic and cook for another minute. Transfer to a crock pot.
4. Add the seasonings, cover and cook on Low for 7-9 hours.
5. Sprinkle with Parmesan cheese before serving.

Smoky Beans, Beef and Sausage

Prep Time: 20 minutes, Cook Time: 4-6 hours, Serves: 10 to 12

INGREDIENTS:

- 1 lb. ground beef, browned
- ½-1 lb. small smoky link sausages
- 16-oz. (454 g) can kidney beans, drained
- 15-oz. (425 g) can pork and beans
- 15-oz. (425 g) can ranch-style beans, drained
- 1 large onion, chopped
- 1 cup ketchup
- 2 tbsps. brown sugar
- 2 tbsps. hickory-flavored barbecue sauce
- 1 tbsp. prepared mustard
- 1 tsp. salt

DIRECTIONS:

1. In a skillet, cook ground beef and onion until browned. Drain. Transfer to the crock pot and heat on High.
2. Put the remaining ingredients in the cooker. Mix well.
3. Turn to Low and cook 4-6 hours. Absorb oil that's risen to the top with a paper towel before stirring and serving.

Nutrition Info per Serving:

Calories: 285, Protein: 18.72 g, Fat: 13.74 g, Carbohydrates: 21.89 g

Black Bean, Tomato and Lentil Burritos

Prep Time: 15 minutes, Cook Time: 8 hours, Serves: 6

INGREDIENTS:

- 2 (15-ounce, 425 g) cans diced tomatoes
- 2 (15-ounce, 425 g) cans black beans, drained and rinsed
- 1 cup brown rice
- 2½ cups vegetable broth
- ½ cup lentils
- ½ cup corn, fresh, frozen, or canned
- ¼ cup salsa
- 2 tbsps. taco seasoning
- 2 chipotle peppers in adobo sauce, finely chopped
- 1 tsp. ground cumin
- 1 tsp. salt
- 12 whole wheat tortillas
- Additional toppings, such as more salsa, avocado or guacamole, and black olives

DIRECTIONS:

1. In a crock pot, combine the beans, salsa, tomatoes, corn, rice, taco seasoning, chipotles, cumin, salt, and broth. Cover and cook on low for 6 to 8 hours or on high for 3 to 4 hours.
2. Cook until 40 minutes left, add the lentils. Continue cooking until the lentils are tender. The rice will be tender and most of the liquid will be absorbed. This is the filling.
3. Lay out the tortillas and place about ⅓ to ½ cup of the filling on each tortilla. Spread the filling down through the center of the tortilla. Fold each end about 1½ inches over the point edge of the beans. And roll up the tortilla along the long edge.
4. Stack up and serve with more avocado, salsa or guacamole, and black olives.

Smoky Mixed Bean Chili

Prep Time: 10 minutes, Cook Time: 6-8 hours, Serves: 1

INGREDIENTS:

- 1 (16-ounce, 454 g) can mixed beans, drained and rinsed
- 1 cup frozen roasted corn kernels, thawed
- 1 cup canned fire-roasted diced tomatoes, undrained
- ½ cup diced onion
- 2 garlic cloves, minced
- 1 tsp. ground cumin
- 1 tsp. smoked paprika
- 1 tsp. dried oregano
- ⅛ tsp. sea salt

DIRECTIONS:

1. In the crock pot, add all of the ingredients. Stir quickly to combine.
2. Cover the cooker and set on low, cook for 6 to 8 hours.

Nutrition Info per Serving:

Calories: 257, Saturated Fat: 0 g, Trans Fat: 0 g, Carbohydrates: 58 g, Protein: 13 g, Fiber: 17 g

Apple, Sausage and Bean Stew

Prep Time: 15 minutes, Cook Time: 3½-4½ hours, Serves: 12

INGREDIENTS:

- 53-oz. (1502 g) can baked beans, well drained
- 1 pkg. smoky cocktail sausages
- 3 tart apples, peeled and chopped
- 1 large onion, chopped
- ½ cup barbecue sauce
- ½ cup firmly packed brown sugar

DIRECTIONS:

1. In a crock pot, combine beans, onions, and apples. Mix well.
2. Add barbecue sauce, brown sugar, and sausages to the cooker. Stir.
3. Cover and cook on Low for 3-4 hours, and then set it on High for 30 minutes.
4. Serve warm.

Nutrition Info per Serving:

Calories: 83, Protein: 2.73 g, Fat: 0.88 g, Carbohydrates: 18.99 g

Simple Crock Pot Beans

Prep Time: 10 minutes, Cook Time: 6 to 8 hours on low, Serves: 6

INGREDIENTS:

- 1 pound (454 g) dry beans (any type), rinsed
- Enough water to cover the beans in your crock pot by about 2 inches

DIRECTIONS:

1. Add beans to your crock pot.
2. Pour enough water over the beans to cover them by about 2 inches.
3. Cook on low for 6 to 8 hours.
4. Cool the beans and then store them in the fridge for a week or in the freezer for up to 3 months.

Nutrition Info per Serving:

Calories: 255, Total fat: <1 g, Protein: 17 g, Sodium: 9 mg, Fiber: 12 g

Simple Fava Beans

Prep Time: 5 minutes, Cook Time: 8 to 10 hours, Serves: 12

INGREDIENTS:

- 1 tbsp. olive oil
- 1 pound (454 g) fava beans, soaked overnight and rinsed
- 1 tsp. garlic powder
- ¼ tsp. sea salt
- 1 tsp. ground cumin

DIRECTIONS:

1. Mix the beans, garlic powder, salt, olive oil and cumin in your crock pot.
2. Add enough water to cover the beans by 2 inches.
3. Cover and cook on low for 8 to 10 hours until the beans are soft.

Nutrition Info per Serving:

Calories: 140, Total Fat: 2g, Saturated Fat: 0g, Carbohydrates: 22g, Protein: 10g, Fiber: 10g

White Bean and Spinach Casserole

Prep Time: 10 minutes, Cook Time: 8 hours, Serves: 6

INGREDIENTS:

- 4 cups baby spinach
- 2 cups dried white beans, soaked overnight and rinsed
- 1 onion, finely chopped
- 6 cups (1440 ml) vegetable broth
- 2 tsps. garlic powder
- Zest of 1 orange
- ½ tsp. sea salt
- ¼ tsp. freshly ground black pepper
- 1 tbsp. dried rosemary

DIRECTIONS:

1. Mix the beans, onion, rosemary, garlic powder, orange zest, broth, salt, and pepper in a crock pot.
2. Cover and cook on low for 8 hours.
3. About half an hour before serving, stir in the spinach.

Nutrition Info per Serving:

Calories: 256, Total Fat: 1g, Saturated Fat: 0g, Carbohydrates: 49g, Protein: 17g, Fiber: 11g

Cheesy Lentil Tacos

Prep Time: 15 minutes, Cook Time: 3-6 hours, Serves: 6

INGREDIENTS:

- 1 tsp. canola oil
- ½ lb. (227 g) dry lentils, picked clean of stones and floaters
- ¾ cup finely chopped onions
- ⅛ tsp. garlic powder
- 2 tsps. ground cumin
- 1 tbsp. chili powder
- 1 tsp. dried oregano
- 2 cups fat-free, low-sodium chicken broth
- 1 cup salsa
- 12 taco shells
- shredded lettuce
- chopped tomatoes
- shredded, reduced-fat cheddar cheese
- fat-free sour cream
- taco sauce

DIRECTIONS:

1. In a skillet, add the canola oil and onion, sprinkle over with the garlic powder and sauté until tender. Add the lentils, cumin, chili powder and oregano. Cook and stir for 1 minute, then transfer into the crock pot.
2. Pour the broth in the cooker.
3. Cover and cook on Low for 3 hours for somewhat-crunchy lentils, or on Low for 6 hours for soft lentils.
4. After cooking, add the salsa.
5. Spoon about ¼ cup into each taco shell. Place the lettuce, tomatoes, cheese, sour cream, and taco sauce on the top and serve.

Nutrition Info per Serving:

Calories: 340, Total Fat: 11 g, Total Carbohydrate: 42 g, Protein: 19 g, Sugar: 12 g, Fiber: 5 g, Sodium: 600 mg

Cheesy Mushroom and Green Bean Casserole

Prep Time: 15 minutes, Cook Time: 6 hours on low, Serves: 6

INGREDIENTS:

- 2 pounds (907 g) green beans, cut into 2-inch pieces
- ¼ cup butter, divided
- 1 cup sliced button mushrooms
- 8 ounces (227 g) cream cheese
- ½ sweet onion, chopped
- 1 cup chicken broth
- ¼ cup grated Parmesan cheese
- 1 tsp. minced garlic

DIRECTIONS:

1. Use 1 tablespoon of the butter to lightly grease the insert of the crock pot.
2. Melt the remaining butter in a large skillet over medium-high heat. Stir in the mushrooms, onion, and garlic, sauté for 5 minutes, until the vegetables are softened.
3. Add the green beans into the skillet, stir well and transfer the mixture to the insert.
4. Add the cream cheese and broth to a small bowl, whisk them together until smooth.
5. Transfer the cheese mixture into the vegetables and stir. Place the Parmesan over the combined mixture.
6. Cover the cooker and cook on low for 6 hours.
7. Serve warm.

Nutrition Info per Serving:

Calories: 274, Total Fat: 22 g, Total Carbs: 10 g, Net Carbs: 5 g, Protein: 9 g, Fiber: 5 g

Sweet and Sour Beans with Bacon

Prep Time: 10 minutes, Cook Time: 6-8 hours, Serves: 8

INGREDIENTS:

- 16-oz. can low-sodium lima beans, drained
- 16-oz. can low-sodium baked beans, undrained
- 16-oz. can low-sodium kidney beans, drained
- 4 slices lean bacon
- 1 onion, chopped
- 1 tsp. prepared mustard
- 1 clove garlic, crushed
- ¼ cup brown sugar
- ½ tsp. salt
- ¼ cup vinegar

DIRECTIONS:

1. In a nonstick skillet, cook bacon until browned.
2. Add bacon, 2 tbsps. drippings from bacon, onion, mustard, garlic, brown sugar, salt, and vinegar into a crock pot. Mix well.
3. Add beans into the cooker.
4. Cover lid and cook on Low for 6-8 hours.
5. Serve warm.

Nutrition Info per Serving:

Calories: 210, Protein: 11 g, Fat: 2 g, Carbohydrates: 40 g, Fiber: 9 g, Sodium: 570 mg

Green Beans with Cranberry and Walnut Mung

Prep Time: 20 minutes, Cook Time: 5-7 hours, Serves: 8

INGREDIENTS:

- 2 pounds (907g) fresh green beans
- ⅓ cup orange juice
- 1 onion, chopped
- ⅛ tsp. freshly ground black pepper
- 1 cup dried cranberries
- 1 cup coarsely chopped toasted walnuts
- ½ tsp. salt

DIRECTIONS:

1. Place green beans, onions, cranberries, orange juice, salt, and pepper in a 6-quart crock pot. Cook on low heat for 5 to 7 hours, close the lid until the green beans are soft.
2. Sprinkle walnuts at the end and serve immediately.

Nutrition Info per Serving:

Calories: 100, Fat: 3g, Saturated Fat: 0g, Protein: 2g, Carbohydrates: 18g, Sugar: 11g, Fiber: 3g

Sausage and Beans Lunch

Prep Time: 30 minutes, Cook Time: 2-4 hours, Serves: 6 to 12

INGREDIENTS:

- 2-3 tbsps. olive oil
- 1 lb. (454 g) sausage, cut into thin slices, or casings removed and crumbled
- 1-lb. (454 g) can red kidney beans, drained, with liquid reserved
- 1-lb. (454 g) can lima or butter beans, drained, with liquid reserved
- 1-lb. (454 g) can garbanzo beans, drained, with liquid reserved
- 1 large onion, chopped
- 10-oz. (283 g) can tomatoes with green chili peppers
- 1½ tsps. dry mustard
- ¼ cup honey
- 1 rib celery, sliced
- 1 tbsp. Worcestershire sauce

DIRECTIONS:

1. In a skillet, brown the sausage and onion in the oil.
2. In 6-quart crock pot, or divide between 2 4-quart cookers, add all of the ingredients and stir to combine. Add reserved juice from kidney, garbanzo beans and lima if there's enough room in the cookers.
3. Cover the cooker and cook on Low for 2 to 4 hours.

Nutrition Info per Serving:

Calories: 404, Fat: 21.33 g, Carbohydrates: 39.36 g, Protein: 20.02 g

CHAPTER 6

VEGETABLES

Cabbage Rolls with Worcestershire Sauce

Prep Time: 15 minutes, Cook Time: 8 hours, Serves: 6

INGREDIENTS:

- FOR THE SAUCE:
- 3 (14-ounce, 397 g) cans crushed tomatoes
- 1 onion, finely chopped
- 3 garlic cloves, minced
- 1 tbsp. low-sodium Worcestershire sauce
- ½ tsp. sea salt
- FOR THE CABBAGE ROLLS:
- 1 pound (454 g) fresh mushrooms, finely chopped
- 3 cups cooked brown rice
- 1 onion, finely chopped
- 3 garlic cloves, minced
- Nonstick cooking spray
- 1 egg, beaten
- 1 tbsp. low-sodium Worcestershire sauce
- 1 tsp. dried thyme
- ½ tsp. sea salt
- 1 large head napa cabbage, separated into leaves

DIRECTIONS:

To Make the Sauce:
1. Mix the tomatoes, Worcestershire sauce, onion, garlic, and salt in a large bowl, mixing well to form a sauce. Set aside.

To Make the Cabbage Rolls:
1. Spray the jar of your crock pot with nonstick cooking spray.
2. In another bowl, mix the cooked rice, mushrooms, onion, garlic, egg, Worcestershire sauce, thyme, and salt.
3. Scoop up some rice mixture and drop it in the center of a cabbage leaf. Roll the cabbage leaf around the filling, making sure all the edges are tucked in. Repeat until you have used up all the filling.
4. Place the cabbage rolls in the crock pot, covering each layer with tomato sauce.
5. Cover and cook on low for 8 hours.

Nutrition Info per Serving:

Calories: 309, Total Fat: 2g, Saturated Fat: 0g, Carbohydrates: 62g, Protein: 13g, Fiber: 11g

Easy Caramelized Onions

Prep Time: 15 minutes, Cook Time: 10 hours on low, Serves: 2 cups

INGREDIENTS:

- 2 tbsps. extra-virgin olive oil
- 4 large onions (white or sweet), sliced very thin
- ½ tsp. sea salt

DIRECTIONS:

1. Add the olive oil, onions and sea salt into the crock pot, stir to coat the onions with the oil.
2. Cover the cooker and cook for 10 hours on low. Drain the liquid and serve.

Nutrition Info per Serving:

Calories: 234, Total Fat: 14g, Saturated Fat: 1g, Protein: 3g, Total Carbs: 26g, Fiber: 5g, Sugars: 13g

Vegetable Tempeh Carnitas

Prep Time: 15 minutes, Cook Time: 6 hours (low), 3 hours (high), Serves: 6

INGREDIENTS:

- Cooking spray
- 5 garlic cloves
- 1½ pounds (680 g) tempeh, cut into bite-size cubes
- 1 tsp. dried oregano
- 1 tsp. ground cumin
- 1 tsp. chipotle powder
- ½ tsp. smoked paprika
- ½ tsp. sea salt
- 2 tbsps. fresh lime juice
- ¾ cup fresh orange juice
- 3 tbsps. chopped
- chipotles in adobo
- 12 flour tortillas
- FOR THE TOPPINGS:
- 1 medium onion, chopped
- 2 medium avocados, chopped
- 1 cup chopped fresh cilantro
- 3 jalapeños, seeded and chopped
- 6 lime wedges
- Salsa

DIRECTIONS:

1. Use cooking spray to spray the crock pot. Add the garlic, tempeh, oregano, cumin, chipotle powder, smoked paprika, and salt.
2. Combine the lime juice, orange juice, and chipotles to a medium bowl, mashing the chipotles into the liquids. Pour over the ingredients in the crock pot with this mixture.
3. Cover the cooker and cook on low for 6 hours or on high for 3 hours.
4. Add the tortillas to a dry skillet, warm over medium heat or in the microwave. Fill the warm tortillas with the filling and top with your choice toppings.
5. Squeeze the lime wedges over the carnitas and serve.

Mushroom and Snow Pea Pot

Prep Time: 15 minutes, Cook Time: 8 hours, Serves: 6

INGREDIENTS:

- 1 pound (454 g) fresh shiitake mushrooms, sliced
- 2 cups snow peas
- ¼ cup chopped fresh cilantro
- 8 cups (1920 ml) vegetable broth
- 8 scallions, sliced
- 1 tbsp. low-sodium soy sauce
- 2 tbsps. grated fresh ginger
- 1 tsp. garlic powder
- ½ tsp. sea salt
- 1 tbsp. sesame-chili oil

DIRECTIONS:

1. Mix the mushrooms, snow peas, broth, soy sauce, scallions, ginger, garlic powder, and salt in your crock pot.
2. Cover and cook on low for 8 hours.
3. Stir in the sesame-chili oil and cilantro before serving.

Nutrition Info per Serving:

Calories: 104, Total Fat: 1g, Saturated Fat: 0g, Carbohydrates: 24g, Protein: 4g, Fiber: 4g

Braised Cabbage with Onions

INGREDIENTS:

- 1 tbsps olive oil
- 1 large head green cabbage, cored and chopped
- 3 onions, chopped
- ½ cup roasted vegetable broth
- 6 garlic cloves, minced
- 2 tbsps. apple cider vinegar
- 2 tbsps. honey
- ½ tsp. salt

DIRECTIONS:

1. Combine all the ingredients in a 6-quart crock pot. Cover the lid and cook for about 6 to 7 hours, until the cabbage and onion are soft. Serve immediately!

Nutrition Info per Serving:

Calories: 75, Fat, 2g, Saturated Fat: 0g, Protein: 2g, Carbohydrates: 14g, Sugar: 10g, Fiber: 3g, Sodium: 171mg

Cheesy Spinach Black Bean and Corn Enchiladas

INGREDIENTS:

- 2 cups chopped fresh spinach
- 2 cups cooked black or pinto beans
- 2 cups fresh or frozen corn
- 2 tbsps. chopped chipotles in adobo
- 1 medium onion, chopped
- 1 tsp. ground cumin
- Sea salt
- 2½ cups Fire-Roasted Enchilada Sauce
- 12 corn tortillas
- 2 cups queso quesadilla or Monterey Jack cheese
- Cooking spray

DIRECTIONS:

The Night Before:

1. Add the spinach, beans, corn, chipotles in adobo, onion and cumin into a large bowl, combine well. Mix gently. Taste and add salt if necessary.
2. Heat the enchilada sauce in a large saucepan over medium heat. Dip each tortilla in the sauce and lay it on a flat surface, next add 2 tablespoons of the bean mixture, sprinkle the cheese over, and roll it up. Cover the enchiladas and place in the refrigerator to chill overnight. Store the remaining enchilada sauce and cheese for use in the morning.

In the Morning:

1. Use cooking spray to spray the crock pot. Lay the enchiladas in the crock pot, seam-side down. Add more layers to the top if you can't fit them all in one layer.
2. Place the remaining enchilada sauce to cover the enchiladas. Sprinkle any remaining cheese over top.
3. Cover the cooker and cook for 6 hours on low or 3 hours on high.
4. Serve the enchiladas hot from the crock pot.

Maple Braised Carrot Purée

INGREDIENTS:

- 8 large carrots, peeled and sliced
- 1 red onion, chopped
- ¼ cup maple syrup
- 2 tbsps. grated fresh ginger root
- ¼ cup canned coconut milk
- ½ tsp. salt

DIRECTIONS:

1. Put all ingredients in a 6-quart crock pot and stir to combine. Cover the lid and cook on low heat for 6 to 8 hours, until the carrots are very tender.
2. Then take the mixture out, put it in a potato masher or immersion blender, and stir to the desired consistency. Serve immediately!

Nutrition Info per Serving:

Calories: 80, Fat: 2g, Saturated Fat: 1g, Protein: 1g, Carbohydrates: 16g Sugar: 11g, Fiber: 2g, Sodium: 203mg

Buttery Braised Red Cabbage

INGREDIENTS:

- 1 tbsp. extra-virgin olive oil
- ½ sweet onion, thinly sliced
- 1 small red cabbage, coarsely shredded (about 6 cups)
- ¼ cup apple cider vinegar
- 2 tsps. minced garlic
- 3 tbsps. granulated erythritol
- ½ tsp. ground nutmeg
- ⅛ tsp. ground cloves
- 2 tbsps. butter
- Freshly ground black pepper, for seasoning
- Salt, for seasoning
- ½ cup crumbled blue cheese, for garnish
- ½ cup chopped walnuts, for garnish
- Pink peppercorns, for garnish (optional)

DIRECTIONS:

1. Use the olive oil to lightly grease the insert of the crock pot.
2. In the insert, add the onion, cabbage, apple cider vinegar, garlic, erythritol, nutmeg, and cloves, stirring to mix well.
3. Break off little slices of butter and scatter them over the cabbage mixture.
4. Cover the cooker and set on low, cook for 7 to 8 hours.
5. Season with pepper and salt.
6. Top with the blue cheese, walnuts, and peppercorns (if desired), and serve.

Nutrition Info per Serving:

Calories: 152, Total Fat: 12 g, Total Carbs: 4 g, Net Carbs: 3 g, Protein: 7 g, Fiber: 1 g

Crock Pot Buttery Spaghetti Squash

Prep Time: 15 minutes, Cook Time: 6 hours on low, Serves: 8

INGREDIENTS:

- ½ cup chicken stock
- 1 small spaghetti squash, washed
- ¼ cup butter
- Freshly ground black pepper, for seasoning
- Salt, for seasoning

DIRECTIONS:

1. In the insert of the crock pot, add the chicken stock and squash. The squash should not touch the sides of the insert.
2. Set on low and cook for 6 hours.
3. After cooking, allow the squash to cool for 10 minutes and cut in half.
4. Use a fork to scrape out the squash strands into a bowl. When finished, stir in the butter and toss to combine.
5. Season with pepper and salt, and serve.

Nutrition Info per Serving:

Calories: 98, Total Fat: 7 g, Total Carbs: 6 g, Net Carbs: 3 g, Protein: 1 g, Fiber: 3 g

Creamy Mushroom Stroganoff

Prep Time: 15 minutes, Cook Time: 6 hours on low, Serves: 6

INGREDIENTS:

- 3 tbsps. extra-virgin olive oil, divided
- 14 ounces (397 g) mushrooms, sliced
- ½ cup sour cream
- ½ cup heavy (whipping) cream
- 2 cups beef broth
- 2 tbsps. butter
- 2 tsps. minced garlic
- ½ sweet onion, diced
- 1 tbsp. tomato paste
- 3 tbsps. paprika
- 2 tbsps. chopped parsley, for garnish

DIRECTIONS:

1. Use 1 tablespoon of the olive oil to lightly grease the insert of the crock pot.
2. Heat the remaining 2 tablespoons of the olive oil and the butter in a large skillet over medium heat. Stir in the garlic, onion and mushrooms, sauté for 5 minutes, until they are softened.
3. Place the mushroom mixture into the insert and stir in the tomato paste, broth and paprika.
4. Cover the cooker and cook on low for 6 hours.
5. Add the sour cream and heavy cream, stir well.
6. Top with the parsley and serve.

Nutrition Info per Serving:

Calories: 236, Total Fat: 20 g, Total Carbs: 7 g, Net Carbs: 4 g, Protein: 7 g, Fiber: 3 g

Greek Eggplant and Chickpeas

Prep Time: 15 minutes, Cook Time: 8 hours, Serves: 6

INGREDIENTS:

- 2 eggplants, peeled and chopped
- 2 (14-ounce, 397 g) cans crushed tomatoes
- 2 cups cooked chickpeas, rinsed
- 2 onions, chopped
- 2 tsps. garlic powder
- 1 tsp. dried oregano
- ¼ tsp. ground cinnamon
- 3 ounces (85 g) low-fat feta cheese
- ½ tsp. sea salt
- ¼ tsp. freshly ground black pepper

DIRECTIONS:

1. Mix the eggplant, tomatoes, chickpeas, onions, garlic powder, oregano, salt, pepper, and cinnamon in your crock pot.
2. Cover and cook on low for 8 hours.
3. Garnish the feta cheese over the top just before serving.

Nutrition Info per Serving:

Calories: 191, Total Fat: 3g, Saturated Fat: 1g, Carbohydrates: 33g, Protein: 11g, Fiber: 13g

Healthy Stuffed Tomato Crock Pot

Prep Time: 20 minutes, Cook Time: 6 to 7 hours, Serves: 6

INGREDIENTS:

- 6 large tomatoes
- ¾ cup low-sodium whole-wheat bread crumbs
- 1 yellow bell pepper, stemmed, seeded, and chopped
- 3 garlic cloves, minced
- ½ cup roasted vegetable broth
- 1½ cups shredded Colby cheese
- ¼ cup finely chopped flat-leaf parsley
- 1 red onion, finely chopped
- 1 tsp. dried thyme leaves

DIRECTIONS:

1. Process the tomatoes. Cut off the top of the tomato and use a serrated spoon to core the tomato, leaving only the pulp. Set aside the tomatoes for later use.
2. Stir and combine the onion, bell pepper, garlic, breadcrumbs, cheese, parsley, thyme and reserved tomato pulp in a medium bowl.
3. Fill the tomatoes with the mixture and place them in a 6-quart crock pot. Pour the vegetable soup.
4. Put the lid on and cook on low heat for 6 to 7 hours, until the tomatoes are soft. Serve immediately!

Nutrition Info per Serving:

Calories: 187, Fat: 7g, Saturated Fat: 4g, Protein: 9g, Carbohydrates: 22g, Sugar: 6g, Fiber: 4g, Sodium: 143mg

Simple Mushroom Stroganoff

INGREDIENTS:

- 2 pounds (907 g) fresh portobello mushrooms, gills and stems removed, caps cut into ½-inch-thick slices
- 1 pound frozen pearl onions
- 3 cups cooked whole-wheat egg noodles
- 1½ cups (360 ml) vegetable broth
- ¼ cup (60 ml) dry white wine
- 1 tsp. garlic powder
- 1 tbsp. low-sodium Worcestershire sauce
- 1 tbsp. Dijon mustard
- 2 cups (480 ml) fat-free sour cream

DIRECTIONS:

1. Mix the mushrooms, pearl onions, and garlic powder in the crock pot.
2. Combine together the broth, wine, Worcestershire sauce, and mustard in a medium bowl. Add to the crock pot.
3. Cover and cook on low for 8 hours.
4. Stir in the sour cream. Serve over the egg noodles.

Nutrition Info per Serving:

Calories: 353, Total Fat: 2g, Saturated Fat: 1g, Carbohydrates: 63g, Protein: 17g, Fiber: 7g

Moroccan Vegetable Stew

INGREDIENTS:

- 1 tbsp. extra-virgin olive oil
- 2 cups chopped cauliflower
- 2 cups diced pumpkin
- ½ sweet onion, diced
- 1 red bell pepper, diced
- 2 cups coconut milk
- 2 tsps. minced garlic
- 2 tbsps. natural peanut butter
- 1 tsp. ground coriander
- 1 tbsp. ground cumin
- ¼ cup chopped cilantro, for garnish

DIRECTIONS:

1. Use the olive oil to lightly grease the insert of the crock pot.
2. In the insert, add the cauliflower, pumpkin, onion, bell pepper, and garlic.
3. Add the peanut butter, coconut milk, coriander and cumin to a small bowl, whisk them together until smooth.
4. Over the vegetables in the insert, pour with the coconut milk mixture.
5. Cover the cooker and cook on low for 7 to 8 hours.
6. Top with the cilantro and serve.

Nutrition Info per Serving:

Calories: 415, Total Fat: 35 g, Total Carbs: 14 g, Net Carbs: 7 g, Protein: 11 g, Fiber: 7 g

Flavory Caramelized Onion Dip Crock Pot

INGREDIENTS:

- 6 garlic cloves, minced
- 3 onions, sliced
- 2 cups sliced cremini mushrooms
- 2 tbsps. balsamic vinegar
- 2 white onions, chopped
- 1 bay leaf
- 2 tbsps. unsalted butter
- 1 tsp. dried thyme leaves
- 2 tbsps. cornstarch
- 2½ cups grated Gruyère cheese

DIRECTIONS:

1. Combine the onion, mushrooms, garlic, butter, bay leaf, thyme, and balsamic vinegar in a 6-quart crock pot.
2. Boil on low heat and cover, about 8 to 10 hours, until the onions are deep golden brown and very soft. Remove the mixture from the pot and remove the bay leaves.
3. In a medium bowl, add cheese and cornstarch, then add to the crock pot.
4. Put the lid on and cook for another 20 to 30 minutes on low heat until the cheese is melted.
5. Finally, take it out and enjoy with raw pancakes and corn flakes.

Nutrition Info per Serving:

Calories: 263, Fat: 17g, Saturated Fat: 11g, Protein: 15g, Carbohydrates: 9g, Sugar: 4g, Fiber: 1g, Sodium: 386mg

Summer Vegetable Medley

INGREDIENTS:

- ¼ cup balsamic vinegar
- ½ cup extra-virgin olive oil
- 1 tsp. dried thyme
- 1 tbsp. dried basil
- ¼ tsp. salt
- 2 zucchinis, diced into 1-inch pieces
- 2 cups cauliflower florets
- 1 cup halved button mushrooms
- 1 yellow bell pepper, cut into strips

DIRECTIONS:

1. Add the vinegar, oil, thyme, basil and salt to a large bowl, whisk them together until blended.
2. Place the zucchinis, cauliflower, mushrooms and bell pepper in the bowl, and toss to coat.
3. Place the vegetables into the insert of a crock pot.
4. Cover the cooker and cook on low for 6 hours.
5. Serve warm.

Nutrition Info per Serving:

Calories: 189, Total Fat: 18 g, Total Carbs: 5 g, Net Carbs: 4 g, Protein: 1 g, Fiber: 1 g

Buffalo Cauliflower with Navy Beans

Prep Time: 5 minutes, Cook Time: 8 hours, Serves: 2

INGREDIENTS:

- 1 head cauliflower, cut into small florets
- 3 cups cooked navy beans, rinsed
- ½ cup (120 ml) poultry broth
- ½ cup (120 ml) Louisiana hot sauce
- 1 tbsp. chili powder
- 2 tsps. ground cumin
- 1 red onion, finely chopped
- 2 celery stalks, diced
- ½ tsp. sea salt
- Pinch cayenne pepper
- ¼ cup crumbled blue cheese

DIRECTIONS:

1. Mix the cauliflower, onion, celery, navy beans, broth, hot sauce, chili powder, cumin, salt, and cayenne in your crock pot.
2. Cover and cook on low for 8 hours.
3. Garnished with the blue cheese. Serve.

Nutrition Info per Serving:

Calories: 190, Total Fat: 3g, Saturated Fat: 1g, Carbohydrates: 33g, Protein: 11g, Cholesterol: 4mg, Fiber: 13g

Creamy Cauliflower and Broccoli Casserole

Prep Time: 15 minutes, Cook Time: 6 hours on low, Serves: 6

INGREDIENTS:

- 1 tbsp. extra-virgin olive oil
- 1 pound (454 g) broccoli, cut into florets
- 1 pound (454 g) cauliflower, cut into florets
- 2 cups coconut milk
- 1½ cups shredded ground cheese, divided
- ¼ cup almond flour
- ½ tsp. ground nutmeg
- Pinch freshly ground black pepper

DIRECTIONS:

1. Use the olive oil to lightly grease the insert of the crock pot.
2. Add the cauliflower and broccoli to the insert.
3. Add the coconut milk, almond flour, nutmeg, 1 cup of the cheese and pepper to a small bowl, stir them together.
4. Over the vegetables pour with the coconut milk mixture, and place the remaining ½ cup of the cheese over the casserole.
5. Cover the cooker and cook on low for 6 hours.
6. Serve warm.

Nutrition Info per Serving:

Calories: 377, Total Fat: 32 g, Total Carbs: 12 g, Net Carbs: 6 g, Protein: 16 g, Fiber: 6 g

Curry Red Lentil and Spinach Napa Rolls

Prep Time: 10 minutes, Cook Time: 8 hours, Serves: 6

INGREDIENTS:

- 1½ cups dried red lentils, soaked overnight and rinsed
- 4 cups (960 ml) vegetable broth
- 1 tsp. ground cumin
- ½ tsp. ground coriander
- ½ tsp. curry powder
- ¼ tsp. sea salt
- 1 onion, chopped
- 6 garlic cloves, minced
- 2 cups chopped baby spinach
- 1 large head napa cabbage, separated into leaves

DIRECTIONS:

1. Mix the lentils, broth, cumin, coriander, onion, garlic, curry powder, and salt in your crock pot.
2. Cover and cook on low for 8 hours.
3. Mash the lentils with a potato masher. Stir in the baby spinach.
4. Serve with the napa cabbage leaves for wrapping.

Nutrition Info per Serving:

Calories: 202, Total Fat: 1g, Saturated Fat: 0g, Carbohydrates: 37g, Protein: 14g, Fiber: 17g

Healthy Curried Vegetables

Prep Time: 20 minutes, Cook Time: 6 to 8 hours, Serves: 8

INGREDIENTS:

- 4 large carrots, peeled and cut into chunks
- 3 cups broccoli florets
- 1 (8 ounce, 227g) package button mushrooms, sliced
- 2 medium sweet potatoes, peeled and cut into chunks
- 2 red bell peppers, stemmed, seeded, and chopped
- 2 medium zucchinis, cut into 1-inch slices
- 2 onions, chopped
- 3 garlic cloves, minced
- 1 cup canned coconut milk
- 5 cups roasted vegetable broth
- 2 to 4 tbsps. yellow curry paste

DIRECTIONS:

1. Put all the ingredients in a 6-quart crock pot and stir to combine with a spoon. Then put the lid on, put the crock pot on the stove and cook on low heat for 6 to 8 hours, until the vegetables are soft.
2. Transfer the mixed soup from the pot to the bowl and serve warm!

Nutrition Info per Serving:

Calories: 161, Fat: 6g, Saturated Fat: 5g, Protein: 4g, Carbohydrates: 32g, Sugar: 9g, Fiber: 6g, Sodium: 662mg

Garlic Bacon and Kale

Prep Time: 15 minutes, Cook Time: 6 hours on low, Serves: 8

INGREDIENTS:

- 2 tbsps. bacon fat
- 2 pounds (907 g) kale, rinsed and chopped roughly
- 12 bacon slices, cooked and chopped
- 2 cups vegetable broth
- 2 tsps. minced garlic
- Freshly ground black pepper, for seasoning
- Salt, for seasoning

DIRECTIONS:

1. Use bacon fat to grease the insert of the crock pot generously.
2. Place the garlic, bacon, kale, and broth into the insert. Toss to mix.
3. Cover the cooker and set on low, cook for 6 hours.
4. Season with pepper and salt, and serve hot.

Nutrition Info per Serving:

Calories: 147, Total Fat: 10 g, Total Carbs: 7 g, Net Carbs: 4 g, Protein: 7 g, Fiber: 3 g

Crock Pot Caramelized Onions

Prep Time: 10 minutes, Cook Time: 9 to 10 hours on low, Serves: 3

INGREDIENTS:

- ¼ cup extra-virgin olive oil
- 6 sweet onions, sliced
- ½ tsp. salt

DIRECTIONS:

1. Add the oil, onions and salt to a large bowl, toss them together. Place the mixture to the insert of the crock pot.
2. Cover the cooker and set on low, cook for 9 to 10 hours.
3. Serve, or cool in a sealed container, and store in the refrigerator for up to 5 days.

Nutrition Info per Serving:

Calories: 64, Total Fat: 5 g, Total Carbs: 5 g, Net Carbs: 3 g, Protein: 1 g, Fiber: 2 g

Roasted Bell Crock Pot

Prep Time: 20 minutes, Cook Time: 5-6 hours, Serves: 8

INGREDIENTS:

- 1 tsp. dried thyme leaves
- 1 red onion, chopped
- 8 to 10 bell peppers of different colors, stemmed, seeded, and halved
- 1 tbsp. olive oil

DIRECTIONS:

1. Place bell peppers in a 6-quart crock pot. Don't overfill it. Then drizzle with olive oil, sprinkle with red onion and thyme. Put the lid on and simmer for 5 to 6 hours. Stir once during cooking until the peppers are very tender and slightly browned on the edges.
2. If necessary, you may need to remove the bell pepper skin. They fall off easily. Serve immediately!

Nutrition Info per Serving:

Calories: 59, Fat: 2g, Saturated Fat: 0g, Protein: 2g, Carbohydrates: 9g, Sugar: 5g, Fiber: 3g, Sodium: 6mg

Low Carb Ratatouille

Prep Time: 15 minutes, Cook Time: 6 hours on low, Serves: 6

INGREDIENTS:

- 3 tbsps. extra-virgin olive oil, divided
- 1 cup diced pumpkin
- 2 zucchinis, diced
- 1 yellow bell pepper, diced
- 1 red bell pepper, diced
- 3 tsps. minced garlic
- ½ sweet onion, diced
- ¼ tsp. salt
- ¼ tsp. freshly ground black pepper
- Pinch red pepper flaskes
- 1 (14-ounce, 397 g) can diced tomatoes
- 1 cup crumbled goat cheese, for garnish

DIRECTIONS:

1. Use 1 tablespoon of the olive oil to lightly grease the insert of the crock pot.
2. In the insert, add the pumpkin, zucchini, red and yellow bell peppers, garlic, onion, salt, pepper, and red pepper flakes, toss to combine.
3. Stir in the remaining 2 tablespoons of the olive oil and the tomatoes.
4. Cover the cooker and set on low, cook for 6 hours.
5. Top with the goat cheese and serve.

Nutrition Info per Serving:

Calories: 232, Total Fat: 18 g, Total Carbs: 11 g, Net Carbs: 6 g, Protein: 7 g, Fiber: 5 g

Coconut Curry Vegetable Stew with Avocado

Prep Time: 15 minutes, Cook Time: 7 to 8 hours on low, Serves: 6

INGREDIENTS:

- 1 tbsp. extra-virgin olive oil
- 1 cup cauliflower florets
- 1 cup diced pumpkin
- 4 cups coconut milk
- 1 zucchini, diced
- 1 red bell pepper, diced
- 1 sweet onion, chopped
- 2 tsps. minced garlic
- 2 tsps. grated fresh ginger
- 1 tbsp. curry powder
- 2 cups shredded spinach
- 1 avocado, diced, for garnish

DIRECTIONS:

1. Use olive oil to lightly grease the insert of the crock pot.
2. Stir in the cauliflower, pumpkin, coconut milk, zucchini, bell pepper, onion, garlic, ginger, and curry powder.
3. Cover the cooker and set on low, cook for 7 to 8 hours.
4. Add the spinach and stir.
5. Garnish with avocado and serve.

Nutrition Info per Serving:

Calories: 502, Total Fat: 44 g, Total Carbs: 19 g, Net Carbs: 9 g, Protein: 7 g, Fiber: 10 g

Crock Pot Garlic Mushrooms

Prep Time: 10 minutes, Cook Time: 6 hours on low, Serves: 8

INGREDIENTS:

- 3 tbsps. extra-virgin olive oil
- 1 pound (454 g) button mushrooms, wiped clean and halved
- 2 tbsps. chopped fresh parsley
- 2 tsps. minced garlic
- ¼ tsp. salt
- ⅛ tsp. freshly ground black pepper

DIRECTIONS:

1. In the insert of the crock pot, add the olive oil, garlic, mushrooms, salt, and pepper, toss to coat.
2. Cover the cooker and set on low, cook for 6 hours.
3. Add the parsley and toss well before serving.

Nutrition Info per Serving:

Calories: 58, Total Fat: 5 g, Total Carbs: 2 g, Net Carbs: 1 g, Protein: 2 g, Fiber: 1 g

Mixed Vegetable Vindaloo

Prep Time: 15 minutes, Cook Time: 6 hours on low, Serves: 6

INGREDIENTS:

- 1 tbsp. extra-virgin olive oil
- 1 carrot, diced
- 4 cups cauliflower florets
- 1 red bell pepper, diced
- 1 zucchini, diced
- ½ sweet onion, chopped
- 1 dried Chipotle pepper, chopped
- 2 cups coconut milk
- 1 tbsp. grated fresh ginger
- 2 tsps. minced garlic
- 2 tsps. ground cumin
- 1 tsp. ground coriander
- ½ tsp. turmeric
- ¼ tsp. cardamom
- ¼ tsp. cayenne pepper
- 2 tbsps. chopped cilantro, for garnish
- 1 cup Greek yogurt, for garnish

DIRECTIONS:

1. Use the olive oil to lightly grease the insert of the crock pot.
2. In the insert, add the carrot, cauliflower, bell pepper and zucchini.
3. Add the remaining ingredients except for the yogurt and cilantro to a small bowl, whisk them together until well blended.
4. Pour the coconut milk mixture into the insert and combine well.
5. Cover the cooker and cook on low for 6 hours.
6. Top with the cilantro and yogurt, and serve.

Nutrition Info per Serving:

Calories: 299, Total Fat: 23 g, Total Carbs: 14 g, Net Carbs: 9 g, Protein: 9 g, Fiber: 5 g

Cheesy Zucchini and Tomato Casserole

Prep Time: 20 minutes, Cook Time: 4½ hours, Serves: 4

INGREDIENTS:

- 1 tbsp. extra-virgin olive oil
- 4 medium zucchinis, sliced
- One (15-ounce, 425 g) can diced tomatoes, with the juice
- 1 medium red onion, sliced
- 1 green bell pepper, cut into thin strips
- ¼ cup grated Parmesan cheese
- ½ tsp. basil
- 1 tsp. sea salt
- ½ tsp. black pepper

DIRECTIONS:

1. In the crock pot, add the zucchini slices, tomatoes, onion slices and bell pepper strips. Sprinkle with the basil, salt and pepper.
2. Cover the cooker and cook on low for 3 hours.
3. Drizzle over the casserole with the olive oil and sprinkle with the Parmesan. Cover the cooker and cook on low for another 1½ hours. Serve hot.

Healthy Root Vegetable Tagine

Prep Time: 20 minutes, Cook Time: 9 hours, Serves: 8

INGREDIENTS:

- 1 pound (454 g) carrots, peeled and chopped into bite-size pieces
- 1 pound (454 g) parsnips, peeled and chopped into bite-size pieces
- 1 pound (454 g) turnips, peeled and chopped into bite-size pieces
- 2 medium yellow onions, chopped into bite-size pieces
- 6 dried apricots, chopped
- 6 figs, chopped
- 1¾ cups vegetable stock
- ½ tsp. ground ginger
- 1 tsp. ground cumin
- 1 tsp. ground turmeric
- ½ tsp. ground cinnamon
- 1 tbsp. dried parsley
- ¼ tsp. cayenne pepper
- 1 tbsp. dried cilantro (or 2 tbsps. chopped fresh cilantro)

DIRECTIONS:

1. In the crock pot, combine the carrots, onions, parsnips, turnips, apricots, and fig. Sprinkle with the ginger, cumin, turmeric, cinnamon, parsley, cayenne pepper, and cilantro.
2. Pour in the vegetable stock. Cover and cook on Low for 9 hours. the vegetables will be very tender. Serve hot.

Crock Pot Carrots and Parsnips

Prep Time: 20 minutes, Cook Time: 5-7 hours, Serves: 8

INGREDIENTS:

- 2 tbsps. olive oil
- 6 large carrots, peeled and cut into 2-inch pieces
- 5 large parsnips, peeled and cut into 2-inch pieces
- 2 red onions, chopped
- 4 garlic cloves, minced
- 1 tbsp. honey
- ½ tsp. salt

DIRECTIONS:

1. Combine all the ingredients and gently stir in a 6-quart crock pot, stirring gently until fully combined. Cook on low heat for 5 to 7 hours, and cover until the vegetables are tender. Enjoy now!

Nutrition Info per Serving:

Calories: 138, Fat: 4g, Saturated Fat: 1g, Protein: 2g, Carbohydrates: 26g, Sugar: 10g, Fiber: 6g, Sodium: 199mg

Tasty Vegan Enchilada Casserole with Tempeh

Prep Time: 10 minutes, Cook Time: 6 hours (low) or 3½ hours (high), Serves: 6

INGREDIENTS:

- Cooking spray
- 2 pounds (907 g) tempeh, chopped
- 8 Roma tomatoes, chopped, or 1 (28-ounce, 784 g) can diced fire-roasted tomatoes
- 2 zucchinis, diced
- 2 cups fresh or frozen corn
- 1 medium onion, chopped
- 1½ medium jalapeños, seeded and chopped, or more as desired
- ½ cup chopped fresh cilantro
- 6 blue corn or other corn tortillas
- 1 tsp. ground cumin
- 1 tsp. ancho chili powder
- ½ tsp. garlic powder
- ½ cup sliced black olives

DIRECTIONS:

1. Use cooking spray to spray the crock pot.
2. Add all the ingredients into a large bowl, except the tortillas. On the bottom of the crock pot, spoon a thin layer of the vegetable mixture. Place a layer of tortillas to cover the mixture.
3. On the tortillas, spoon a thicker layer of the vegetable mixture. Cover with another layer of tortillas and repeat until the ingredients are used up, ending with a layer of tortillas.
4. Cover the cooker and cook on low for 6 hours or on high for 3½ hours.
5. Cut the casserole into slices and serve hot.

Dill Bacon and Asparagus

Prep Time: 10 minutes, Cook Time: 4 to 5 hours on low, Serves: 8

INGREDIENTS:

- 1 tbsp. extra-virgin olive oil
- 10 eggs
- 2 cups chopped asparagus spears
- 1 cup chopped cooker bacon
- ¾ cup coconut milk
- 2 tsps. chopped fresh dill
- ½ tsp. salt
- ¼ tsp. fresh ground black pepper

DIRECTIONS:

1. Use olive oil to lightly grease the insert of the crock pot.
2. Add the coconut milk, eggs, dill, salt and pepper into a medium bowl, whisk them together. Then stir in the bacon and asparagus. Transfer the mixture into the crock pot.
3. Cover the cooker and set on low, cook for 4 to 5 hours.
4. Serve warm.

Nutrition Info per Serving:

Calories: 225, Total Fat: 18 g, Total Carbs: 3 g, Net Carbs: 2 g, Protein: 14 g, Fiber: 1 g

Healthy Parmesan Eggplant

Prep Time: 20 minutes, Cook Time: 8-9 hours, Serves: 8

INGREDIENTS:

- 2 tbsps. olive oil
- 5 large eggplants, peeled and sliced ½-inch thick
- 2 (8-ounce, 227g) BPA-free cans low-sodium tomato sauce
- 2 onions, chopped
- 6 garlic cloves, minced
- ½ cup chopped toasted almonds
- ½ cup grated Parmesan cheese
- 1 tsp. dried Italian seasoning

DIRECTIONS:

1. Layer the sliced eggplants with onion and garlic in a 6-quart crock pot.
2. Combine tomato sauce, olive oil and Italian seasoning in a medium bowl. Then pour the ketchup mixture into the crock pot.
3. Cook on low heat for 8 to 9 hours, and cover until the eggplant is soft.
4. Mix Parmesan cheese and almonds in a small bowl. Sprinkle it on the eggplant mixture and serve.

Nutrition Info per Serving:

Calories: 206, Fat: 8g, Saturated Fat: 3g, Protein: 10g, Carbohydrates: 28g, Sugar: 14g, Fiber: 11g, Sodium: 283mg

Spiced Corn and Tomatoes

Prep Time: 20 minutes, Cook Time: 5-6 hours, Serves: 8

INGREDIENTS:

- 5 cups frozen corn
- 4 large tomatoes, seeded and chopped
- 2 onions, chopped
- 4 garlic cloves, minced
- 2 jalapeño peppers, minced
- ½ tsp. salt
- ⅛ tsp. cayenne pepper
- 1 tbsp. chili powder

DIRECTIONS:

1. Put all the ingredients in a 6-quart crock pot and stir to combine. Cover the lid and cook for 5 to 6 hours on low heat until the vegetables are soft. Serve immediately!

Nutrition Info per Serving:

Calories: 124, Fat: 1g, Saturated Fat: 0g, Protein: 4g, Carbohydrates: 29g, Sugar: 14g, Fiber: 5g, Sodium: 167mg

Crock Pot Quinoa Lentil Tacos

Prep Time: 5 minutes, Cook Time: 10 hours (low) or 5 hours (high), Serves: 6

INGREDIENTS:

- 1 tsp. smoked paprika
- 1 tbsp. Taco Seasoning Mix
- 1½ cups quinoa
- 1½ cups red lentils
- 6 cups vegetable stock
- 2 tbsps. chopped chipotles in adobo, or more as desired
- Whole-wheat tortillas
- FOR THE TOPPINGS:
- Chopped tomatoes
- Salsa

DIRECTIONS:

1. Add all the taco ingredients except the tortillas and the toppings to the crock pot, combine together.
2. Cover the cooker and cook on low for 10 hours or on high for 5 hours.
3. Place the tortillas in a dry skillet, warm over medium heat. Fill the warm tortillas with the filling and top with your choice toppings. Fold in half to serve.

Italian Roasted Beets and Tomato

Prep Time: 20 minutes, Cook Time: 5-7 hours, Serves: 8

INGREDIENTS:

- 10 medium beets, peeled and sliced
- 2 onions, chopped
- 4 garlic cloves, minced
- 4 large tomatoes, seeded and chopped
- 2 tbsps. olive oil
- 1 tsp. dried oregano leaves
- ½ tsp. salt
- 1 tsp. dried basil leaves

DIRECTIONS:

1. Combine the beets, tomatoes, onions, and garlic in a 6-quart crock pot. Drizzle with olive oil, sprinkle with dried herbs and salt for seasoning, stir until fully combined.
2. Turn on a low heat, close the lid, and cook for 5 to 7 hours until the beets are soft. Serve immediately!

Nutrition Info per Serving:

Calories: 100, Fat: 4g, Saturated Fat: 0g, Protein: 3g, Carbohydrates: 16g, Sugar: 10g, Fiber: 4g, Sodium: 215mg

Crock Pot Garlic

Prep Time: 10 minutes, Cook Time: 8 hours on low, Serves: 2

INGREDIENTS:

- ¼ cup extra-virgin olive oil
- 6 heads garlic
- Salt, for seasoning

DIRECTIONS:

1. On the counter, lay with a large sheet of aluminum foil.
2. Cut the heads of garlic the top off, exposing the cloves. Put the garlic on the foil, cut side up, and drizzle in the olive oil. Use salt to lightly season the garlic.
3. Use the foil to loosely fold around the garlic to form a packet. Transfer the packet in the insert of the crock pot.
4. Cover the cooker and cook on low for 8 hours.
5. After cooking, allow the garlic to cool for 10 minutes and then squeeze the cloves out of the papery skins.
6. Place the garlic in a sealed container, and store in the refrigerator for up to 1 week.

Nutrition Info per Serving:

Calories: 25, Total Fat: 2 g, Total Carbs: 2 g, Net Carbs: 2 g, Protein: 0 g, Fiber: 0 g

Spicy Vegetable Broth

Prep Time: 5 minutes, Cook Time: 8 to 12 hours,
Serves: 10 cups

INGREDIENTS:

- 4 ounces (113 g) fresh mushrooms
- 1 onion, roughly chopped
- 1 head garlic, halved crosswise
- 2 celery stalks (leaves included), roughly chopped
- 2 carrots, roughly chopped
- 2 fresh thyme sprigs
- 10   peppercorns

DIRECTIONS:

1. In your crock pot, mix all the ingredients. Fill the crock pot with water two-thirds of the way.
2. Cover and set on low. Cook for 8 to 12 hours.
3. Strain the broth through a fine-mesh colander, discarding the solids.
4. Store the broth in an airtight container in the refrigerator for up to 5 days or in the freezer for up to 1 year.

Nutrition Info per Serving:

Calories: 35, Total Fat: 0g, Saturated Fat: 0g, Carbohydrates: 4g, Protein: 0g, Fiber: 0g

Thai Green Vegetables and Soybean

Prep Time: 20 minutes, Cook Time: 3 to 3½ hours,
Serves: 10

INGREDIENTS:

- 1½   pounds (680g) green beans
- 3 bulbs fennel, cored and chopped
- 3 cups fresh soybeans
- 1 jalapeño pepper, minced
- ½ cup canned coconut milk
- 2 tbsps. lime juice
- 1 lemongrass stalk
- ½ tsp. salt
- ⅓ cup chopped fresh cilantro

DIRECTIONS:

1. Combine green beans, soybeans, fennel, jalapeno, lemongrass, coconut milk, lime juice, and salt in a 6-quart crock pot. Simmer on low heat for 3 to 3½ hours, close the lid until the vegetables are tender.
2. Take out the lemongrass and sprinkle with coriander. Enjoy!

Nutrition Info per Serving:

Calories: 115, Fat: 5g, Saturated Fat: 3g, Protein: 6g, Carbohydrates, 11g, Sugar: 4g, Fiber: 6g, Sodium: 154mg

Sweet Root Vegetables

Prep Time: 20 minutes, Cook Time: 6 to 8 hours on low,
Serves: 10

INGREDIENTS:

- 3 tbsps. honey
- 6 large carrots, cut into chunks
- 3 sweet potatoes, peeled and cut into chunks
- 2 medium rutabagas, peeled and cut into chunks
- 2 onions, chopped
- ½ tsp. salt
- ⅛ tsp. freshly ground black pepper

DIRECTIONS:

1. Combine all the ingredients and gently stir in a 6-quart crock pot. Cook on low heat for 6 to 8 hours, and cover until the vegetables are tender. Enjoy now!

Nutrition Info per Serving:

Calories: 102, Fat: 0g, Saturated Fat: 0g, Protein: 2g, Carbohydrates: 25g, Sugar: 14g, Fiber: 4g, Sodium: 177mg

Tender Vegetable Lasagna

Prep Time: 20 minutes, Cook Time: 7 to 8 hours on low,
Serves: 6

INGREDIENTS:

- 3 tbsps. extra-virgin olive oil, divided
- 8 ounces (227 g) Ricotta cheese
- 8 ounces (227 g) goat cheese
- 2 cups shredded Mozzarella cheese
- 1 cup sliced mushrooms
- 2 zucchini, thinly sliced lengthwise
- 2 cups shredded kale
- 1 tbsp. chopped basil
- 2 cups simple marinara sauce

DIRECTIONS:

1. Use 1 tablespoon olive oil to lightly grease the insert of the crock pot.
2. Heat the remaining 2 tablespoons of the olive oil in a large skillet over medium-high heat. Stir in the mushrooms and sauté for 5 minutes, until they are softened.
3. Add the marinara sauce into the skillet and stir to combine.
4. Pour into the insert with about one-third of the sauce. Arrange one-third of the zucchini strips over the sauce. Place one-third of the kale over the zucchini. Then over the kale sprinkle with half of both the ricotta and goat cheese. Repeat with the sauce, zucchini, kale, ricotta, and goat cheese to create another layer.
5. Place the remaining zucchini strips and the sauce on the top. Sprinkle over with the mozzarella cheese.
6. Cover the cooker and cook on low for 7 to 8 hours.
7. Serve warm.

Nutrition Info per Serving:

Calories: 345, Total Fat: 25 g, Total Carbs: 10 g, Net Carbs: 7 g, Protein: 21 g, Fiber: 3 g

Mushrooms and Carrots with Pearl Barley

Prep Time: 10 minutes, Cook Time: 8 hours, Serves: 6

INGREDIENTS:

- 3 large carrots, peeled and chopped
- 8 ounces (227 g) shiitake mushrooms, sliced
- 1 cup fresh or frozen peas
- 2 cups pearl barley
- 1 onion, peeled and chopped
- 5 cups (1200 ml) vegetable broth
- ½ tsp. salt
- 1 tsp. dried rosemary
- ⅛ tsp. black pepper

DIRECTIONS:

1. Mix the barley, broth, onion, salt, rosemary, carrots, mushrooms and pepper in your crock pot.
2. Cover and cook on low for 7½ hours.
3. Stir in the peas. Cover and cook for additional half an hour.

Nutrition Info per Serving:

Calories: 351, Total Fat: 2g, Saturated Fat: 1g, Carbohydrates: 72g, Protein: 14g, Fiber 15g

Tasty Red Cabbage Crock Pot

Prep Time: 20 minutes, Cook Time: 5-7 hours, Serves: 8

INGREDIENTS:

- 1 Granny Smith apple, peeled and chopped
- 1 medium head red cabbage, cored and chopped (about 8 cups)
- 3 tbsps. honey
- Pinch ground cloves
- ¼ cup apple cider vinegar
- 1 red onion, chopped
- ½ tsp. salt
- ⅛ tsp. freshly ground black pepper

DIRECTIONS:

1. Combine all the ingredients in a 6-quart crock pot and cover. Turn on a low heat and cook for 5 to 7 hours, until the cabbage is soft. Serve immediately!

Nutrition Info per Serving:

Calories: 60, Fat: 0g, Saturated Fat: 0g, Protein: 1g, Carbohydrates: 15g, Sugar: 11g, Fiber: 3g, Sodium: 161mg

Honey Glazed Turnips

Prep Time: 20 minutes, Cook Time: 6 to 8 hours on low, Serves: 8

INGREDIENTS:

- 4 pounds (1.8kg) turnips, peeled and sliced
- 4 cups chopped turnip greens
- 1 bulk fennel, cored and chopped
- ¼ cup honey
- ¼ cup roasted vegetable broth
- 2 garlic cloves, minced
- ½ tsp. salt

DIRECTIONS:

1. Put all the ingredients in a 6-quart crock pot and mix well. Cover the lid, place the pot on the stove and cook on low heat for 6 to 8 hours, until the radishes are soft and the vegetables are soft. Serve immediately!

Nutrition Info per Serving:

Calories: 86, Fat: 0g, Saturated Fat: 0g, Protein: 3g, Carbohydrates: 20g, Sugar: 13g, Fiber: 5g, Sodium: 232mg

CHAPTER 7

BEEF

Potato and Beef Casserole

Prep Time: 25 minutes, Cook Time: 4 hours, Serves: 8

INGREDIENTS:

- 1 pound (454 g) ground beef
- 1 package (32 ounces, 896 g) frozen cubed hash brown potatoes, thawed
- 1 can (10 ¾ ounces, 304 g) condensed cheddar cheese soup, undiluted
- ½ pound (227 g) sliced fresh mushrooms
- 2 jars (14 ounces each, 397 g) pizza sauce
- 2 cups (8 ounces, 227 g) shredded Italian cheese blend
- 1 small onion, chopped
- 1 medium green pepper, chopped
- 1 tsp. Italian seasoning
- ½ cup 2% milk
- ½ tsp. garlic salt
- ¼ tsp. crushed red pepper flakes
- 1 tsp. Italian seasoning

DIRECTIONS:

1. Add the onion, beef, green pepper and mushrooms into a large skillet, cook until the meat is no longer pink, drain.
2. While the beef is cooking, add the soup, pizza sauce, Italian seasoning, milk, garlic salt and pepper flakes into a large bowl, combine them together. Stir in the pepperoni, potatoes, and beef mixture.
3. Place half of the meat mixture into a 5-qt. crock pot. Sprinkle with half of the cheese, repeat layers. Cover the cooker and cook on low for 4-5 hours or until potatoes are tender.

Crock Pot Pesto Beef

Prep Time: 5 minutes, Cook Time: 9 to 10 hours on low, Serves: 8

INGREDIENTS:

- 1 tbsp. extra-virgin olive oil
- 2 pounds (907 g) beef chuck roast
- ½ cup beef broth
- ¾ cup prepared pesto

DIRECTIONS:

1. Use the olive oil to grease the insert of the crock pot lightly.
2. Use the pesto to slather all over of the beef. In the insert, add the beef and pour in the broth.
3. Cover the cooker and set on low, cook for 9 to 10 hours.
4. After cooking, serve warm.

Nutrition Info per Serving:

Calories: 530, Total Fat: 43 g, Total Carbs: 2 g, Net Carbs: 2 g, Protein: 32 g, Fiber: 0 g

Delicious Beef Pot Roast

Prep Time: 20 minutes, Cook Time: 8-10 hours, Serves: 8

INGREDIENTS:

- 1 (3-pound, 1.4kg) grass-fed chuck shoulder roast or tri-tip roast
- 8 Yukon Gold potatoes, cut into chunks
- 4 large carrots, peeled and cut into chunks
- 2 onions, chopped
- 1 leek, sliced
- 1 cup beef stock
- 8 garlic cloves, sliced
- 1 tsp. dried marjoram
- ½ tsp. salt
- ¼ tsp. freshly ground black pepper

DIRECTIONS:

1. Combine potatoes, carrots, onions, leeks, and garlic in a 6-quart crock pot.
2. Put the beef on the mixed vegetables and pour in the appropriate marjoram, salt and pepper.
3. Pour beef broth in the crock pot and cover.
4. Cook on low heat for 8 to 10 hours, until the beef is very tender. Take out the beef and serve with vegetables.

Nutrition Info per Serving:

Calories: 567, Fat: 31g, Saturated Fat: 12g, Protein: 37g, Carbohydrates: 36g, Sugar: 5g, Fiber: 4g

Steak Diane Slow Cooked

Prep Time: 20 minutes, Cook Time: 8-10 hours, Serves: 8

INGREDIENTS:

- 1 (3-pound, 1.4kg) grass-fed chuck shoulder roast or tri-tip roast, cut into 2-inch pieces
- 5 large carrots, sliced
- 2 cups sliced cremini mushrooms
- 2 onions, sliced
- 4 garlic cloves, sliced
- 1 cup low-sodium beef broth
- 2 shallots, peeled and sliced
- 1 tsp. dried marjoram leaves
- 2 tbsps. chopped fresh chives
- 2 tbsps. butter

DIRECTIONS:

1. Combine the onions, garlic, shallots, mushrooms, and carrots in a 6-quart crock pot.
2. Place the beef on the vegetables in the crock pot and stir gently. Sprinkle with chives and marjoram, then drizzle the beef broth over all the mixture.
3. Cook on low heat for 8 to 10 hours, and cover until the beef is very tender. Drizzle with butter, mix well and serve.

Nutrition Info per Serving:

Calories: 381, Fat: 19g, Saturated Fat: 8g, Protein: 38g, Carbohydrates: 11g, Sugar: 5g, Fiber: 2g

Korean Braised Short Ribs with Carrots

Prep Time: 10 minutes, Cook Time: 8 hours, Serves: 1

INGREDIENTS:

- 1 tsp. toasted sesame oil
- 8 ounces (227 g) short ribs, trimmed of fat
- 4 carrots, cut into 2-inch pieces
- 2 cups low-sodium beef broth
- 1 tbsp. fish sauce
- 1 tbsp. low-sodium soy sauce
- 1 tbsp. rice wine vinegar
- 1 tsp. minced garlic
- 1 tsp. Sriracha
- 1 tsp. minced fresh ginger
- 1 scallion, white and green parts, sliced thin, for garnish

DIRECTIONS:

1. Add the sesame oil, fish sauce, soy sauce, vinegar, garlic, Sriracha and ginger into a small bowl, whisk them together. Spread onto the short ribs with this mixture to coat thoroughly. You can do this one day ahead and keep the short ribs in the refrigerator.
2. In the crock pot, add the carrots and then over the top set with the short ribs. Pour in the beef broth.
3. Cover the cooker and set on low, cook for 8 hours. Garnish the short ribs with the scallions and serve.

Nutrition Info per Serving:

Calories: 532, Saturated Fat: 18 g, Trans Fat: 0 g, Carbohydrates: 15 g, Protein: 18 g, Fiber: 3 g

Spicy Moroccan Beef Taging

Prep Time: 20 minutes, Cook Time: 8-10 hours, Serves: 8

INGREDIENTS:

- 1 (3-pound, 1.4kg) grass-fed beef sirloin roast, cut into 2-inch pieces
- 3 carrots, cut into chunks
- 2 onions, chopped
- 2 jalapeño peppers, minced
- 1 cup chopped dates
- 1 cup beef stock
- 6 garlic cloves, minced
- 1 tsp. ground turmeric
- 2 tbsps. honey
- 2 tsps. ground cumin

DIRECTIONS:

1. Put the onions, garlic, jalapenos, carrots, and dates in a 6-quart crock pot and mix. Put on the beef again.
2. Put honey, beef stock, cumin and turmeric in a small bowl and mix well. Pour into a crock pot.
3. Cook on low heat for 8 to 10 hours, until the beef is very tender. Serve immediately!

Nutrition Info per Serving:

Calories: 452, Fat: 21g, Saturated Fat: 9g, Protein: 35g, Carbohydrates: 29g, Sugar: 22g, Fiber: 4g

Crock Pot Balsamic Glazed Roast Beef

Prep Time: 15 minutes, Cook Time: 7 to 8 hours on low, Serves: 8

INGREDIENTS:

- 3 tbsps. extra-virgin olive oil, divided
- 2 pounds (907 g) boneless beef chuck roast
- 1 cup beef broth
- ½ cup balsamic vinegar
- 1 tbsp. minced garlic
- 1 tbsp. granulated erythritol
- ½ tsp. red pepper flakes
- 1 tbsp. chopped fresh thyme

DIRECTIONS:

1. Use 1 tablespoon of the olive oil to grease the insert of the crock pot lightly.
2. Heat the remaining 2 tablespoons of the olive oil in a large skillet over medium-high heat. Place the beef in the skillet and brown on all sides, about 7 minutes total. Transfer to the insert.
3. Add the remaining ingredients to a small bowl, whisk them together until blended.
4. Pour over the beef with the sauce.
5. Cover the cooker and set on low, cook for 7 to 8 hours.
6. After cooking, turn off the heat and serve warm.

Nutrition Info per Serving:

Calories: 476, Total Fat: 39 g, Total Carbs: 1 g, Net Carbs: 1 g, Protein: 28 g, Fiber: 0 g

Italian Braised Veal Shanks and Vegetables

Prep Time: 10 minutes, Cook Time: 8 hours, Serves: 1

INGREDIENTS:

- 1 veal shank, about 1 pound (454 g)
- 1 cup low-sodium chicken or beef broth
- ½ cup diced carrot
- ½ cup diced onion
- ½ cup diced celery
- ½ cup dry red wine
- 1 tsp. fresh thyme
- 1 tsp. minced garlic
- 1 tsp. fresh rosemary
- ½ tbsp. tomato paste
- ⅛ tsp. sea salt
- Freshly ground black pepper
- ½ tsp. orange zest

DIRECTIONS:

1. Add the thyme, garlic, rosemary, tomato paste, salt and a few grinds of the black pepper into a small bowl, combine them together. Coat the veal shank in this mixture. You can do this a day ahead and place the veal in the refrigerator.
2. In the crock pot, add the carrot, onion, celery, wine, orange zest, and broth. Stir thoroughly. Nestle the veal shank in the vegetable and wine mixture.
3. Cover the cooker and set on low, cook for 8 hours.

Nutrition Info per Serving:

Calories: 526, Saturated Fat: 5 g, Trans Fat: 0 g, Carbohydrates: 10 g, Protein: 74 g, Fiber: 2 g

Crock Pot Beef and Zucchini Soup

Prep Time: 20 minutes, Cook Time: 6 hours on low, Serves: 6

INGREDIENTS:

- 3 tbsps. extra-virgin olive oil, divided
- 1 pound (454 g) ground beef
- 1 (28-ounce, 784 g) can diced tomatoes, undrained
- 4 cups beef broth
- ½ sweet onion,
- chopped
- 4 ounces (113 g) cream cheese
- 1 zucchini, diced
- 1 cup shredded mozzarella
- 2 tsps. minced garlic
- 1½ tbsps. dried basil
- 2 tsps. dried oregano

DIRECTIONS:

1. Use 1 tablespoon of the olive oil to lightly grease the insert of the crock pot.
2. Heat the remaining 2 tablespoons of the olive oil in a large skillet over medium-high heat. Stir in the ground beef and sauté for 6 minutes, until it is cooked through.
3. Stir in the garlic and onion, sauté for another 3 minutes.
4. Place the meat mixture to the insert.
5. Add the tomatoes, broth, basil, zucchini, and oregano, stir well.
6. Cover the cooker and cook on low for 6 hours.
7. Add the cream cheese and mozzarella, stir well and serve.

Nutrition Info per Serving:

Calories: 472, Total Fat: 36 g, Total Carbs: 9 g, Net Carbs: 6 g, Protein: 30 g, Fiber: 3 g

Healthy BBQ Beef Brisket

Prep Time: 20 minutes, Cook Time: 8-11 hours, Serves: 8

INGREDIENTS:

- 1 (3-pound, 1.4kg) grass-fed beef brisket, trimmed
- 2 (8-ounce, 227g) BPA-free cans no-salt-added tomato sauce
- 3 onions, chopped
- ⅓ cup natural mustard
- 8 garlic cloves, minced
- 3 tbsps. honey
- 2 tsps. paprika
- 1 tsp. dried marjoram leaves
- 1 tsp. dried oregano leaves
- ½ tsp. cayenne pepper

DIRECTIONS:

1. In a 6-quart crock pot, add onions and garlic.
2. Combine paprika, oregano, marjoram, and cayenne in a small bowl. Spread this mixture on the sirloin to make it delicious.
3. In another small bowl, add ketchup, mustard, and honey, and mix well.
4. Put the beef in the crock pot. Pour the tomato mixture on the beef.
5. Cook on low heat for 8 to 11 hours, until the beef is very tender. Serve immediately! You can eat beef slices or chop it up as steamed buns.

Nutrition Info per Serving:

Calories: 303, Fat: 10g, Saturated Fat: 3g, Protein: 37g, Carbohydrates: 18g, Sugar: 12g, Fiber: 2g

Bread Crumbs and Beef Stuffed Bell Peppers

Prep Time: 10 minutes, Cook Time: 8 hours, Serves: 1

INGREDIENTS:

- 1 tsp. extra-virgin olive oil
- 4 narrow red bell peppers
- ½ cup diced onion
- 1 tsp. ground fennel seed
- 1 egg, beaten
- 2 tbsps. bread crumbs
- 8 ounces (227 g) lean ground beef
- 2 tbsps. tomato paste
- 1 tsp. minced garlic
- 1 tbsp. Italian herb blend
- ¼ cup grated Parmesan cheese

DIRECTIONS:

1. Use olive oil to grease the inside of the crock pot.
2. Cut each of the red peppers the tops off and set the tops to the side. Remove the membranes and seeds from the interior of each pepper.
3. Add the remaining ingredients into a large bowl, and mix the ingredients together thoroughly with your hands. Fill the mixture into each of the peppers. Upright to stand the peppers in the crock pot, and place the tops on each pepper.
4. Cover the cooker and set on low, cook for 8 hours.

Nutrition Info per Serving:

Calories: 438, Saturated Fat: 6 g, Trans Fat: 0 g, Carbohydrates: 27 g, Protein: 46 g, Fiber: 7 g, Sodium: 314 mg

Homomede Beef Broth

Prep Time: 5 minutes, Cook Time: 24 to 48 hours, Serves: 10 cups

INGREDIENTS:

- 2 to 3 pounds (907 g to 1.4 kg) beef bones and trimmings
- 1 carrot, roughly chopped
- 4 ounces (113 g) fresh mushrooms or 1 ounce dried mushrooms
- 1 celery stalk (leaves
- included), roughly chopped
- 1 onion, roughly chopped
- 1 head garlic, halved crosswise
- 1 fresh rosemary sprig
- 1 fresh thyme sprig
- 14 peppercorns

DIRECTIONS:

1. In your crock pot, mix all the ingredients. Fill the crock pot with water two-thirds of the way.
2. Cover and set on low. Cook for 24 to 48 hours.
3. Strain the broth through a fine-mesh colander, discarding the solids.
4. Cover the broth and refrigerate it for 2 to 3 hours.
5. Use a spoon to skim the fat from the top of the stock and discard it.
6. Store the broth in an airtight container in the refrigerator for up to 5 days or in the freezer for up to 1 year.

Nutrition Info per Serving:

Calories: 56, Total Fat: 0g, Saturated Fat: 0g, Carbohydrates: 3g, Protein: 5g, Fiber: 0g

Thai Beef with Vegetables

Prep Time: 20 minutes, Cook Time: 8-10 hours, Serves: 8

INGREDIENTS:

- 2½ pounds (1.1kg) grass-fed beef sirloin roast, cut into 2-inch pieces
- 3 large carrots, shredded
- 3 onions, chopped
- 3 large tomatoes, seeded and chopped
- 1 cup canned coconut milk
- ¾ cup peanut butter
- ½ cup beef stock
- 6 garlic cloves, minced
- 2 tbsps. grated fresh ginger root
- 3 tbsps. lime juice
- 1 small red chili pepper, minced

DIRECTIONS:

1. Pour the onions, garlic, carrots, ginger root, and tomatoes in a 6-quart crock pot and mix.
2. Combine peanut butter, coconut milk, chili, lime juice and beef broth in a medium bowl.
3. Put the roast on top of the vegetables in the crock pot and drizzle with peanut butter.
4. Cook on low heat for 8 to 10 hours, until the beef is very tender. Serve immediately!

Nutrition Info per Serving:

Calories: 530, Fat: 35g, Protein: 36g, Carbohydrates: 18g, Sugar: 8g, Fiber: 5g

Corned Beef with Potato and Carrot

Prep Time: 20 minutes, Cook Time: 9 hours, Serves: 5

INGREDIENTS:

- 6 medium red potatoes, quartered
- 4 cups water
- 2 medium carrots, cut into chunks
- 2 corned beef briskets with spice packets (3 pounds each, 1.4 kg)
- 1 large onion, sliced
- 2 tbsps. sugar
- ¼ cup packed brown sugar
- 2 tbsps. whole peppercorns
- 2 tbsps. coriander seeds

DIRECTIONS:

1. Add the carrots, onion and potatoes into a 6-qt. crock pot. Then add briskets (discard spice packets from corned beef or save for another use). Over the meat, sprinkle with the sugar, brown sugar, peppercorns and coriander. Pour water to cover.
2. Cover the cooker and cook on low for 9-11 hours or until vegetables and meat are tender.
3. After cooking, take the meat and vegetables out and place onto a serving platter. Thinly slice one brisket across the grain and serve with vegetables. Save the remaining brisket for Reuben sandwiches, strata or save for another use.

Sloppy Joes in Lettuce

Prep Time: 15 minutes, Cook Time: 8 hours, Serves: 4

INGREDIENTS:

- 1 pound (454 g) extra-lean ground beef
- 1 (14-ounce, 397 g) can crushed tomatoes
- 2 onions, chopped
- 2 green bell peppers, seeded and chopped
- ½ cup (120 ml) apple cider vinegar
- 2 tbsps. honey
- Juice and zest of 1 orange
- ¼ tsp. sea salt
- ¼ tsp. cayenne pepper
- 4 large iceberg lettuce leaves

DIRECTIONS:

1. Put the ground beef in your crock pot.
2. Mix the honey, tomatoes, onions, bell peppers, vinegar, orange juice and orange zest, salt, and cayenne.
3. Cover and cook on low for 8 hours.
4. Spoon the mixture into the lettuce leaves. Serve.

Nutrition Info per Serving:

Calories: 261, Total Fat: 5g, Saturated Fat: 2g, Carbohydrates: 26g, Protein: 28g, Fiber: 6g

Spiced Short Ribs Vindaloo

Prep Time: 30 minutes, Cook Time: 8 ¼ hours, Serves: 4

INGREDIENTS:

- 2 pounds (907 g) bone-in beef short ribs
- 1 cup fresh sugar snap peas, halved
- 1 tbsp. butter
- 8 garlic cloves, minced
- 1 medium onion, finely chopped
- ½ cup red wine vinegar
- 2 tsps. coriander seeds
- 1 tbsp. cumin seeds
- 1 tbsp. minced fresh gingerroot
- ½ tsp. ground cloves
- 2 tsps. mustard seed
- ¼ tsp. ground cinnamon
- ¼ tsp. kosher salt
- ¼ tsp. cayenne pepper
- 4 bay leaves
- Hot cooked rice and plain yogurt

DIRECTIONS:

1. Add coriander and cumin into a dry small skillet, toast them over medium heat, until aromatic, stirring frequently. Allow it to cool. Coarsely crush seeds in a spice grinder or use a mortar and pestle to crush.
2. Heat butter in a large saucepan over medium heat. Stir in the garlic, onion, and ginger, cook and stir for 1 minute. Add the cloves, mustard seed, cinnamon, salt, cayenne pepper and crushed seeds, cook and stir for 1 minute longer. Allow it to cool completely.
3. Combine the onion mixture, vinegar and bay leaves in a large resealable plastic bag. Add ribs, seal bag and turn to coat. Place in the refrigerator to chill overnight.
4. In a 4-qt. crock pot, add the rib mixture. Cover the cooker and cook on low for 8-10 hours or until meat is tender. Add peas and stir well, cook for another 8 to 10 minutes or until peas are crisp-tender. Skim fat, discard bay leaves. Serve the rib mixture with rice and yogurt.

Spicy Skirt Steak Fajitas

Prep Time: 10 minutes, Cook Time: 6-8 hours, Serves: 1

INGREDIENTS:

- 1 tbsp. extra-virgin olive oil
- 12 ounces (340 g) skirt steak, sliced thin
- 2 bell peppers, assorted colors, cored and cut into thin strips
- 1 small avocado, sliced, for garnish
- ½ onion, halved and cut into thin half circles
- 1 tbsp. minced garlic
- 1 tbsp. freshly squeezed lime juice
- 2 tbsps. minced chipotles in adobo
- ⅛ tsp. sea salt
- 4 corn tortillas

DIRECTIONS:

1. Add the olive oil, garlic, lime juice, chipotles and salt into a small bowl, whisk them together. Place the skirt steak into the bowl and toss to coat the meat thoroughly. You can marinate this overnight in the refrigerator if you wish.
2. In the crock pot, add the steak, onions and peppers.
3. Cover the cooker and cook on low for 6 to 8 hours, until the vegetables and meat are very tender.
4. Garnish with the avocado slices, and serve in warmed corn tortillas.

Nutrition Info per Serving:

Calories: 791, Saturated Fat: 12 g, Trans Fat: 0 g, Carbohydrates: 46 g, Protein: 52 g, Fiber: 15 g

Curried Coconut Beef

Prep Time: 10 minutes, Cook Time: 7 to 8 hours on low, Serves: 6

INGREDIENTS:

- 1 tbsp. extra-virgin olive oil
- 1 pound (454 g) beef chuck roast, cut into 2-inch pieces
- 2 cups coconut milk
- 1 cup shredded baby bok choy
- 1 sweet onion, chopped
- 1 red bell pepper, diced
- 1 tbsp. coconut aminos
- 2 tbsps. hot curry powder
- 2 tsps. minced garlic
- 2 tsps. grated fresh ginger

DIRECTIONS:

1. Use the olive oil to grease the insert of the crock pot lightly.
2. In the insert of the crock pot, add the onion, beef, and bell pepper.
3. Add the remaining ingredients except the bok choy to a medium bowl, whisk them together. Pour the sauce into the insert and combine well.
4. Cover the cooker and cook on low for 7 to 8 hours.
5. Add the bok choy, stir well and allow it to stand for 15 minutes.
6. After cooking, turn off the heat and serve warm.

Nutrition Info per Serving:

Calories: 504, Total Fat: 42 g, Total Carbs: 10 g, Net Carbs: 7 g, Protein: 23 g, Fiber: 3 g

Turkey and Beef Meatloaf

Prep Time: 10 minutes, Cook Time: 8 hours, Serves: 1

INGREDIENTS:

- 1 tsp. extra-virgin olive oil
- 8 ounces (227 g) lean ground beef
- 4 ounces (113 g) ground turkey
- ½ cup whole-grain bread crumbs
- ½ cup minced onion
- 1 egg
- 1 tsp. minced fresh thyme
- 1 tsp. minced garlic
- ¼ cup minced fresh parsley
- ¼ cup ketchup
- ⅛ tsp. sea salt
- Freshly ground black pepper

DIRECTIONS:

1. Add all of the ingredients except the olive oil into a large bowl, combine them together. Mix all the ingredients together thoroughly with your hands.
2. Use the olive oil to grease the inside of the crock pot. In the crock, add the meatloaf mixture and form it into a loaf-like shape.
3. Cover the cooker and set on low, cook for 8 hours.

Nutrition Info per Serving:

Calories: 525, Saturated Fat: 5 g, Trans Fat: 0 g, Carbohydrates: 36 g, Protein: 57 g, Fiber: 4 g

Crock Pot Beef and Cabbage Roll Casserole

Prep Time: 15 minutes, Cook Time: 7 to 8 hours on low, Serves: 4

INGREDIENTS:

- 3 tbsps. extra-virgin olive oil, divided
- 1 pound (454 g) ground beef
- 4 cups shredded cabbage
- 2 cups finely chopped cauliflower
- 2 cups simple marinara sauce
- ½ cup cream cheese
- 1 sweet onion, chopped
- 1 tsp. dried thyme
- ¼ tsp. salt
- ¼ tsp. freshly ground black pepper
- 2 tsps. minced garlic

DIRECTIONS:

1. Use tablespoon of the olive oil to grease the insert of the crock pot slightly.
2. Along bottom of the insert, press with the ground beef.
3. Heat the remaining 2 tablespoons of the olive oil in a medium skillet over medium-high heat. Add the garlic, cauliflower, onion, thyme, salt, and pepper, and sauté for 3 minutes, until the onion is softened.
4. Stir in the cabbage and sauté for another 5 minutes.
5. Transfer the cabbage mixture to the insert, then pour the marinara sauce to cover the cabbage, and place the cream cheese on the top.
6. Cover the cooker and set on low, cook for 7 to 8 hours.
7. Stir well and serve.

Nutrition Info per Serving:

Calories: 547, Total Fat: 42 g, Total Carbs: 10 g, Net Carbs: 6 g, Protein: 34 g, Fiber: 4 g

Beef, Mushroom and Barley Soup

Prep Time: 10 minutes, Cook Time: 2 hour 45 minutes, Serves: 6

INGREDIENTS:

- 1 pound (454 g) beef stew meat, cubed
- 8 ounces (227 g) sliced mushrooms
- 4 cups low-sodium beef broth
- 2 carrots, chopped
- 3 celery stalks, chopped
- ½ cup pearl barley
- 1 onion, chopped
- 6 garlic cloves, minced
- 1 cup water
- ¼ tsp. freshly ground black pepper
- ½ tsp. dried thyme
- ¼ tsp. salt
- 1 tbsp. extra-virgin olive oil

DIRECTIONS:

1. Season the meat with salt and pepper.
2. In a large pot, heat oil over medium-high heat, sear the meat on all sides, remove it from the pot, and set aside.
3. Add the mushrooms to the pot and cook briefly for 1 or 2 minutes. Take it out and set aside.
4. Add onion, carrot and celery to the pot and sauté until tender. Add garlic and sauté until fragrant. Add the beef and mushrooms back to the pot, along with the thyme, beef broth and water. Bring to a boil, reduce the heat, then cover and simmer for 1.5 to 2 hours, until the meat starts to soften.
5. Add the barley and cook for another 30 to 40 minutes until it is soft. If needed, add another 1 cup of water during the cooking process to achieve the desired consistency. Serve warm.

Nutrition Info per Serving:

Calories: 245, Total Fat: 9g, Protein: 21g, Carbohydrates: 19g, Sugars: 3g, Fiber: 4g, Sodium: 516mg

Beef Curry

Prep Time: 10 minutes, Cook Time: 8 hours, Serves: 6

INGREDIENTS:

- 1 pound (454 g) stew beef, trimmed and cut into 1-inch pieces
- 1 pound (454 g) red potatoes, scrubbed and cut into 1-inch pieces
- 2 (15-ounce, 425 g) cans diced tomatoes, with their juice
- 1 onion, sliced
- 4 large carrots, peeled and cut into 1-inch pieces
- 1 tbsp. grated fresh ginger
- 1 tsp. garlic powder
- ½ tsp. sea salt
- 2 tbsps. curry powder
- 1 tsp. ground cumin

DIRECTIONS:

1. Mix all the ingredients in your crock pot.
2. Cover and cook on low for 8 hours.
3. Skim the fat from the surface of the curry with a large spoon and discard.

Nutrition Info per Serving:

Calories: 229, Total Fat: 5g, Saturated Fat: 0g, Carbohydrates: 26g, Protein: 20g, Cholesterol: 0mg, Fiber: 6g

Crock Pot Caribbean Pot Beef Roast

Prep Time: 30 minutes, Cook Time: 6 hours, Serves: 10

INGREDIENTS:

- 1 boneless beef chuck roast (2 ½ pounds, 1.1 kg)
- 2 large carrots, sliced
- 1 can (15 ounces, 425 g) tomato sauce
- 2 medium sweet potatoes, cubed
- ¼ cup chopped celery
- 1 tbsp. canola oil
- 1 large onion, chopped
- 2 garlic cloves, minced
- 1 tbsp. sugar
- 1 tbsp. all-purpose flour
- 1 tbsp. brown sugar
- 1 tsp. ground cumin
- ¾ tsp. ground coriander
- ¾ tsp. salt
- ½ tsp. dried oregano
- ¾ tsp. chili powder
- ⅛ tsp. ground cinnamon
- ¾ tsp. grated orange peel
- ¾ tsp. baking cocoa

DIRECTIONS:

1. In a 5-qt. crock pot, add the carrots, potatoes, and celery. Place oil and beef in a large skillet, brown the meat on all sides. Then transfer meat to crock pot.
2. Saute the onion in drippings in the same skillet until tender. Stir in the garlic, cook for 1 minute. Add the brown sugar, flour, seasonings, orange peel and cocoa, combine well. Stir in tomato sauce, add to skillet and heat through. Pour over beef.
3. Cover the cooker and set on low, cook for 6-8 hours or until vegetables and beef are tender.

Tender Pot Roast

Prep Time: 10 minutes, Cook Time: 8 hours, Serves: 1

INGREDIENTS:

- 16 ounces (454 g) chuck roast, trimmed of visible fat
- 2 carrots, cut into 2-inch pieces
- 2 red potatoes, quartered
- 1 onion, cut into 8 wedges
- 1 cup low-sodium beef broth
- 1 tsp. minced rosemary
- ⅛ tsp. sea salt
- Freshly ground black pepper

DIRECTIONS:

1. Combine the salt and a few grinds of the black pepper in a bowl, the use this mixture to season the roast. Then place it into the crock pot. Arrange the carrots, onion, potatoes, and rosemary around the sides and on top of the meat.
2. Pour in the beef broth.
3. Cover the cooker and set on low, cook for 8 hours, until the meat is meltingly tender.

Nutrition Info per Serving:

Calories: 696, Saturated Fat: 7 g, Trans Fat: 0 g, Carbohydrates: 46 g, Protein: 81 g, Fiber: 7 g, Sodium: 524 mg

Vegetable and Beef Stuffed Peppers

Prep Time: 25 minutes, Cook Time: 6 hours on low, Serves: 4

INGREDIENTS:

- 3 tbsps. extra-virgin olive oil, divided
- 1 pound (454 g) ground beef
- 4 bell peppers, tops cut off and seeded
- 1 tomato, diced
- ½ cup finely chopped cauliflower
- 1 cup shredded

- Cheddar cheese
- ½ sweet onion, chopped
- ½ cup chicken broth
- 2 tsps. minced garlic
- 2 tsps. dried oregano
- 1 tsp. dried basil
- 1 tbsp. basil, sliced into thin strips, for garnish

DIRECTIONS:

1. Use 1 tablespoon of the olive oil to lightly grease the insert of the crock pot.
2. Heat the remaining 2 tablespoons of the olive oil in a large skillet over medium-high heat. Stir in the beef and sauté for 10 minutes, until it is cooked through.
3. Then stir in the garlic, tomato, cauliflower, onion, oregano, and basil. Sauté for another 5 minutes.
4. Stuff the meat mixture into the bell peppers, and place the cheese on the top.
5. In the crock pot, add the peppers and pour the broth into the bottom.
6. Cover the cooker and set on low, cook for 6 hours.
7. Top with the basil and serve warm.

Nutrition Info per Serving:

Calories: 571, Total Fat: 41 g, Total Carbs: 12 g, Net Carbs: 9 g, Protein: 38 g, Fiber: 3 g

Crock Pot Beef with Cheese Dip

Prep Time: 20 minutes, Cook Time: 2 hours (low), Serves: 16

INGREDIENTS:

- Cooking spray
- 1 pound (454 g) lean ground beef
- 8 ounces (227 g) queso quesadilla or cream cheese, cut into 1-inch cubes
- 1 large tomato, seeded and chopped
- 1 medium onion, chopped
- 3 medium roasted

- jalapeños, peeled, seeded, and chopped
- 1 cup whole milk
- 1 cup grated Monterey Jack cheese
- ½ cup grated Cheddar cheese
- 1 tbsp. Taco Seasoning Mix
- 1 to 2 chipotles in adobo, chopped to a paste, to taste

DIRECTIONS:

1. Add the tomato, onion, ground beef, and jalapeños to a large bowl, stir well. Mix in the seasoning mix and then the chopped chipotles, and stir again.
2. Use cooking spray to spray the inside of the crock pot. Place the meat-vegetable mixture in the cooker and then add the cheeses and milk, use a wooden spoon to stir well.
3. Cover the cooker and set on low, cook for 2 hours. Stir well the cheese and serve.

Veggie and Beef Bourguignon with Egg Noodles

Prep Time: 20 minutes, Cook Time: 8 hours, Serves: 8

INGREDIENTS:

- 2 pounds (907 g) lean beef stew meat
- 16 ounces (454 g) pearl onions, peeled fresh or frozen, thawed
- 8 ounces (227 g) mushrooms, stems removed
- 6 tbsps. all-purpose flour
- 2 large carrot cut into 1-inch slices

- 2 garlic cloves, minced
- ¾ cup beef stock
- ½ cup dry red wine
- ¼ cup tomato paste
- 8 ounces (227 g) uncooked egg noodles
- 1½ tsps. sea salt
- ½ tsp. dried rosemary
- ¼ tsp. dried thyme
- ½ tsp. black pepper
- ¼ cup chopped fresh thyme leaves

DIRECTIONS:

1. In a medium bowl, add the beef, sprinkle with the flour, and toss well to coat.
2. In the crock pot, add the beef mixture, onions, carrots, garlic and mushrooms.
3. In a small bowl, combine the wine, stock, tomato paste, rosemary, salt, thyme, and black pepper. Stir into the beef mixture.
4. Cover the cooker and cook on low for 8 hours.
5. According to package directions to cook the noodles, omitting any salt.
6. Top the noodles with the beef mixture, sprinkled with the thyme and serve.

Spiced Creamy Beef Goulash

Prep Time: 15 minutes, Cook Time: 9 to 10 hours on low, Serves: 6

INGREDIENTS:

- 1 tbsp. extra-virgin olive oil
- ½ sweet onion, chopped
- 1½ pounds (680 g) beef, cut into 1-inch pieces
- 1 cup sour cream
- 1 red bell pepper, diced
- 1 carrot, cut into ½-inch-thick slices
- 1 cup beef broth
- ¼ cup tomato paste
- 2 tsps. minced garlic
- 1 tbsp. Hungarian paprika
- 1 bay leaf
- 2 tbsps. chopped fresh parsley, for garnish

DIRECTIONS:

1. Use the olive oil to grease the insert of the crock pot lightly.
2. In the insert of the crock pot, add the onion, beef, red bell pepper, carrot, broth, garlic, paprika, tomato paste and bay leaf.
3. Cover the cooker and cook on low for 9 to 10 hours.
4. After cooking, remove the bay leaf, add the sour cream and stir well.
5. Top with the parsley and serve.

Nutrition Info per Serving:

Calories: 548, Total Fat: 42 g, Total Carbs: 8 g, Net Carbs: 6 g, Protein: 32 g, Fiber: 2 g

Italian Beef and Vegetables

Prep Time: 25 minutes, Cook Time: 10 hours (low) or 5 hours (high), Serves: 6

INGREDIENTS:

- 1 large onion, cut into wedges
- 1 bone-in beef chuck or other pot roast (5 pounds, 2.3 kg)
- 3 carrots, halved and cut into chunks
- 6 small Yukon Gold or other yellow-fleshed potatoes, peeled
- 1 fennel bulb, halved, trimmed, and cut into wedges
- ⅔ cup beef broth, or water
- 1 tbsp. Italian seasoning, crushed
- 1½ tbsps. dried parsley
- 1 tsp. garlic salt
- 1 tbsp. fennel seeds, crushed
- 1 tsp. black pepper
- 1 tbsp. avocado oil or extra-virgin olive oil
- 2 tbsps. quick-cooking tapioca, crushed

DIRECTIONS:

1. In a 4-quart crock pot, add the onion, carrots, potatoes, and fennel bulb.
2. Add the Italian seasoning, parsley, garlic salt, fennel seeds, and pepper into a small bowl, stir well and rub the mixture on all sides of the beef.
3. Add the oil to a large skillet, heat it over medium-high heat. Stir in the beef and brown on all sides. Place the beef into the crock pot. Place ⅓ cup of the broth into the hot skillet and bring to a boil, stirring to scrape up any browned bits from the bottom of the skillet. Pour over the beef in the crock pot with the hot broth. In a bowl, combine the remaining ⅓ cup broth and the tapioca and pour into the crock pot.
4. Cover the cooker and cook on low for 10 to 12 hours or on high for 5 to 6 hours.
5. Equally divide the beef roast into four pieces, removing and discarding the bone. In a serving platter, place one piece and store the remaining three pieces into separate storage containers. Transfer two of the potatoes and one-third of the other vegetables to the serving platter with a slotted spoon. Transfer the four remaining potatoes and ½ cup of the other vegetables to one storage container and the remaining vegetables to another storage container. Skim the fat from the sauce in the crock pot, spoon half the sauce over the vegetables in the ragout Remix container. Seal the containers, label with the designated Remix recipe, and refrigerate.
6. Drizzle over the meat and vegetables with the remaining sauce on the serving platter and serve immediately.

Homemade Beef Hot Dogs

Prep Time: 15 minutes, Cook Time: 2 hours, Serves: 8

INGREDIENTS:

- 1 lb. (454 g) all-beef hot dogs
- 10-oz. (283 g) jar grape jelly
- ¼ tsp. dry mustard
- ¼ cup red wine
- ⅓ cup prepared mustard

DIRECTIONS:

1. Cut hot dogs into ½-inch slices. Place in the crock pot.
2. Add the jelly, dry mustard, red wine and prepared mustard into the hot dogs in the cooker, stir well.
3. Cover the cooker and cook on Low for 2 hours.
4. After cooking, serve in rolls or over cooked pasta.

Nutrition Info per Serving:

Calories: 84, Fat: 0.67 g, Carbohydrates: 20.28 g, Protein: 1.5 g

Beef and Mushroom Lo Mein

Prep Time: 20 minutes, Cook Time: 8½ to 10½ hours, Serves: 8

INGREDIENTS:

- 2 pounds, 2.3 kg) grass-fed beef chuck roast, cut into 2-inch pieces
- 1 (8-ounce, 227g) package whole-wheat spaghetti pasta, broken in half
- 2 cups shiitake mushrooms, sliced
- 2 onions, chopped
- 1 jalapeño pepper, minced
- 3 cups beef stock
- 4 garlic cloves, minced
- 2 tbsps. honey
- 2 tbsps. low-sodium soy sauce
- 1 tbsp. grated fresh ginger root

DIRECTIONS:

1. Combine the onion, mushrooms, garlic, ginger root, and jalapeno in a 6-quart crock pot. Add beef cubes and stir.
2. Pour the beef broth, soy sauce and honey into a medium-sized bowl until well mixed. Pour the mixed beef broth into a crock pot.
3. Cook on low heat and cover, about 8 to 10 hours, until the beef is very tender.
4. Turn the crock pot to high temperature. Add the pasta and stir gently, making sure all the pasta is covered with beef broth.
5. Cook on high heat for about 20 to 30 minutes, until the pasta is soft and serve while it is hot.

Nutrition Info per Serving:

Calories: 355, Fat: 14g, Saturated Fat: 5g, Protein: 28g, Carbohydrates: 33g, Sugar: 8g, Fiber: 4g

Chinese-style Beef Meatballs

Prep Time: 40 minutes, Cook Time: 3 hours, Serves: 6

INGREDIENTS:

- 1 lb. (454 g) ground beef
- 1 can water chestnuts, drained
- 1 egg
- 2 cups pineapple juice
- 6 slices pineapple, cut into halves
- ¾ cup water
- ½ cup sugar
- ½ cup wine vinegar
- 1 green pepper, cut in strips
- canned chow mein noodles
- 2 tbsps. soy sauce
- 5 tbsps. cornstarch, divided
- ½ tsp. salt
- 2 tbsps. minced onions

DIRECTIONS:

1. Mix beef, salt, egg, 1 tbsp. cornstarch, and onions well. Shape into 1-inch meatballs. Brown on all sides under broiler.
2. Combine remaining cornstarch with pineapple juice.
3. When smooth, add water, soy sauce, vinegar, and sugar. Bring to boil. Simmer and stir until thickened. Combine meatballs and sauce in crock pot.
4. Cover and cook on Low for 2 hours.
5. Add green peppers and water chestnuts.
6. Cover and cook for 1 hour.
7. Serve over chow mein noodles and garnish with pineapple slices.

Nutrition Info per Serving:

Calories: 375, Carbohydrates: 42.98 g, Protein: 23.25 g, Fat: 11.92 g

CHAPTER 8

FISH AND SEAFOOD

Tex-Mex Lemon Fish

Prep Time: 10 minutes, Cook Time: 3-4 hours, Serves: 6

INGREDIENTS:

- 1½ lbs. (680 g) frozen firm-textured fish fillets, thawed
- 2 lemons, divided
- 2 onions, thinly sliced
- 2 tbsps. butter, melted
- 1 bay leaf
- 2 tsps. salt
- 4 whole peppercorns
- 1 cup water

DIRECTIONS:

1. Cut the fillets into serving portions.
2. In a bowl, add 1 sliced lemon, the onion slices, butter, bay leaf, salt, and peppercorns, mix well and pour into the crock pot.
3. Place the fillets over the lemon and onion slices. Add water.
4. Cover the cooker and cook on High for 3 to 4 hours.
5. Use slotted spoon to carefully remove the fish fillets before serving. Place on heatproof plate.
6. Sprinkle with the juice of half of the second lemon. Garnish with remaining lemon slices.

Nutrition Info per Serving:

Calories: 160, Total Fat: 5 g, Total Carbohydrate: 7 g, Protein: 22 g, Sugar: 3 g, Fiber: 2 g

Curried Shrimp with Mushroom Soup

Prep Time: 5 to 10 minutes, Cook Time: 4-6 hours, Serves: 4 to 5

INGREDIENTS:

- 2 cups cooked shrimp
- 1 small onion, chopped
- 10¾-oz. (304 g) can cream of mushroom soup
- 1 cup sour cream
- 1 tsp. curry powder

DIRECTIONS:

1. In the crock pot, add the shrimp, onion, soup and curry powder, mix well.
2. Cover the cooker and cook on Low for 2 to 3 hours.
3. Stir in the sour cream 10 minutes before serving.
4. Serve over the puff pastry or rice.

Nutrition Info per Serving:

Calories: 153, Fat: 7.9 g, Carbohydrates: 7.56 g, Protein: 12.89 g

Buttery Dijon-Lemon Fish

Prep Time: 10 minutes, Cook Time: 3 hours, Serves: 4

INGREDIENTS:

- 1½ lbs. (680 g) orange roughy fillets
- 3 tbsps. butter, melted
- 2 tbsps. Dijon mustard
- 1 tbsp. lemon juice
- 1 tsp. Worcestershire sauce

DIRECTIONS:

1. Cut the fillets to fit in the crock pot.
2. Combine the butter, Dijon, lemon juice and Worcestershire sauce in a bowl, and pour over the fish. (If you have to stack the fish, spoon a portion of the sauce over the first layer of fish before adding the second layer.)
3. Cover the cooker and cook on Low for 3 hours, or until the fish flakes easily but is not dry or overcooked.

Nutrition Info per Serving:

Calories: 166, Fat: 9.11 g, Carbohydrates: 20.63 g, Protein: 1.55 g

Herbed Lemon Flounder

Prep Time: 5 minutes, Cook Time: 3-4 hours, Serves: 6

INGREDIENTS:

- 2 lbs. (907 g) flounder fillets, fresh or frozen
- ¾ cup chicken broth
- 4 tbsps. chopped fresh parsley
- 2 tbsps. dried minced onion
- 2 tbsps. dried chives
- 2 tbsps. lemon juice
- ½ tsp. salt
- ½-1 tsp. leaf marjoram

DIRECTIONS:

1. Use the paper towel to wipe the fish as dry as possible. Cut fish into portions to fit your crock pot.
2. Sprinkle over the fish with the salt.
3. In a bowl, combine the lemon juice and broth. Stir in the onion, chives, parsley and leaf marjoram.
4. Place a meat rack in the crock pot. Lay fish on the rack. Pour over each portion with the liquid mixture.
5. Cover the cooker and cook on High for 3 to 4 hours.

Nutrition Info per Serving:

Calories: 160, Total Fat: 2.5 g, Total Carbohydrate: 5 g, Protein: 29 g, Sugar: 2 g, Fiber: 0.5 g

Simple White Fish Risotto

Prep Time: 20 minutes, Cook Time: 3½ to 4 hours 45 minutes, Serves: 6

INGREDIENTS:

- 6 (5-ounce, 142g) tilapia fillets
- 8-ounces (227g) cremini mushrooms, sliced
- 6 cups roasted vegetable broth or fish stock
- 2 onions, chopped
- 2 cups short-grain brown rice
- 2 cups baby spinach leaves
- ½ cup grated Parmesan cheese
- 5 garlic cloves, minced
- 1 tsp. dried thyme leaves
- 2 tbsps. unsalted butter

DIRECTIONS:

1. Combine mushrooms, onions, garlic, rice, thyme and vegetable broth in a 6-quart crock pot. Cook on low heat for 3 to 4 hours, until the rice absorbs the soup and becomes soft.
2. Put fish on the rice. Put the lid on and continue to cook for 25 to 35 minutes, until the fillets are cooked through.
3. Stir the fish into the risotto. Put on baby spinach leaves.
4. Stir in butter and cheese. Simmer on low heat for 10 minutes. Serve immediately!

Nutrition Info per Serving:

Calories: 469, Fat: 12g, Saturated Fat: 5g, Protein: 34g, Carbohydrate: 61g, Sugar: 2g, Fiber: 5g, Sodium: 346mg

Chicken, Mushroom and Shrimp Casserole

Prep Time: 15-20 minutes, Cook Time: 3-8 hours, Serves: 6

INGREDIENTS:

- 2 tbsps. butter, melted
- 3 cups cut-up, cooked skinless chicken breast
- 2 (4-oz. 113 g) cans sliced mushrooms, drained
- 3 cups fat-free, low-sodium chicken broth
- 12-oz. (340 g) pkg. shelled frozen shrimp
- 1¼ cups rice, uncooked
- ⅔ cup slivered almonds
- ⅓ cup light soy sauce
- 1 cup water
- 8 green onions, chopped, 2 tbsps. reserved

DIRECTIONS:

1. In the crock pot, add the butter and rice. Stir to coat the rice well.
2. Add the remaining ingredients except the almonds and 2 tbsps. green onions to the cooker.
3. Cover and cook on Low for 6 to 8 hours, or on High for 3 to 4 hours, until the rice is tender.
4. After cooking, sprinkle the almonds and green onions over top before serving.

Nutrition Info per Serving:

Calories: 410, Total Fat: 15 g, Total Carbohydrate: 26 g, Protein: 42 g, Sugar: 10 g, Fiber: 5 g

Buttery Seafood Medley

Prep Time: 20 minutes, Cook Time: 3-4 hours, Serves: 10 to 12

INGREDIENTS:

- 1 lb. (454 g) shrimp, peeled and deveined
- 1 lb. (454 g) bay scallops
- 1 lb. (454 g) crabmeat
- 2 (10¾-oz. 304 g) cans cream of celery soup
- 2 soup cans milk
- 2 tbsps. butter, melted
- 1 tsp. Old Bay seasoning
- ¼-½ tsp. salt
- ¼ tsp. pepper

DIRECTIONS:

1. In the crock pot, layer the shrimp, crab, and scallops.
2. In a bowl, combine the milk and soup. Pour over the seafood.
3. In a separate bowl, add the butter, salt, pepper and Old Bay seasoning, mix well and pour over the top in the crock pot.
4. Cover and cook on Low for 3 to 4 hours.
5. After cooking, serve over the noodles or rice.

Nutrition Info per Serving:

Calories: 346, Fat: 16.29 g, Carbohydrates: 45.86 g, Protein: 13.89 g

Healthy Salmon and Veggies Ratatouille

Prep Time: 20 minutes, Cook Time: 6½ to 7½ hours, Serves: 8

INGREDIENTS:

- 2 tbsps. olive oil
- 2 pounds (907g) salmon fillets
- 5 large tomatoes, seeded and chopped
- 2 eggplants, peeled and chopped
- 2 cups sliced button mushrooms
- 2 red bell peppers, stemmed, seeded, and chopped
- 2 onions, chopped
- 5 garlic cloves, minced
- 1 tsp. dried herbes de Provence

DIRECTIONS:

1. Combine eggplants, tomatoes, mushrooms, onions, bell peppers, garlic, olive oil and Provencal herbs in a 6-quart crock pot. Cover the lid and cook on low heat for 6 to 7 hours, until the vegetables are soft.
2. Put the salmon in the crock pot. Cook on low heat for another 30 to 40 minutes, until the salmon fillets are tested with a fork.
3. Mix the cooked salmon with the vegetables and stir gently. Serve immediately!

Nutrition Info per Serving:

Calories: 342, Fat: 16g, Saturated Fat: 2g, Protein: 32g, Carbohydrates: 18g, Sugar: 10g, Fiber: 7g, Sodium: 218mg

Boiled Fish with Carrots

Prep Time: 20 minutes, Cook Time: 7½ to 9½ hours, Serves: 6

INGREDIENTS:

- 6 (5-ounce, 142g) trout fillets
- 4 large orange carrots, peeled and sliced
- 3 purple carrots, peeled and sliced
- 3 yellow carrots, peeled and sliced
- ½ cup roasted vegetable broth or fish stock
- 2 onions, chopped
- 4 garlic cloves, minced
- 1 tsp. dried marjoram leaves
- 1 bay leaf
- ½ tsp. salt

DIRECTIONS:

1. Combine carrots, onions, garlic, vegetable broth, marjoram, bay leaf, and salt in a 6-quart crock pot. Simmer for 7 to 9 hours on low heat, and cover until the carrots are tender.
2. Discard the bay leaves. Place trout fillets in a crock pot. Continue to cook for 20 to 30 minutes until the fillet is peeled off with a fork test.

Nutrition Info per Serving:

Calories: 263, Fat: 9g, Saturated Fat: 3g, Protein: 28g, Carbohydrates: 19g, Sugar: 9g, Fiber: 5g

Crock Pot Shrimp with Grits

Prep Time: 20 minutes, Cook Time: 5½ to 7½ hours, Serves: 8

INGREDIENTS:

- 2 pounds (907g) raw shrimp, peeled and deveined
- 4 large tomatoes, seeded and chopped
- 2 onions, chopped
- 2 green bell peppers, stemmed, seeded, and chopped
- 2½ cups stone-ground grits
- 8 cups chicken stock or roasted vegetable broth
- 1½ cups shredded Cheddar cheese
- 5 garlic cloves, minced
- 1 bay leaf
- 1 tsp. Old Bay Seasoning

DIRECTIONS:

1. Combine grits, onions, garlic, tomatoes, sweet peppers, chicken broth, bay leaves, and seasonings in a 6-quart crock pot. Cook on low heat for 5 to 7 hours, and cover until the coarse grains are soft and most of the liquid is absorbed.
2. Add shrimp. Put the lid on and continue to cook for 30 to 40 minutes until the shrimp turns pink.
3. Stir in the cheese and serve immediately.

Nutrition Info per Serving:

Calories: 415, Fat: 10g, Saturated Fat: 4g, Protein: 33g, Carbohydrates: 51g, Sugar: 5g, Fiber: 5g, Sodium: 415mg

Lemon Crawfish Poppers

Prep Time: 15 minutes, Cook Time: 30 minutes, Serves: 4

INGREDIENTS:

- 1 pound (450 g) raw crawfish tails (langoustine tails), coarsely chopped
- 1 medium yellow summer squash, grated
- 1 small carrot, finely chopped
- 1 zucchini, finely chopped
- 1 cup ground split peas
- 1 cup chickpea flour
- ½ small red bell pepper, finely chopped
- 4 medium egg whites
- 1 garlic clove, minced
- 1 tbsp. red wine vinegar
- 1 tsp. Creole Seasoning
- 1 tsp. baking powder
- 1 tsp. ketchup
- 1 tbsp. tahini
- 1 tbsp. freshly squeezed lemon juice
- 1 lemon, cut into wedges, for serving

DIRECTIONS:

1. Mix the ground split peas, chickpea flour, Creole seasoning, and baking powder in a medium bowl and mix well.
2. Mix the crawfish tails, summer squash, carrot, zucchini, bell pepper, garlic, and egg whites in a large bowl.
3. Add the crawfish mixture into the dry ingredients, pour in water as needed, ¼ cup at a time. The mix is ready to be formed when it resembles a batter-like consistency and no dry flour is visible.
4. Working in two or three batches with wet hand, form golf ball-size nuggets and put in the basket of an air fryer.
5. Turn the air fryer to 350°F(180ºC), close, and cook for 10 minutes. Place the poppers to a plate. Repeat with the rest of the batter.
6. To make the dipping sauce, whisk together the vinegar, ketchup, tahini, and lemon juice in a small bowl and toss to coat well.
7. Serve with the lemon wedges.

Nutrition Info per Serving:

Calories: 321, Total Fat: 3g, Sodium: 165mg, Total Carbohydrates: 31g, Sugar: 8g, Fiber: 7g, Protein: 41g

Crab, Scallop and Shrimp Pasta

Prep Time: 15 minutes, Cook Time: 1-2 hours, Serves: 4 to 6

INGREDIENTS:

- 2 tbsps. butter, melted
- 1 lb. (454 g) medium shrimp, cooked and peeled
- ½ lb. (227 g) bay scallops, lightly cooked
- ½ lb. (227 g) crabmeat or imitation flaked crabmeat
- 2 cups sour cream
- 3 cups shredded Monterey Jack cheese
- ⅛ tsp. pepper

DIRECTIONS:

1. In the crock pot, add the butter, sour cream and cheese, mix well.
2. Stir in the scallops, crabmeat, shrimp and pepper.
3. Cover the cooker and cook on Low for 1 to 2 hours.
4. After cooking, serve immediately over the linguine. Garnish with fresh parsley.

Nutrition Info per Serving:

Calories: 628, Fat: 45.13 g, Carbohydrates: 9.1 g, Protein: 46.4 g

Salmon and Mushroom Casserole

INGREDIENTS:

- 14¾-oz. (418 g) can salmon with liquid
- 4-oz. (113 g) can mushrooms, drained
- 1½ cups bread crumbs
- 1 cup shredded fat-free cheese
- 1 tbsp. minced onion
- ⅓ cup eggbeaters
- 1 tbsp. lemon juice

DIRECTIONS:

1. In a bowl, flake the fish and remove the bones. Add the bead crumbs, mushrooms, onion, eggbeaters, lemon juice and cheese. Pour into a lightly greased crock pot.
2. Cover the cooker and cook on Low for 2½ to 3½ hours.

Nutrition Info per Serving:

Calories: 150, Total Fat: 4 g, Total Carbohydrate: 9 g, Protein: 19 g, Sugar: 1 g, Fiber: 1 g

Moroccan Sea Bass

INGREDIENTS:

- 2 tbsps. extra-virgin olive oil
- 2 pounds (907 g) fresh sea bass fillets
- One (15-ounce, 425 g) can diced tomatoes, with the juice
- 4 garlic cloves, minced
- 1 large yellow onion, finely chopped
- 1 medium red bell pepper, cut into ½-inch strips
- 1 medium yellow bell pepper, cut into ½-inch strips
- 1½ tsps. sweet paprika
- 1 tsp. saffron threads, crushed in the palm of your hand
- ¼ tsp. hot paprika or ¼ tsp. smoked paprika (or pimentón)
- ½ tsp. ground ginger
- ¼ cup fresh orange juice
- ¼ cup finely chopped fresh cilantro
- ¼ cup finely chopped fresh flat-leaf parsley
- Sea salt
- Black pepper
- 1 Navel orange, thinly sliced, for garnish

DIRECTIONS:

1. Heat the olive oil in a large skillet over medium-high heat. Add the garlic, onion, red and yellow bell peppers, sweet paprika, saffron, hot or smoked paprika, and ginger, and cook for 3 minutes, or until the onion begins to soften, stirring often.
2. Stir in the tomatoes and cook for another 2 minutes, to blend the flavors.
3. Transfer the mixture to the crock pot and add the orange juice, stir well.
4. Place over the tomato mixture with the sea bass fillets, and spoon some of the mixture over the fish. Cover the cooker and cook on high for 2 hours, or on low for 3 to 4 hours. Cook until the center of the sea bass is opaque.
5. Use a spatula to carefully lift the fish out of the crock pot and transfer to a serving platter. Use aluminum foil to cover loosely.
6. Skim off any excess fat from the sauce, stir in the cilantro and parsley, and season with salt and pepper.
7. Spoon over the fish with some of the sauce, and garnish with the orange slices. Serve hot, passing the remaining sauce on the side.

Cheesy Salmon Soufflé

INGREDIENTS:

- 15-oz. (425 g) can salmon, drained and flaked
- 1 cup shredded cheddar cheese
- 2 eggs, beaten well
- 2 cups seasoned croutons
- 1 cup boiling water
- 2 chicken bouillon cubes
- ¼ tsp. dry mustard, optional

DIRECTIONS:

1. Use nonstick cooking spray to grease the interior of your cooker.
2. In the crock pot, add the eggs, salmon, croutons, and cheese, mix well.
3. In a small bowl, dissolve the bouillon cubes in boiling water. Add mustard, if you wish, and stir. Pour over salmon mixture and lightly stir them together.
4. Cover the cooker and cook on High for 2 to 3 hours, or until the mixture appears to be set. Let stand for 15 minutes before serving.

Nutrition Info per Serving:

Calories: 309, Fat: 14.32 g, Carbohydrates: 13.48 g, Protein: 29.47 g

Savory Salmon and Barley Bake

INGREDIENTS:

- 6 (5-ounce, 142g) salmon fillets
- 1 (8-ounce, 227g) package cremini mushrooms, sliced
- 2 cups hulled barley, rinsed
- 5 cups roasted vegetable broth
- 2 fennel bulbs, cored and chopped
- 2 red bell peppers, stemmed, seeded, and chopped
- ⅓ cup grated Parmesan cheese
- 4 garlic cloves, minced
- 1 tsp. dried tarragon leaves
- ⅛ tsp. freshly ground black pepper

DIRECTIONS:

1. Combine barley, fennel, bell peppers, garlic, mushrooms, vegetable broth, tarragon and pepper in a 6-quart crock pot. Cook on low heat for 7 to 8 hours, until the barley has absorbed most of the mixed soup and softened and the vegetables have also softened.
2. Put salmon fillets in a crock pot. Cover the lid and continue to cook for 20 to 40 minutes, until the salmon fillets are tested with a fork.
3. Sprinkle with Parmesan cheese, stir in salmon, and serve.

Nutrition Info per Serving:

Calories: 609, Fat: 20g, Saturated Fat: 4g, Protein: 49g, Carbohydrates: 55g, Sugar: 4g, Fiber: 13g, Sodium: 441mg

Creamy Potato and Fish Bake

Prep Time: 20 minutes, Cook Time: 1-2 hours, Serves: 4

INGREDIENTS:

- 1-lb. (454 g) perch fillet, fresh or thawed
- 10¾-oz. (304 g) can cream of celery soup
- 2 cups cooked, diced potatoes, drained
- ¼ cup grated Parmesan cheese
- ½ cup water
- 1 tbsp. chopped parsley
- ½ tsp. dried basil
- ¼ tsp. dried oregano
- ½ tsp. salt

DIRECTIONS:

1. In a bowl, mix the soup and water. Pour half in the crock pot. On top of the soup spread with the fillet. Place the potatoes over the fillet. Pour the remaining soup mix over the top.
2. In a bowl, add the cheese, parsley, basil, oregano and salt, mix well and sprinkle over the ingredients in the crock pot.
3. Cover the cooker and cook on High for 1 to 2 hours, not to overcook the fish.

Nutrition Info per Serving:

Calories: 348, Fat: 23.93 g, Carbohydrates: 16.05 g, Protein: 28.72 g

Ham Shrimp Jambalaya

Prep Time: 15 minutes, Cook Time: 2¼ hours, Serves: 8

INGREDIENTS:

- 2 tbsps. margarine
- 1 lb. (454 g) shelled, deveined, medium-sized shrimp
- 28-oz. (784 g) can low-sodium chopped tomatoes
- 3 ribs celery, chopped
- 1 cup chopped, cooked lean ham
- 2 medium onions, chopped
- 2 green bell peppers, chopped
- 1½ cups fat-free low sodium beef broth
- 1½ cups minute rice, uncooked
- 2 garlic cloves, chopped
- 2 tbsps. chopped parsley, fresh or dried
- ½ tsp. dried thyme
- 1 tsp. dried basil
- ⅛ tsp. cayenne pepper
- ¼ tsp. black pepper
- 1 tbsp. chopped parsley for garnish

DIRECTIONS:

1. One-half hour before assembling the recipe, in the crock pot, melt the margarine on High. Add the garlic, ham, onions, celery and peppers. Cook for 30 minutes.
2. Add the rice. Cover and cook for 15 minutes.
3. Stir in the tomatoes, broth, 2 tbsps. parsley, thyme, basil, cayenne pepper and black pepper. Cover and cook on High for 1 hour.
4. Add the shrimp. Cover and cook on High for 30 minutes, or until the liquid is absorbed.
5. After cooking, garnish with 1 tbsp. parsley before serving.

Nutrition Info per Serving:

Calories: 160, Total Fat: 4 g, Total Carbohydrate: 23 g, Protein: 9 g, Sugar: 5 g, Fiber: 3 g

Fish Feast with Mixed Veggies

Prep Time: 10 minutes, Cook Time: 2-3 hours, Serves: 8

INGREDIENTS:

- 3 lbs. (1.4 kg) red snapper fillets
- 14-oz. (397 g) can low-sodium diced tomatoes
- 2 unpeeled zucchinis, sliced
- 1 green bell pepper, cut in 1-inch pieces
- 1 large onion, sliced
- ¼ cup dry white wine or white grape juice
- 1 tbsp. garlic, minced
- ½ tsp. dried oregano
- ½ tsp. dried basil
- ¼ tsp. salt
- ¼ tsp. black pepper

DIRECTIONS:

1. Use non-fat cooking spray to spray the crock pot.
2. Rinse snapper and use paper towel to pat dry. Place in the crock pot.
2. In a large bowl, combine all of the remaining ingredients together and pour over the fish in the crock pot.
3. Cover and cook on High for 2 to 3 hours, not to overcook the fish.

Nutrition Info per Serving:

Calories: 200, Total Fat: 2.5 g, Total Carbohydrate: 7 g, Protein: 36 g, Sugar: 3 g, Fiber: 2 g

Spicy Lime Fish Tacos

Prep Time: 5 minutes, Cook Time: 1½ hours (low), Serves: 6

INGREDIENTS:

- 2 tbsps. olive oil, plus 1 tbsp. for greasing the crock pot
- 1½ pounds (680 g) tilapia or sea bass fillets
- 2 roasted poblano chiles, diced
- 2 tbsps. Taco Seasoning Mix
- ½ tsp. sea salt
- Zest of 1 lime
- 2 tbsps. fresh lime juice
- ½ cup chopped fresh
- cilantro
- 2 garlic cloves, minced
- 12 blue corn tortillas
- FOR THE TOPPINGS:
- 2 avocados, diced
- Green Salsa or Pico de Gallo
- 3 cups shredded cabbage
- ¾ cup chopped scallions
- Lime wedges

DIRECTIONS:

1. Use 1 tablespoon of olive oil to rub the inside of the crock pot.
2. Use the taco seasoning and salt to season the fish, and then transfer it into the crock pot.
3. Add 2 tablespoons of olive oil, chiles, lime zest, lime juice, cilantro and garlic into a medium bowl, combine them together. Pour over the fish fillets in the crock pot with this mixture.
4. Cover the cooker and cook on low for 1½ hours, or until a meat thermometer inserted in the fish reads 145°F(63°C).
5. Add the tortillas into a dry skillet, warm over medium heat. Break the fish apart and divide it among the warm tortillas.
6. To each taco, add avocado, salsa, cabbage, scallions, and a squeeze of lime. Serve with Cilantro and Lime Rice.

Salmon with Root Vegetables

Prep Time: 20 minutes, Cook Time: 7½ to 9½ hours, Serves: 6

INGREDIENTS:

- 6 (5-ounce, 142g) salmon fillets
- 4 large carrots, sliced
- 4 Yukon Gold potatoes, cubed
- 2 sweet potatoes, peeled and cubed
- 2 onions, chopped
- ⅓ cup grated Parmesan cheese
- ⅓ cup roasted vegetable broth or fish stock
- 1 tsp. dried thyme leaves
- 3 garlic cloves, minced
- ½ tsp. salt

DIRECTIONS:

1. Combine carrots, sweet potatoes, Yukon golden potatoes, onions, garlic, vegetable broth, thyme, and salt in a 6-quart crock pot. Turn on a low heat and cook for about 7 to 9 hours, until the vegetables are soft.
2. Put the salmon fillets in the pot and sprinkle some cheese. Put the lid on and cook on low heat for another 30 to 40 minutes, until the salmon fillets are cooked through. Serve immediately!

Nutrition Info per Serving:

Calories: 491, Fat: 19g, Saturated Fat: 4g, Protein: 42g, Carbohydrates: 38g, Sugar: 8g, Fiber: 5g

Shrimp Scampi with Vegetable

Prep Time: 20 minutes, Cook Time: 5½ to 7½ hours, Serves: 8

INGREDIENTS:

- 2 tbsps. butter
- 2 pounds (907g) raw shrimp, shelled and deveined
- 1 pound (454g) cremini mushrooms, sliced
- 8 garlic cloves, minced
- 2 onions, chopped
- 2 leeks, chopped
- ¼ cup freshly squeezed lemon juice
- 1 cup fish stock
- 1 tsp. dried basil leaves

DIRECTIONS:

1. Combine mushrooms, onions, leeks, garlic, fish broth, lemon juice, and basil in a 6-quart crock pot. Turn on low heat and cook for 5 to 7 hours, and cover until the vegetables are soft.
2. Put the shrimp in the pot. Continue to cook on high heat for 30 to 40 minutes, until the shrimp is pink.
3. Stir in the butter, close the lid and let stand for 10 minutes. Serve immediately!

Nutrition Info per Serving:

Calories: 158, Fat: 4g, Saturated Fat: 2g, Protein: 22g, Carbohydrates: 10g, Sugar: 3g, Fiber: 2g, Sodium: 275mg

Buttery White Fish with Lime

Prep Time: 5 minutes, Cook Time: 2 hours (low), Serves: 6

INGREDIENTS:

- 1 tbsp. olive oil
- 6 sea bass (or other firm white fish) fillets
- 3 tbsps. unsalted butter, melted
- ¼ tsp. sea salt
- Zest of 1 lime
- ¼ cup fresh lime juice
- ½ cup chopped fresh cilantro
- 2 tbsps. chopped jalapeño
- Lime wedges, for garnish

DIRECTIONS:

1. Use the olive oil to rub the inside of the crock pot.
2. Use the melted butter to lightly brush the fish, sprinkle it with salt, and then place it in the bottom of the crock pot.
3. Add the lime zest, lime juice, cilantro and jalapeño into a medium bowl, combine them together, then spoon the mixture over the fish.
4. Cover the cooker and cook on low for 2 hours, or until a meat thermometer inserted in the fish reads 145°F(63°C).
5. Serve the fish with rice, warm whole-wheat tortillas, and a salad. Garnish with lime wedges.

Crabmeat with Pasta Sauce

Prep Time: 15 minutes, Cook Time: 4-6 hours, Serves: 4 to 6

INGREDIENTS:

- ½ lb. (227 g) fresh mushrooms, sliced
- 1 medium onion, chopped
- 6-oz. (170 g) can tomato paste
- 2 (12-oz. 340 g) cans low-sodium tomato sauce, or 1 12-oz. (340 g) can low-sodium tomato sauce and 1 (12-oz. 340 g) can low-sodium chopped tomatoes
- ½ tsp. dried basil
- ½ tsp. dried oregano
- ½ tsp. garlic powder
- ½ tsp. salt
- 1 lb. (454 g) crabmeat
- 16 oz. (454 g) angel-hair pasta, cooked

DIRECTIONS:

1. In a nonstick skillet, sauté the mushrooms and onions over low heat. When wilted, transfer into the crock pot.
2. Add the tomato paste, tomato sauce, basil, oregano, garlic powder and salt into the cooker, mix well. Then stir in the crabmeat.
3. Cover the cooker and cook on Low for 4 to 6 hours.
4. After cooking, serve over the angel-hair pasta.

Nutrition Info per Serving:

Calories: 550, Total Fat: 5 g, Total Carbohydrate: 88 g, Protein: 42 g, Sugar: 12 g, Fiber: 9 g

Cheesy Crab Meat Sauce

Prep Time: 10 minutes, Cook Time: 5 to 6 hours on low, Serves: 4

INGREDIENTS:

- 12 ounces (340 g) crab meat, flaked
- 8 ounces (227 g) goat cheese
- 8 ounces (227 g) cream cheese
- ½ cup grated Asiago cheese
- 1 sweet onion, finely chopped
- 1 cup sour cream
- 1 scallion, white and green parts, chopped
- 1 tbsp. granulated erythritol
- 2 tsps. minced garlic

DIRECTIONS:

1. Add all of the ingredients to a large bowl, stir them together until well mixed.
2. In an 8-by-4-inch loaf pan, add the mixture and transfer the pan in the insert of the crock pot.
3. Cover the cooker and cook on low for 5 to 6 hours.
4. After the cooking, turn off the heat and serve warm.

Nutrition Info per Serving:

Calories: 361, Total Fat: 28 g, Total Carbs: 10 g, Net Carbs: 8 g, Protein: 17 g, Fiber: 2 g, Cholesterol: 88 mg

Crock Pot Lime Tilapia Veracruz

Prep Time: 5 minutes, Cook Time: 2 to 4 hours (low), Serves: 6

INGREDIENTS:

- Cooking spray
- 6 tilapia fillets (about 6 ounces each, 170 g)
- 1 tbsp. olive oil
- 2 large tomatoes, chopped
- 1 bell pepper (any color), seeded and thinly sliced
- ½ cup sliced pimento-stuffed green olives
- 1 medium pepperoncino, seeded and diced
- 1 large onion, chopped
- 6 lime wedges
- ¼ tsp. sea salt
- ½ tsp. freshly ground black pepper
- 4 garlic cloves, sliced
- 2 tbsps. drained capers

DIRECTIONS:

1. Use cooking spray to spray the crock pot.
2. With olive oil to brush the tilapia fillets and lightly sprinkle salt and pepper over them. Lay the fillets on the bottom of the crock pot.
3. Add the remaining ingredients except the lime wedges to a medium bowl, combine them together. Then spoon over the fillets with this mixture.
4. Cover the cooker and cook on low for 2 to 4 hours, or until a meat thermometer inserted in the fish reads 145°F(63°C).
5. Remove the fillets to warm plates and spoon some of the vegetables and sauce over each before serving. Top with lime wedges.

Classic Shrimp Marinara with Spaghetti

Prep Time: 15 minutes, Cook Time: 6¼-7¼ hours. Serves: 6

INGREDIENTS:

- 1 lb. (454 g) shrimp, cooked and shelled
- 16-oz. (454 g) can low-sodium tomatoes, cut up
- 3 cups spaghetti
- 6-oz. (170 g) can tomato paste
- 1 clove garlic, minced
- 2 tbsps. minced parsley
- 1 tsp. dried oregano
- grated Parmesan cheese
- ½ tsp. dried basil
- ½ tsp. salt
- ¼ tsp. black pepper
- ½ tsp. seasoned salt

DIRECTIONS:

1. In the crock pot, add the tomatoes, garlic, parsley, tomato paste, basil, salt, pepper, and seasoned salt, mix well.
2. Cover the cooker and cook on Low for 6 to 7 hours.
3. Stir the shrimp into the sauce.
4. Cover and cook on Low for another 10 to 15 minutes.
5. After cooking, serve over the cooked spaghetti. Top with the Parmesan cheese.

Nutrition Info per Serving:

Calories: 210, Total Fat: 1.5 g, Total Carbohydrate: 29 g, Protein: 21 g, Sugar: 4 g, Fiber: 4 g

Tuna with Celery

Prep Time: 10 minutes, Cook Time: 4-10 hours, Serves: 4

INGREDIENTS:

- 12-oz. (340 g) can tuna, drained
- 1 medium green pepper, finely chopped
- 1 rib celery, chopped
- 2 cups tomato juice
- 2 tbsps. onion flakes
- 2 tbsps. Worcestershire sauce
- 3 tbsps. vinegar
- 2 tbsps. sugar
- 1 tbsp. prepared mustard
- ½ tsp. cinnamon
- dash chili powder
- dash of hot sauce, optional

DIRECTIONS:

1. In the crock pot, combine all of the ingredients.
2. Cover the cooker and cook on Low for 8 to 10 hours, or on High for 4 to 5 hours. Add ½ cup tomato juice if the mixture becomes too dry during cooking.
3. After cooking, serve on buns.

Nutrition Info per Serving:

Calories: 138, Fat: 1.36 g, Carbohydrates: 14.43 g, Protein: 18.3 g

Salmon and Potato Casserole

Prep Time: 10 minutes, Cook Time: 8 hours, Serves: 1

INGREDIENTS:

- 1 tsp. butter, at room temperature, or extra-virgin olive oil
- 2 medium russet potatoes, peeled and sliced thin
- 4 ounces (113 g) smoked salmon
- 1 cup 2% milk
- 2 eggs
- 1 tsp. dried dill
- ⅛ tsp. sea salt
- Freshly ground black pepper

DIRECTIONS:

1. Use the butter to grease the inside of the crock pot.
2. Add the milk, eggs, dill, salt and a few grinds of the black pepper to a small bowl, whisk them together.
3. In a single layer on the bottom of the crock pot, spread one-third of the potatoes and top them with one-third of the salmon. Over the salmon, pour in one-third of the egg mixture. Repeat this layering with the remaining potatoes, salmon, and egg mixture.
4. Cover the cooker and set on low, cook for 8 hours or overnight.

Nutrition Info per Serving:

Calories: 355, Saturated Fat: 5 g, Trans Fat: 0 g, Carbohydrates: 40 g, Protein: 24 g, Fiber: 5 g

Spiced Jambalaya

Prep Time: 20 minutes, Cook Time: 7½ to 9½ hours, Serves: 8

INGREDIENTS:

- 1½ pounds (680g) raw shrimp, shelled and deveined
- 10 (4-ounce, 113g) boneless, skinless chicken thighs, cut into 2-inch pieces
- 5 celery stalks, sliced
- 2 jalapeño peppers, minced
- 2 green bell peppers, stemmed, seeded, and chopped
- 2 onions, chopped
- 2 cups chicken stock
- 1 tbsp. Cajun seasoning
- 6 garlic cloves, minced
- ¼ tsp. cayenne pepper

DIRECTIONS:

1. Mix chicken, onion, garlic, jalapeno, bell pepper, celery, chicken broth, cajun seasoning and cayenne in a 6-quart crock pot. Turn on a low heat and cook for 7 to 9 hours. Cover the lid until the chicken turns white.
2. Put the shrimp in the crock pot. Cook for another 30 to 40 minutes, until the shrimp turns pink. Serve immediately!

Nutrition Info per Serving:

Calories: 417, Fat: 20g, Saturated Fat: 5g, Protein: 34g, Carbohydrates: 27g, Sugar: 3g, Fiber: 3g, Sodium: 385mg

Slow-Cooked Mediterranean Cod au Gratin

Prep Time: 20 minutes, Cook Time: 1 to 1½ hours, Serves: 6

INGREDIENTS:

- 6 tbsps. olive oil
- 3 pounds (1.4 kg) Pacific cod fillets
- ⅓ cup grated Asiago cheese
- ⅓ cup grated Parmesan cheese
- ⅓ cup grated Romano cheese
- 1¼ cups milk
- 3 tbsps. all-purpose flour
- 1 tsp. rosemary
- 1½ tsps. sea salt
- ½ tbsp. dry mustard
- ¼ tbsp. ground nutmeg
- 2 tsps. lemon juice

DIRECTIONS:

1. In a small saucepan, add the olive oil and heat over medium heat. Stir in the mustard, flour, rosemary, salt, and nutmeg.
2. Add the milk gradually, stirring constantly until thickened.
3. Stir in the lemon juice, and the Asiago, Parmesan, and Romano cheeses to the saucepan. Stir until the cheeses are melted.
4. In the crock pot, add the fish, and spoon over the fish with the cheese sauce. Cover the cooker and cook on high for 1 to 1½ hours or until the fish flakes. Serve hot.

Chinese Vegetable and Shrimp Casserole

Prep Time: 10-15 minutes, Cook Time: 45 minutes, Serves: 10

INGREDIENTS:

- 2 cups cooked or canned shrimp
- 1 cup cooked or canned chicken
- 1-lb. (454 g) can (2 cups) Chinese vegetables
- ½ cup chopped green peppers
- 4 cups rice, cooked
- 10¾-oz. (304 g) can cream of celery soup
- ½ cup milk
- 1 tbsp. soy sauce
- can of Chinese noodles

DIRECTIONS:

1. In the crock pot, add all of the ingredients except the noodles, mix well.
2. Cover the cooker and cook on Low for 45 minutes.
3. After cooking, top with the noodles just before serving.

Nutrition Info per Serving:

Calories: 511, Fat: 52.2 g, Carbohydrates: 5.4 g, Protein: 8.52 g

CHAPTER 9

LAMB

Tunisian Pumpkin and Lamb Stew

Prep Time: 15 minutes, Cook Time: 8 hours on low, Serves: 6

INGREDIENTS:

- ¼ cup extra-virgin olive oil
- 1½ pounds (680 g) lamb shoulder, cut into 1-inch chunks
- 4 cups pumpkin, cut into 1-inch pieces
- 1 (14.5-ounce, 411 g) can diced tomatoes
- 2 carrots, diced
- 1 sweet onion, chopped
- 3 cups beef broth
- 1 cup Greek yogurt
- 1 tbsp. minced garlic
- 2 tbsps. ras el hanout
- 1 tsp. hot chili powder
- 1 tsp. salt

DIRECTIONS:

1. Use 1 tablespoon olive oil to lightly grease the crock pot insert.
2. Heat the remaining oil in a large skillet over medium-high heat.
3. Add the lamb to the skillet, and brown for 6 minutes, then add the garlic and onion.
4. Sauté for another 3 minutes, then place the vegetables and lamb into the insert.
5. In the insert, add the broth, pumpkin, tomatoes, carrots, ras el hanout, chili powder, and salt, and stir to combine.
6. Cover the cooker and set on low, cook for 8 hours
7. Top with yogurt and serve.

Nutrition Info per Serving:

Calories: 447, Total Fat: 35 g, Total Carbs: 12 g, Net Carbs: 9 g, Protein: 22 g, Fiber: 3 g

Wash-Day Lamp Bean Stew

Prep Time: 10 minutes, Cook Time: 6-7 hours, Serves: 8 to 10

INGREDIENTS:

- 1½-2 lbs. (680 to 907 g) lean lamb or beef, cubed
- 2 (15-oz. 425 g) cans white beans, drained
- 2 (15-oz. 425 g) cans garbanzo beans, drained
- 2 medium onions, peeled and quartered
- 1 tomato, peeled and quartered
- 1 quart water
- 1 tsp. salt
- 1 tsp. turmeric
- 3 tbsps. fresh lemon juice
- 8-10 pita bread pockets

DIRECTIONS:

1. In a crock pot, add all of the ingredients.
2. Cover the cooker and cook on High for 6 to 7 hours.
3. Use a strainer spoon to lift stew from the cooker and stuff in pita bread pockets.

Nutrition Info per Serving:

Calories: 203, Fat: 4.71 g, Carbohydrates: 22.75 g, Protein: 18.11 g

Garlicky Lamb Meatballs with Avocado Dill Sauce

Prep Time: 15 minutes, Cook Time: 7-8 hours, Serves: 12 meatballs

INGREDIENTS:

- 1½ pounds (680 g) ground lamb
- 1 large egg
- 1 small white onion, minced
- 1 cup Avocado-Dill Sauce
- 1 tsp. garlic powder
- ½ tsp. ground cumin
- ½ tsp. pumpkin pie spice
- ½ tsp. paprika
- ½ tsp. sea salt
- ¼ tsp. freshly ground black pepper

DIRECTIONS:

1. Add all of the ingredients except the avocado-dill sauce into a large bowl, combine them together well. Shape the lamb mixture into about 12 meatballs. In the bottom of the crock pot, arrange with the meatballs.
2. Cover the cooker and cook on low for 7 to 8 hours.
3. Serve with the avocado-dill sauce.

Nutrition Info per Serving:

Calories: 200, Total Fat: 17 g, Total Carbs: 2 g, Sugar: 0 g, Fiber: 1 g, Protein: 10 g, Sodium: 138 mg

Rosemary Garlic Lamb Shoulder Chops

Prep Time: 15 minutes, Cook Time: 6 hours on low, Serves: 4

INGREDIENTS:

- 3 tbsps. extra-virgin olive oil, divided
- 1½ pounds (680 g) lamb shoulder chops
- 1 sweet onion, sliced
- ½ cup chicken broth
- Freshly ground black
- pepper, for seasoning
- Salt, for seasoning
- 2 tsps. minced garlic
- 1 tsp. dried thyme
- 2 tsps. dried rosemary

DIRECTIONS:

1. Use 1 tablespoon of the olive oil to lightly grease the insert of the crock pot.
2. Heat the remaining 2 tablespoons of the olive oil in a large skillet over medium-high heat.
3. Use pepper and salt to season the lamb. In the skillet, add the lamb and brown for 6 minutes, turning once.
4. Transfer the lamb to the insert, and stir in the garlic, broth, onion, thyme and rosemary.
5. Cover the cooker and set on low, cook for 6 hours.
6. Turn off the heat and serve warm.

Nutrition Info per Serving:

Calories: 380, Total Fat: 27 g, Total Carbs: 3 g, Net Carbs: 2 g, Protein: 31 g, Fiber: 1 g

Irish Lamb Stew with Root Vegetables

Prep Time: 10 minutes, Cook Time: 8 hours, Serves: 1

INGREDIENTS:

- 12 ounces (340 g) boneless lamb shoulder or stew meat, cut into 1-inch pieces
- 1 cup diced and peeled potatoes
- 1 cup diced and peeled parsnips
- ½ cup diced onions
- 1 cup low-sodium beef broth
- ½ cup dark beer, such as Guinness Stout
- ⅛ tsp. sea salt
- Freshly ground black pepper
- 1 tbsp. minced garlic
- ½ tbsp. tomato paste

DIRECTIONS:

1. Use the salt and a few grinds of the black pepper to season the lamb. In the crock pot, add the lamb, onions, potatoes, parsnips, and garlic.
2. Add the beer, beef broth and tomato paste into a measuring cup or small bowl, whisk them together. Pour this over the lamb and vegetables.
3. Cover the cooker and set on low, cook for 8 hours.

Nutrition Info per Serving:

Calories: 423, Saturated Fat: 5 g, Trans Fat: 0 g, Carbohydrates: 22 g, Protein: 51 g, Fiber: 2 g, Sodium: 454 mg

Spiced Lamb Leg

Prep Time: 15 minutes, Cook Time: 8 hours, Serves: 8

INGREDIENTS:

- 1 (2-pound) boneless leg of lamb, butterflied
- 1 cup beef broth
- ½ tsp. dried marjoram
- ½ tsp. ground cinnamon
- ½ tsp. ground nutmeg
- 2 tsps. dried oregano
- 1 tsp. dried thyme
- 1 tsp. onion powder
- 1 tsp. garlic powder
- ½ tsp. sea salt
- ¼ tsp. freshly ground black pepper

DIRECTIONS:

1. Mix the garlic powder, marjoram, cinnamon, oregano, thyme, onion powder, nutmeg, salt, and pepper in a small bowl. Rub the mixture all over the lamb.
2. Put the lamb in the crock pot and pour the broth over.
3. Cover and cook on low for 8 hours. Slice the lamb and serve.

Nutrition Info per Serving:

Calories: 218, Total Fat: 8g, Saturated Fat: 3g, Carbohydrates: 1g, Protein: 32g, Cholesterol: 102mg, Fiber: 0g

Home-Style Curried Lamb Stew

Prep Time: 15 minutes, Cook Time: 7 to 8 hours on low, Serves: 6

INGREDIENTS:

- 3 tbsps. extra-virgin olive oil, divided
- 1½ pounds (680 g) lamb shoulder chops
- Freshly ground black pepper, for seasoning
- Salt, for seasoning
- ½ sweet onion, sliced
- 3 cups coconut milk
- ¼ cup curry powder
- 2 tsps. minced garlic
- 1 tbsp. grated fresh ginger
- 1 carrot, diced
- 2 tbsps. chopped cilantro, for garnish

DIRECTIONS:

1. Use 1 tablespoon of the olive oil to lightly grease the insert of the crock pot,
2. Heat the remaining 2 tablespoons of the olive oil in a large skillet over medium-high heat.
3. Use pepper and salt to season the lamb. Place the lamb into the skillet and brown for 6 minutes, turning once. Place into the insert.
4. Add the onion, coconut milk, curry, garlic and ginger to a medium bowl, stir them together.
5. Transfer the mixture to the lamb and add the carrot.
6. Cover the cooker and set on low, cook for 7 to 8 hours.
7. Top with the cilantro and serve.

Nutrition Info per Serving:

Calories: 490, Total Fat: 41 g, Total Carbs: 10 g, Net Carbs: 5 g, Protein: 26 g, Fiber: 5 g

Healthy Lamb Chops

Prep Time: 15 minutes, Cook Time: 7-8 hours, Serves: 4 to 6

INGREDIENTS:

- 8 bone-in lamb chops (about 3 pounds, 1.4 kg)
- 1 medium onion, sliced
- 2 tbsps. balsamic vinegar
- 2 tsps. dried rosemary
- 2 tsps. garlic powder
- ½ tsp. dried thyme leaves
- 1 tsp. sea salt
- Freshly ground black pepper

DIRECTIONS:

1. Add onion slices to line the bottom of the crock pot.
2. Add the rosemary, garlic powder, thyme, salt and pepper to a small bowl, stir them together. Use this spice mixture to evenly rub the chops, and transfer them into the crock pot.
3. Drizzle over the top with the vinegar.
4. Cover the cooker and cook on low for 7 to 8 hours and serve.

Nutrition Info per Serving:

Calories: 327, Total Fat: 14 g, Total Carbs: 4 g, Sugar: 1 g, Fiber: 1 g, Protein: 43 g

Authentic Shepherd's Pie

Prep Time: 10 minutes, Cook Time: 8 hours, Serves: 1

INGREDIENTS:

- 8 ounces (227 g) lean ground beef
- 1½ cups prepared mashed potatoes
- 1 cup diced carrots
- 1 cup frozen peas, thawed
- ½ cup diced onions
- 2 tbsps. shredded sharp Cheddar cheese
- ⅛ tsp. sea salt
- Freshly ground black pepper

DIRECTIONS:

1. In the crock pot, add the peas, onions, carrots and beef, and stir together thoroughly. Use the salt and a few grinds of the black pepper to season the mixture.
2. Layer the prepared mashed potatoes over the meat and vegetable mixture evenly.
3. Cover the cooker and set on low, cook for 8 hours.
4. Sprinkle over the shepherd's pie with the Cheddar cheese and serve.

Nutrition Info per Serving:

Calories: 468, Saturated Fat: 6 g, Trans Fat: 0 g, Carbohydrates: 42 g, Protein: 45 g, Fiber: 8 g, Sodium: 403 mg

Moroccan Lamb Stew with Couscous

Prep Time: 15 minutes, Cook Time: 8 hours, Serves: 6

INGREDIENTS:

- 1 pound (454 g) lamb shoulder, trimmed of fat and cut into 1-inch cubes
- 2 cups (480 ml) poultry broth or beef broth
- 1 tbsp. grated fresh ginger
- 2 tsps. ground cumin
- 1 tsp. garlic powder
- ½ tsp. ground cinnamon
- 1 pint cherry tomatoes
- 2 onions, sliced
- ¼ tsp. sea salt
- ¼ tsp. freshly ground black pepper
- 3 cups cooked whole-wheat couscous
- ¼ cup chopped fresh cilantro

DIRECTIONS:

1. In your crock pot, combine the lamb, broth, ginger, cumin, garlic powder, cinnamon, tomatoes, onions, salt, and pepper.
2. Cover and cook on low for 8 hours.
3. Skim any excess fat from the surface of the stew and discard.
4. Garnish with the cilantro and serve over the couscous.

Nutrition Info per Serving:

Calories: 353, Total Fat: 6g, Saturated Fat: 2g, Carbohydrates: 45g, Protein: 28g, Cholesterol: 68mg, Fiber: 5g

Irish Lamb Stew with Carrots and Onions

Prep Time: 15 minutes, Cook Time: 8 hours, Serves: 6

INGREDIENTS:

- 1 pound (454 g) lamb leg, trimmed of fat and cut into 1-inch pieces
- 4 large carrots, peeled and cut into 1-inch chunks
- 2 onions, sliced
- 2 leeks, chopped
- 1 cup fresh or frozen peas
- 3 cups (720 ml) beef broth
- 1 tbsp. dried rosemary
- 1 tsp. ground mustard
- ½ cup uncooked barley
- ½ tsp. sea salt
- ¼ tsp. freshly ground black pepper

DIRECTIONS:

1. Combine all the ingredients in your crock pot.
2. Cover and cook on low for 8 hours.
3. Skim any excess fat from the surface of the stew and discard.

Nutrition Info per Serving:

Calories: 338, Total Fat: 18g, Saturated Fat: 8g, Carbohydrates: 28g, Protein: 18g, Cholesterol: 54mg, Fiber: 7g

Greek Lemon Lamb and Potatoes

Prep Time: 10 minutes, Cook Time: 8-10 hours, Serves: 1

INGREDIENTS:

- 1 tbsp. extra-virgin olive oil
- 1 tbsp. minced fresh rosemary
- 2 bone-in lamb shoulder chops, about 6 ounces each (170 g), trimmed of excess fat
- 4 red potatoes, halved
- 4 garlic cloves, minced, divided
- 1 tbsp. minced fresh oregano
- Juice of 1 lemon
- ¼ tsp. ground cumin
- ½ tsp. ground cinnamon
- ⅛ tsp. sea salt
- Freshly ground black pepper
- Zest of 1 lemon

DIRECTIONS:

1. Add the rosemary, half of the garlic, oregano, lemon juice, cumin, cinnamon, salt and a few grinds of the black pepper into a small bowl, mix them together. Coat this mixture onto the lamb chops and set aside, you can also do this the night before.
2. In the crock pot, add the potatoes along with the remaining garlic, lemon zest, and olive oil. Over the potatoes place with the lamb shoulder.
3. Cover the cooker and set on low, cook for 8 to 10 hours, until the lamb is tender and falling off the bone.

Nutrition Info per Serving:

Calories: 540, Saturated Fat: 3 g, Trans Fat: 0 g, Carbohydrates: 68 g, Protein: 32 g, Fiber: 10 g, Sodium: 226 mg

Crock Pot Vegetables and Lamb

Prep Time: 10 minutes, Cook Time: 6 hours on low, Serves: 4

INGREDIENTS:

- ¼ cup extra-virgin olive oil, divided
- 1 pound (454 g) boneless lamb chops, about ½-inch thick
- 1 zucchini, cut into 1-inch chunks
- ½ fennel bulb, cut into 2-inch chunks
- ½ sweet onion, sliced
- ¼ cup chicken broth
- Freshly ground black pepper, for seasoning
- Salt, for seasoning
- 2 tbsps. chopped fresh basil, for garnish

DIRECTIONS:

1. Use 1 tablespoon of the olive oil to lightly grease the insert of the crock pot.
2. With pepper and salt to season the lamb.
3. Add the remaining 3 tablespoons of the olive oil, fennel, onion and zucchini to a medium bowl, toss them together, then place along with half of the vegetables in the insert.
4. Over the vegetables, add the lamb, then place the remaining vegetables to cover, and add the broth.
5. Cover the cooker and cook on low for 6 hours.
6. Top with the basil and serve.

Nutrition Info per Serving:

Calories: 431, Total Fat: 37 g, Total Carbs: 5 g, Net Carbs: 3 g, Protein: 21 g, Fiber: 2 g

Spiced Lamb Stew with Couscous and Apricots

Prep Time: 30 minutes, Cook Time: 5 hours, Serves: 5

INGREDIENTS:

- 3 tbsps. butter
- 2 pounds (907 g) lamb stew meat, cut into 3/4-inch cubes
- 1 ½ cups chopped sweet onion
- ½ cup orange juice
- ¾ cup dried apricots
- ½ cup chicken broth
- 2 tsps. ground allspice
- 2 tsps. paprika
- 2 tsps. ground cinnamon
- 1 ½ tsps. salt
- 1 tsp. ground cardamom
- Hot cooked couscous
- Chopped dried apricots, optional

DIRECTIONS:

1. Add butter and lamb into a large skillet, brown the meat in batches. Transfer to a 3-qt. crock pot with a slotted spoon. Add the onion into the same skillet, saute in drippings until tender. Add the orange juice, apricots, broth, allspice, paprika, cinnamon, salt and cardamom, pour the mixture over lamb.
2. Cover the cooker and set on high, cook for 5-6 hours or until meat is tender. Serve with couscous. Sprinkle with more chopped apricots if desired.

Lamb Shanks with Mushroom and Carrot

Prep Time: 15 minutes, Cook Time: 7 to 8 hours on low, Serves: 6

INGREDIENTS:

- 3 tbsps. extra-virgin olive oil, divided
- 2 pounds (907 g) lamb shanks
- ½ pound (227 g) wild mushrooms, sliced
- 2 celery stalks, chopped
- 1 leek, thoroughly cleaned and chopped
- 1 carrot, diced
- 1 (15-ounce, 425 g) can crushed tomatoes
- 1 tbsp. minced garlic
- ½ cup beef broth
- 2 tbsps. apple cider vinegar
- 1 tsp. dried rosemary
- ½ cup sour cream, for garnish

DIRECTIONS:

1. Use 1 tablespoon of the olive oil to lightly grease the insert of the crock pot.
2. Heat the remaining 2 tablespoons of the olive oil in a large skillet over medium-high heat. Place the lamb in the skillet and brown for 6 minutes, turning once, and transfer to the insert.
3. Add the leek, mushrooms, carrot, celery and garlic to the skillet, sauté for 5 minutes.
4. Transfer the vegetables to the insert, the add the broth, tomatoes, apple cider vinegar, and rosemary.
5. Cover the cooker and cook on low for 7 to 8 hours.
6. Top with the sour cream and serve.

Nutrition Info per Serving:

Calories: 475, Total Fat: 36 g, Total Carbs: 11 g, Net Carbs: 6 g, Protein: 31 g, Fiber: 5 g

Crock Pot Lamb Leg

Prep Time: 15 minutes, Cook Time: 5-6 hours, Serves: 4 to 6

INGREDIENTS:

- 1 tsp. garlic powder
- 1 tsp. dried rosemary
- 1 tsp. Dijon mustard
- 1 tsp. dried thyme leaves
- 1½ tsps. sea salt
- ½ tsp. freshly ground
- black pepper
- 1 (4-pound, 1.8 kg) bone-in lamb leg
- 2 cups broth of choice
- 1 small onion, roughly chopped

DIRECTIONS:

1. Add the garlic powder, rosemary, mustard, thyme, salt and pepper into a small bowl, stir them together to make a paste. Use this paste to evenly rub the lamb, and transfer it into the crock pot.
2. Place the onion and broth around the lamb in the cooker.
3. Cover the cooker and cook on low for 5 to 6 hours and serve.

Nutrition Info per Serving:

Calories: 780, Total Fat: 41 g, Total Carbs: 3 g, Sugar: 1 g, Fiber: 0 g, Protein: 93 g, Sodium: 1,023 mg

Spanish Style Lamb Chop and Potato

Prep Time: 10 minutes, Cook Time: 8 hours, Serves: 1

INGREDIENTS:

- 1 tsp. extra-virgin olive oil
- 2 bone-in lamb shoulders, trimmed of fat
- 2 red potatoes, unpeeled, quartered
- ½ cup diced roasted red pepper
- ½ cup diced onion
- 2 tbsps. fresh parsley
- ½ cup red wine
- 1 tsp. minced garlic
- ⅛ tsp. sea salt
- ½ tsp. minced fresh rosemary
- 1 tsp. smoked paprika
- Freshly ground black pepper

DIRECTIONS:

1. Use the olive oil to grease the inside of the crock pot.
2. In the crock pot, add the red pepper, onion, parsley, and wine.
3. Add the garlic, salt, rosemary, paprika and a few grinds of the black pepper into a small bowl, combine well. Rub over the lamb chops with this mixture. Or you can do this one day ahead to allow all the flavors of the rub to permeate the meat. Transfer the chops into the crock pot on top of the onion and wine mixture. The chops may need to overlap slightly one another to fit.
4. Place on top of the lamb with the potatoes.
5. Cover the cooker and set on low, cook for 8 hours.

Nutrition Info per Serving:

Calories: 419, Saturated Fat: 4 g, Trans Fat: 0 g, Carbohydrates: 43 g, Protein: 27 g, Fiber: 6 g, Sodium: 326 mg

Irish-Style Lamb and Vegetables Stew

Prep Time: 10 minutes, Cook Time: 8 hours, Serves: 1

INGREDIENTS:

- 12 ounces (340 g) boneless lamb shoulder or stew meat, cut into 1-inch pieces
- 1 cup diced and peeled parsnips
- 1 cup diced and peeled potatoes
- 1 cup low-sodium beef
- broth
- ½ cup diced onions
- 1 tbsp. minced garlic
- ½ cup dark beer, such as Guinness Stout
- ½ tbsp. tomato paste
- ⅛ tsp. sea salt
- Freshly ground black pepper

DIRECTIONS:

1. Combine the salt and a few grinds of the black pepper in a bowl, and use this mixture to season the lamb. In the crock pot, add the lamb, potatoes, parsnips, garlic and onions.
2. Add the beer, beef broth and tomato paste into a measuring cup or small bowl, whisk them together. Then pour this over the lamb and vegetables.
3. Cover the cooker and set on low, cook for 8 hours.

Nutrition Info per Serving:

Calories: 423, Saturated Fat: 5 g, Trans Fat: 0 g, Carbohydrates: 22 g, Protein: 51 g, Fiber: 2 g, Sodium: 454 mg

Lamb Shanks with Veggies

Prep Time: 10 minutes, Cook Time: 4-10 hours, Serves: 4 to 6

INGREDIENTS:

- 3 lamb shanks, cracked
- 2 small carrots, cut in thin strips
- 1 medium onion, thinly sliced
- 1 rib celery, chopped
- 8-oz. (227 g) can tomato sauce
- 1-2 cloves garlic, split
- 1½ tsps. salt
- ¼ tsp. pepper
- 1 tsp. dried thyme
- 2 bay leaves, crumbled
- 1 tsp. dried oregano
- ½ cup dry white wine

DIRECTIONS:

1. In the crock pot, add the carrots, onions, and celery.
2. Use garlic to rub the lamb and season with salt and pepper. Place in the crock pot.
3. In a separate bowl, mix all of the remaining ingredients together and add to the meat and vegetables.
4. Cover the cooker and cook on Low for 8 to 10 hours, or on High for 4 to 6 hours.

Nutrition Info per Serving:

Calories: 67, Fat: 3.2 g, Carbohydrates: 3.46 g, Protein: 6.79 g

Tender Lamb Roast

Prep Time: 10 minutes, Cook Time: 7 to 8 hours on low, Serves: 6

INGREDIENTS:

- 1 tbsp. extra-virgin olive oil
- 2 pounds (907 g) lamb shoulder roast
- 1 (14.5-ounces, 411 g) can diced tomatoes
- 1 cup sour cream
- 2 tsps. minced garlic
- 1 tbsp. cumin
- 1 tsp. chili powder
- 1 tsp. paprika
- Freshly ground black pepper, for seasoning
- Salt, for seasoning
- 2 tsps. chopped fresh parsley, for garnish

DIRECTIONS:

1. Use the olive oil to lightly grease the insert of the crock pot.
2. Combine the pepper and salt in a bowl, then use the mixture to lightly season the lamb.
3. In the insert of the crock pot, add the lamb and stir in the garlic, tomatoes, cumin, chili powder and paprika.
4. Cover the cooker and set on low, cook for 7 to 8 hours.
5. Add the sour cream, and stir well.
6. Top with the parsley and serve.

Nutrition Info per Serving:

Calories: 523, Total Fat: 43 g, Total Carbs: 6 g, Net Carbs: 5 g, Protein: 28 g, Fiber: 1 g

Lamb Tagine with Carrots

Prep Time: 40 minutes, Cook Time: 8 hours, Serves: 8

INGREDIENTS:

- 4 tbsps. olive oil, divided
- 3 pounds (1.4 kg) lamb stew meat, cut into 1 ½-inch cubes
- 1 tsp. pepper
- 1 tsp. salt
- 6 garlic cloves, minced
- 6 medium carrots, sliced
- 2 medium onions, chopped
- 2½ cups reduced-sodium chicken broth
- ½ cup pitted dates, chopped
- ½ cup sliced almonds, toasted
- ¼ cup honey
- ¼ cup sweet vermouth
- ¼ cup lemon juice
- 2 tsps. grated lemon peel
- 1 tbsp. minced fresh gingerroot
- 1½ tsps. ground cumin
- 1½ tsps. ground cinnamon
- 1½ tsps. paprika

DIRECTIONS:

1. Sprinkle lamb with pepper and salt. In batches, brown meat with 2 tablespoons oil in a Dutch oven. Then transfer the meat to a 4- or 5-qt. crock pot with a slotted spoon.
2. Add the remaining oil, garlic, onions, carrots and lemon peel into the same pot, saute until crisp-tender. Stir in the ginger, lemon juice, cumin, cinnamon, and paprika, cook and stir for another 2 minutes. Add to the crock pot.
3. Stir in the honey, broth, vermouth, and dates to the crock pot. Cover the cooker and cook on low for 8 to 10 hours or until the lamb is tender. Sprinkle with almonds and serve.

Sweet Soy Lamb and Rice

Prep Time: 10 minutes, Cook Time: 8 hours, Serves: 1

INGREDIENTS:

- 1 tsp. extra-virgin olive oil
- 12 ounces (340 g) boneless lamb shoulder, cut into 1-inch cubes
- 1 cup low-sodium chicken broth or water
- ½ cup brown rice
- 1 scallion, white and green parts, sliced thin on a bias
- 2 tbsps. honey
- 2 tbsps. low-sodium soy sauce
- Pinch red pepper flakes
- 1 tbsp. freshly squeezed lime juice

DIRECTIONS:

1. Use olive oil to grease the inside of the crock pot.
2. In the crock pot, add the broth, brown rice, and scallion. Stir to mix the ingredients and let the rice is submerged in the liquid.
3. Add the remaining ingredients except the lamb into a large bowl, whisk them together. Place the lamb cubes in the bowl and toss to coat them in this mixture. You can prepare the lamb a day ahead if you wish.
4. Transfer the lamb into the crock pot to cover the rice.
5. Cover the cooker and cook on low for 8 hours.

Nutrition Info per Serving:

Calories: 593, Saturated Fat: 5 g, Trans Fat: 0 g, Carbohydrates: 54 g, Protein: 54 g, Fiber: 2 g

CHAPTER 10

PORK

Lentils with Ham and Mixed Veggies

Prep Time: 10 minutes, Cook Time: 8 hours, Serves: 6

INGREDIENTS:

- 1 cup ham, cooked and chopped
- 2 cups dry lentils, rinsed and sorted
- ½ cup chopped carrots
- 1 cup diced tomatoes
- 1 medium onion, chopped
- ½ cup chopped celery
- 2 garlic cloves, minced
- 1 tsp. dried marjoram
- 1 tsp. ground coriander
- salt to taste
- pepper to taste
- 3 cups water

DIRECTIONS:

1. In a crock pot, add all of the ingredients and mix well.
2. Cover the cooker and cook on Low for 8 hours. Check the lentils after 5 hours of cooking. Stir in 1 more cup water if they've absorbed all the water.

Nutrition Info per Serving:

Calories: 51, Fat: 0.51 g, Carbohydrates: 10.6 g, Protein: 3.12 g

Peach Glazed Ham

Prep Time: 10 minutes, Cook Time: 6 hours, Serves: 12

INGREDIENTS:

- 3-lb. (1.4 kg) boneless, fully cooked ham
- ½-¾ cup brown sugar, according to your taste preferences
- ¼ cup peach preserves
- 2 tbsps. prepared mustard

DIRECTIONS:

1. In a crock pot, add the ham.
2. In a bowl, add the mustard, brown sugar and peach preserves, mix well and spread over the ham.
3. Cover the cooker and cook on Low for 6 hours, or until heated through.

Nutrition Info per Serving:

Calories: 238, Fat: 6.54 g, Carbohydrates: 33.92 g, Protein: 10.64 g

Cola Flavored BBQ Ham

Prep Time: 5 minutes, Cook Time: 8 hour, Serves: 6 to 8

INGREDIENTS:

- 1 lb. (454 g) boiled ham, cut into cubes
- 1 cup cola-flavored soda
- 1 cup ketchup

DIRECTIONS:

1. In the crock pot, add the ham. Top with the ketchup and cola-flavored soda.
2. Cover the cooker and cook on Low for 8 hours.
3. After cooking, serve in the hamburger rolls.

Nutrition Info per Serving:

Calories: 88, Fat: 1.96 g, Carbohydrates: 8.77 g, Protein: 9.89 g

Pork Ribs with Sesame Seeds and Onions

Prep Time: 10 minutes, Cook Time: 5-6 hours, Serves: 6

INGREDIENTS:

- 5 lbs. (2.3 kg) country-style pork ribs
- 1 medium onion, sliced
- ¼ cup soy sauce
- ¾ cup packed brown sugar
- ¼ cup honey
- ½ cup ketchup
- 1 tsp. ground ginger
- 2 tbsps. cider or white vinegar
- 3 garlic cloves, minced
- ¼-½ tsp. crushed red pepper flakes
- 2 tbsps. chopped green onions
- 2 tbsps. sesame seeds, toasted

DIRECTIONS:

1. In the bottom of the crock pot, add the onions.
2. In a large bowl, combine the soy sauce, brown sugar, honey, ketchup, ginger, vinegar, garlic, and red pepper flakes. Add the ribs and turn to coat. Place on the top of the onions in the crock pot. Then over the meat pour with the sauce.
3. Cover the cooker and cook on Low for 5 to 6 hours.
4. After cooking, place the ribs on a serving platter. Sprinkle with the green onions and sesame seeds. Serve sauce on the side.

Nutrition Info per Serving:

Calories: 751, Fat: 24.93 g, Carbohydrates: 48.34 g, Protein: 80.27 g

Barbecued Pork Ribs and Sauerkraut

Prep Time: 5 minutes, Cook Time: 8-10 hours, Serves: 10

INGREDIENTS:

- 2½ lbs. (1.1 kg) sauerkraut, rinsed
- 3 lbs. (1.4 kg) lean country-style pork ribs
- 2 cups low-sodium barbecue sauce
- 1 cup water

DIRECTIONS:

1. On the bottom of a crock pot, add the ribs.
2. Top of the ribs, layer with the sauerkraut.
3. In a bowl, combine the water and barbecue sauce. Pour the over the sauerkraut and meat.
4. Cover the cooker and cook on Low for 8 to 10 hours.

Nutrition Info per Serving:

Calories: 230, Total Fat: 9 g, Total Carbohydrate: 19 g, Protein: 17 g, Sugar: 13 g, Fiber: 3 g

Sweet Ham with Apple

Prep Time: 10 minutes, Cook Time: 4-5 hours, Serves: 4

INGREDIENTS:

- 1 slice fully cooked ham (about 1 lb., 454 g)
- 29-oz. (812 g) can sweet potatoes or yams, drained
- 2 apples, thinly sliced
- 2 tbsps. orange juice
- ¼ cup light brown sugar

DIRECTIONS:

1. Cut the ham in cubes, and place in the crock pot.
2. Add the apple, sweet potatoes or yams, orange juice and brown sugar into the crock pot, mix well.
3. Cover and cook on Low for 4 to 5 hours, or until the apples are tender.

Nutrition Info per Serving:

Calories: 460, Total Fat: 7 g, Total Carbohydrate: 73 g, Protein: 28 g, Sugar: 57 g, Fiber: 5 g

Sweet Cranberry Ham

Prep Time: 5 to 10 minutes, Cook Time: 4½ hours, Serves: 4

INGREDIENTS:

- 1-2-lb. (454 to 907 g) fully cooked ham, or 2-inch-thick slice of fully cooked ham
- 1 cup whole cranberry sauce
- 2 tbsps. brown sugar

DIRECTIONS:

1. In a crock pot, add the ham. Pour in the cranberry sauce to cover. Sprinkle over with the brown sugar.
2. Cover and cook on Low for 4½ hours, or until the meat is heated through but not drying out.

Nutrition Info per Serving:

Calories: 236, Fat: 3.96 g, Carbohydrates: 32.03 g, Protein: 19.3 g

Spiced Ham and Apple with Golden Raisin

Prep Time: 10-15 minutes, Cook Time: 4-5 hours, Serves: 6

INGREDIENTS:

- 1½ lbs. (680 g) fully cooked ham
- 21-oz. (595 g) can apple pie filling
- ⅓ cup golden raisins
- ¼ tsp. ground cinnamon
- ⅓ cup orange juice
- 2 tbsps. water

DIRECTIONS:

1. Cut the ham slices into six equal pieces.
2. Add the raisins, pie filling, cinnamon, orange juice, and water into a mixing bowl, mix together well.
3. In the crock pot, place 1 slice of the ham, then spread ⅙ of the apple mixture over the top.
4. Repeat layers until you have used all the ham and raisin-apple mixture.
5. Cover the cooker and cook on Low for 4 to 5 hours.

Nutrition Info per Serving:

Calories: 755, Fat: 56.88 g, Carbohydrates: 42.6 g, Protein: 21.18 g

Ham Cheese and Noodles Casserole

Prep Time: 15-30 minutes, Cook Time: 2-4 hours, Serves: 8 to 10

INGREDIENTS:

- 12- or 16-oz. (340 to 454 g) pkg. medium egg noodles, divided
- 10¾-oz. (304 g) can condensed cream of celery soup
- 2 cups fully cooked ham, cubed, divided
- 2 cups shredded cheese, your choice, divided
- 1 pint sour cream

DIRECTIONS:

1. According to the package instructions to prepare the noodles. Drain.
2. Combine the sour cream and soup in a small bowl until smooth. Set aside.
3. Layer one-third of the cooked noodles, one-third of the ham, and one-third of the cheese in a greased crock pot.
4. Place one-fourth of sour cream mixture on the top.
5. Repeat steps 3 and 4 twice until all of the ingredients are used. The final layer should be the sour cream and soup mixture.
6. Cover and cook on Low for 2 to 4 hours, or until heated through.

Nutrition Info per Serving:

Calories: 172, Fat: 29.79 g, Carbohydrates: 45.14 g, Protein: 13.74 g

Cheesy Ham and Hash Browns

Prep Time: 10 minutes, Cook Time: 4-6 hours, Serves: 4

INGREDIENTS:

- 26-oz. (728 g) pkg. frozen hash browns
- 10¾-oz. (304 g) can cheddar cheese soup
- 2 cups fully cooked ham, cubed
- 2-oz. (57 g) jar diced pimentos, drained
- ¾ cup milk
- ¼ tsp. pepper, optional

DIRECTIONS:

1. Combine the pimentos, ham and hash browns in a crock pot.
2. In a bowl, mix the milk, soup, and pepper if you wish until smooth.Then pour over the ham mixture. Stir well.
3. Cover and cook on Low for 4 to 6 hours, or until the potatoes are tender.

Nutrition Info per Serving:

Calories: 487, Fat: 25.15 g, Carbohydrates: 61.9 g, Protein: 8.16 g

Slow-Cooked Ham

Prep Time: 5 minutes, Cook Time: 7 hours, Serves: 8

INGREDIENTS:

- ½ cup water
- liquid smoke
- 3-4-lb. (1.4 to 1.8 kg) precooked ham

DIRECTIONS:

1. Pour water into a crock pot.
2. Sprinkle the liquid smoke over the ham. Use the foil to wrap. Place in the crock pot.
3. Cover the cooker and cook on High for 1 hour, then on Low for 6 hours.
4. After cooking, remove the ham with the foil and cut into thick chunks or ½-inch slices and serve.

Nutrition Info per Serving:

Calories: 184, Fat: 6.79 g, Carbohydrates: 1.68 g, Protein: 29.17 g

Cranberry Slow Cooked Franks

Prep Time: 10 minutes, Cook Time: 1-2 hours, Serves: 15 to 20

INGREDIENTS:

- 16-oz. (454 g) can jellied cranberry sauce
- 2 pkgs. cocktail wieners or little smoked sausages
- 3 tbsps. brown sugar
- 1 cup ketchup
- 1 tbsp. lemon juice

DIRECTIONS:

1. In the crock pot, add the cranberry sauce, cocktail wieners or little smoked sausages, brown sugar, ketchup and lemon juice, combine together well.
2. Cover the cooker and cook on High for 1 to 2 hours.

Nutrition Info per Serving:

Calories: 93, Fat: 0.7 g, Carbohydrates: 21.98 g, Protein: 0.89 g

Pork Ribs with Tomato Sauce

Prep Time: 20 minutes, Cook Time: 7-8 hours, Serves: 8 to 10

INGREDIENTS:

- 3-3½ lbs. (1.4 to 1.6 kg) country-style pork ribs, cut into serving-size pieces
- 2 (14½-oz. 411 g) cans Italian-seasoned diced tomatoes
- 1 cup frozen pearl onions
- 1½ tsps. Italian seasoning
- 1 tsp. salt
- water as needed

DIRECTIONS:

1. In a nonstick skillet, brown the ribs on top and bottom. You can brown them in batches to make sure that each piece browns well.
2. Use nonstick cooking spray to spray the crock pot.
3. Layer the browned ribs into the crock pot. In a hot skillet, drain the tomatoes and use a wooden spoon to stir up the drippings to deglaze the skillet with the tomato juice.
4. Top the rib layer with the tomatoes, onions, and seasonings. Then pour the deglazed pan drippings into the crock pot. Fill in about 2-inch of water.
5. Cover the cooker and cook on Low for 7 to 8 hours, or until the meat is tender but not overcooked.

Nutrition Info per Serving:

Calories: 341, Fat: 9.28 g, Carbohydrates: 32.59 g, Protein: 35.42 g

Ham, Potatoes and Cabbage

Prep Time: 30 minutes, Cook Time: 6-7 hours, Serves: 4

INGREDIENTS:

- 2 lbs. (907 g) uncooked ham
- 8 medium red potatoes
- 1 medium head green cabbage
- 12 whole cloves
- water

DIRECTIONS:

1. Rinse the ham, then evenly stick the cloves into the ham. Place in the center of the crock pot.
2. Cut potatoes in half. Place in the crock pot around the ham.
3. Quarter the cabbage and remove the center stem. Place in the cooker around the ham.
4. Cover with the water.
5. Cover the cooker and cook on High for 6 to 7 hours, or until the vegetables and meat are tender, but not dry or mushy.
6. After cooking, serve with the butter for the potatoes and mustard for the ham.

Nutrition Info per Serving:

Calories: 1197, Fat: 32.64 g, Carbohydrates: 154.97 g, Protein: 75.4 g

Mustard Kielbasa

Prep Time: 5 minutes, Cook Time: 2½–3 hours, Serves: 6 to 8

INGREDIENTS:

- 2 lbs. (907 g) smoked fully cooked kielbasa, cut into 1-inch pieces
- 1 tbsp. spicy mustard
- 1 cup brown sugar

DIRECTIONS:

1. In the crock pot, add the mustard and brown sugar, mix well.
2. Add the kielbasa to the cooker, stir to coat evenly.
3. Cover and cook on Low for 2½ to 3 hours, stirring occasionally.

Nutrition Info per Serving:

Calories: 306, Fat: 20.02 g, Carbohydrates: 17.01 g, Protein: 14.93 g

Sausage and Green Beans

Prep Time: 5 minutes, Cook Time: 4-5 hours, Serves: 4 to 5

INGREDIENTS:

- 16-oz. (454 g)-pkg. miniature smoked sausage links
- 1 quart green beans, with most of the juice drained
- 1 small onion, chopped
- ½ cup brown sugar
- ¼ cup ketchup

DIRECTIONS:

1. In the crock pot, add the sausage. Place the beans on the top and then the onion.
2. Stir together the ketchup and sugar in a bowl. Spoon over the top in the cooker.
3. Cover and cook on Low for 4 to 5 hours.

Nutrition Info per Serving:

Calories: 396, Fat: 24.75 g, Carbohydrates: 27.52 g, Protein: 17.13 g

Frankfurter Succotash

Prep Time: 10 minutes, Cook Time: 4-6 hours, Serves: 4 to 6

INGREDIENTS:

- 1 lb. (454 g) hot dogs, cut into ½-inch slices
- 2 (10-oz. 283 g) pkgs. frozen succotash, thawed and drained
- 10¾-oz. (304 g) can cheddar cheese soup

DIRECTIONS:

1. In the crock pot, add the succotash, hot dogs and soup, stir well.
2. Cover the cooker and cook on Low for 4 to 6 hours, or until the vegetables are tender.

Nutrition Info per Serving:

Calories: 152, Fat: 2.48 g, Carbohydrates: 30.12 g, Protein: 6.61 g

Pork Ribs and Acorn Squash with Orange Juice

Prep Time: 15 minutes, Cook Time: 6-8 hours, Serves: 6

INGREDIENTS:

- 6 boneless country-style pork ribs, trimmed of fat
- 2 medium acorn squash
- ¾ cup brown sugar
- 2 tbsps. orange juice
- ¾ tsp. Kitchen Bouquet browning and seasoning sauce

DIRECTIONS:

1. On the bottom of a crock pot, add the ribs.
2. Cut each squash in half. Remove seeds and cut each half into 3 slices.
3. Top the ribs, add the squash slices.
4. In a small bowl, mix the orange juice, sauce and brown sugar. Pour the sauce over the squash and ribs.
5. Cover the cooker and cook on Low for 6 to 8 hours, or until the meat is tender.
6. After cooking, serve 2 rings of squash with each pork rib.

Nutrition Info per Serving:

Calories: 441, Fat: 11.26 g, Carbohydrates: 42.59 g, Protein: 42.13 g

Sweet and Sour Pork Ribs with Pineapple

Prep Time: 15 minutes, Cook Time: 8-10 hours, Serves: 8 to 12

INGREDIENTS:

- 3-4 lbs. (1.4 to 1.8 kg) boneless country-style pork ribs
- 2 (8-oz. 227 g) cans tomato sauce
- 20-oz. (567 g) can pineapple tidbits
- ½ cup thinly sliced green peppers
- ½ cup thinly sliced onions
- ½ cup packed brown sugar
- ¼ cup cider vinegar
- ¼ cup tomato paste
- 1 garlic clove, minced
- 2 tbsps. Worcestershire sauce
- 1 tsp. salt
- ½ tsp. pepper

DIRECTIONS:

1. In a crock pot, add the ribs.
2. In a large bowl, mix all of the remaining ingredients and pour the sauce over the ribs.
3. Cover and cook on Low for 8 to 10 hours.
4. Serve over the rice.

Nutrition Info per Serving:

Calories: 300, Fat: 6.62 g, Carbohydrates: 34.85 g, Protein: 24.98 g

Apricot and Soy Sauce Glazed Ham

Prep Time: 20 minutes, Cook Time: 4-6 hours, Serves: 4

INGREDIENTS:

- 4 ham steaks
- ¾-1 cup honey, depending upon how much sweetness you like
- ⅓ cup apricot jam
- ⅓ cup soy sauce
- ¼ tsp. nutmeg

DIRECTIONS:

1. In a crock pot, add the ham.
2. Combine the honey, apricot jam, nutmeg and soy sauce in a bowl, mix them together. Pour over the ham in the cooker.
3. Cover and cook on Low for 4 to 6 hours, or until the meat is heated through but not dry.

Nutrition Info per Serving:

Calories: 348, Fat: 25.9 g, Carbohydrates: 9.43 g, Protein: 128.06 g

Braised Pork Chops with Cream

Prep Time: 15 minutes, Cook Time: 7 to 8 hours on low, Serves: 6

INGREDIENTS:

- ¼ cup extra-virgin olive oil, divided
- 1 cup heavy (whipping) cream
- Freshly ground black pepper, for seasoning
- Salt, for seasoning
- 1½ pounds (680 g) pork loin chops
- 2 tsps. minced garlic
- ½ sweet onion, chopped
- 1 cup chicken broth
- 1 tsp. dried thyme
- 1 tsp. dried oregano
- 1 tsp. chopped fresh basil, for garnish

DIRECTIONS:

1. Use 1 tablespoon of the olive oil to lightly grease the insert of the crock pot.
2. Heat the remaining 3 tablespoons of the olive oil in a large skillet over medium-high heat.
3. With pepper and salt to lightly season the pork. Place the pork into the skillet and brown for about 5 minutes. Then place the chops into the insert.
4. Add the garlic, onion, broth, thyme and oregano into the skillet and cook over medium bowl, stir well.
5. Transfer the broth mixture into the chops.
6. Cover and set on low, cook for 7 to 8 hours.
7. Add the heavy cream and stir well.
8. Top with the basil and serve hot.

Nutrition Info per Serving:

Calories: 522, Total Fat: 45 g, Total Carbs: 2 g, Net Carbs: 2 g, Protein: 27 g, Fiber: 0 g

Ham and Hash Browns with Mushrooms

Prep Time: 15 minutes, Cook Time: 6-8 hours, Serves: 6 to 8

INGREDIENTS:

- 2½ cups cubed cooked ham
- 28-oz. (784 g) pkg. frozen hash brown potatoes
- 2-oz. (57 g) jar pimentos, drained and chopped
- 4-oz. (113 g) can mushrooms, or ¼-lb. (113 g) sliced fresh mushrooms
- 10¾-oz. (304 g) can cheddar cheese soup
- ¾ cup half-and-half
- dash of pepper
- salt to taste

DIRECTIONS:

1. In a crock pot, add the pimentos, potatoes, mushrooms and ham, mix well.
2. Place the soup, half-and-half, pepper and salt in a bowl, combine well and pour over the potatoes mixture.
3. Cover the cooker and cook on Low for 6 to 8 hours. You can also cook the night before, and in the morning, you will get a wonderful breakfast.

Nutrition Info per Serving:

Calories: 165, Fat: 1.67 g, Carbohydrates: 34.47 g, Protein: 4.96 g

Kielbasa and Cabbage with Potato

Prep Time: 15 minutes, Cook Time: 7-8 hours, Serves: 6

INGREDIENTS:

- 1½ lbs. (680 g) Polish kielbasa, cut into 3-inch long links
- 28-oz. (784 g) can cut-up tomatoes with juice
- 2 medium onions, chopped
- 3 medium red potatoes, peeled and cubed
- 1½ lb. (680 g)-head green cabbage, shredded
- 1 red bell pepper, chopped
- 2 garlic cloves, minced
- ⅔ cup dry white wine
- ¾ tsp. caraway seeds
- 1 tbsp. Dijon mustard
- ½ tsp. pepper
- ¾ tsp. salt

DIRECTIONS:

1. In the crock pot, add all of the ingredients, and mix well.
2. Cover the cooker and cook on Low for 7 to 8 hours, or until the cabbage is tender.

Nutrition Info per Serving:

Calories: 501, Fat: 23.63 g, Carbohydrates: 52.06 g, Protein: 24.58 g

Cheesy Ham, Potatoes and Green Beans

Prep Time: 5 minutes, Cook Time: 6-8 hours, Serves: 4

INGREDIENTS:

- 1-lb. (454 g) ham slice, cut in chunks
- 2 cups green beans, frozen or fresh
- 2 cups red-skinned potatoes, quartered, but not peeled
- ½ cup chopped onion
- ½ cup water
- 4 slices American cheese

DIRECTIONS:

1. In a crock pot, add the beans, ham, onion, potatoes and water, gently mix together.
2. Cover the cooker and cook on Low for 6 to 8 hours, or until the vegetables are tender.
3. One hour before the end of the cooking time, lay cheese slices over the top, and continue to cook for 1 hour.

Nutrition Info per Serving:

Calories: 289, Fat: 11.55 g, Carbohydrates: 20.64 g, Protein: 27.18 g

Sausage Mushroom and Sauerkraut

Prep Time: 10 minutes, Cook Time: 3-6 hours, Serves: 8 to 12

INGREDIENTS:

- 2 tbsps. water or oil
- 2 (14½-oz. 411 g) cans diced tomatoes with green peppers
- 2-3 lbs. (907 g to 1.4 kg) smoked sausage, cut into 1-inch pieces
- ½ lb. (227 g) fresh mushrooms, sliced
- 1 quart sauerkraut, drained
- 2 onions, sliced
- 2 bell peppers, chopped
- 2 tbsps. brown sugar
- 1 tsp. salt
- ½ tsp. pepper

DIRECTIONS:

1. Add the sausage in the crock pot. Heat on Low while you prepare the other ingredients.
2. In a saucepan, add the onions, mushrooms and peppers, sauté in a small amount of water or oil, then transfer into the crock pot.
3. Add the tomatoes, sauerkraut, brown sugar, salt and pepper into the cooker, stir well.
4. Cover and cook on Low for 5 to 6 hours, or on High for 3 to 4 hours.
5. After cooking, serve with the mashed potatoes.

Nutrition Info per Serving:

Calories: 552, Fat: 21.11 g, Carbohydrates: 82.26 g, Protein: 22.27 g

Garlicky Brie and Pancetta Stuffed Pork Tenderloin

Prep Time: 20 minutes, Cook Time: 8 hours on low, Serves: 4

INGREDIENTS:

- 1 tbsp. extra-virgin olive oil
- 2 (½-pound, 227 g) pork tenderloins
- 4 ounces (113 g) Pancetta, cooked crispy and chopped
- 4 ounces (113 g) Triple-Cream Brie
- 1 tsp. chopped fresh basil
- 1 tsp. minced garlic
- ⅛ tsp. freshly ground black pepper

DIRECTIONS:

1. Use the olive oil to lightly grease the insert of the crock pot.
2. On a cutting board, cut lengthwise of the pork, holding the knife parallel to the board, through the center of the meat without cutting right through. Open the meat up like a book and use plastic wrap to cover.
3. Use a mallet or rolling pin to pound the meat until each piece is about ½ inch thick. On a clean work surface, lay the butterflied pork well.
4. Add the Brie, pancetta, basil, garlic and pepper into a small bowl, stir them together.
5. Evenly spread the cheese mixture over the tenderloins and leave about 1 inch around the edges.
6. Roll the tenderloin up and use toothpicks to secure.
7. Put the pork in the insert, cover, and cook on low for 8 hours.
8. Take the toothpicks away and serve.

Nutrition Info per Serving:

Calories: 423, Total Fat: 32 g, Total Carbs: 1 g, Net Carbs: 1 g, Protein: 34 g, Fiber: 0 g

Creamy Ham and Potatoes

Prep Time: 20 minutes, Cook Time: 4-5 hours, Serves: 6

INGREDIENTS:

- 1 lb. (454 g) cooked ham, cubed
- 6 cups sliced, raw potatoes
- 10¾-oz. (304 g) can cream of mushroom or celery soup
- salt and pepper to taste
- 1½ cups milk

DIRECTIONS:

1. In a crock pot, add the potatoes. Sprinkle with the salt and pepper of each layer.
2. Combine the milk, soup, and ham together in a bowl. Pour over the potatoes.
3. Cover the cooker and cook on High for 3½ hours. Continue to cook for another ½ to 1½ hours if needed, or until the potatoes are tender.

Nutrition Info per Serving:

Calories: 302, Fat: 7.05 g, Carbohydrates: 38.88 g, Protein: 21.87 g

Sausage, Apples and Sweet Potatoes

Prep Time: 15 to 20 minutes, Cook Time: 4-10 hours, Serves: 4 to 6

INGREDIENTS:

- 1 lb. bulk sausage
- 2 sweet potatoes, peeled and sliced
- 3 apples, peeled and sliced
- 1 tbsp. flour
- 2 tbsps. brown sugar
- ¼ cup water

DIRECTIONS:

1. In a skillet, brown loose the sausage, use a wooden spoon to break up the chunks of meat. Drain well.
2. Layer the sausage, sweet potatoes, and apples in the crock pot.
3. In a bowl, add the flour, brown sugar and water, combine well and pour over the ingredients in the crock pot.
4. Cover the cooker and cook on Low for 8 to 10 hours, or on High for 4 hours.

Nutrition Info per Serving:

Calories: 261, Fat: 13.94 g, Carbohydrates: 24.49 g, Protein: 14.61 g

Sausage and Vegetables

Prep Time: 25 to 30 minutes, Cook Time: 6 hours, Serves: 8 to 10

INGREDIENTS:

- 2-3 lbs. (907 g to 1.4 kg) sweet Italian sausage, cut into 3-inch pieces
- 28 oz. (784 g)-can chopped tomatoes
- 3 medium onions, sliced
- 1 sweet green pepper, sliced
- 1 sweet red pepper, sliced
- 1 sweet yellow pepper, sliced
- 4 garlic cloves, minced
- 1 tbsp. oil
- ½ tsp. red crushed pepper
- 1 tsp. salt

DIRECTIONS:

1. In a skillet, add the garlic, onions and peppers, sauté them in the oil until just softened, transfer into the crock pot.
2. Add the tomatoes, crushed red pepper and salt to the cooker. Mix well.
3. Stir in the sausage links.
4. Cover the cooker and cook on Low for 6 hours.
5. After cooking, serve on the rolls, or over the baked potatoes or pasta.

Nutrition Info per Serving:

Calories: 172, Fat: 9.27 g, Carbohydrates: 7.37 g, Protein: 15.69 g

Ham and Potatoes with Cheese

Prep Time: 20 minutes, Cook Time: 6-8 hours, Serves: 4 to 6

INGREDIENTS:

- 12-oz. (340 g) pkg., or 1 lb. (454 g), cooked ham, cubed, divided
- 2-3 lbs. (907 g to 1.4 kg) potatoes, peeled, sliced, divided
- 2 cups shredded cheddar cheese, divided
- 10¾-oz. (304 g) can cream of celery or mushroom soup
- 1 small onion, chopped, divided

DIRECTIONS:

1. Use nonstick cooking spray to spray the interior of the crock pot.
2. In the cooker, layer with ⅓ each of the potatoes, ham, onion, and cheese.
3. Repeat layers twice.
4. Over the ingredients, spread with the soup.
5. Cover the cooker and cook on Low for 6 to 8 hours, or until the potatoes are tender.

Nutrition Info per Serving:

Calories: 237, Fat: 4.89 g, Carbohydrates: 37.09 g, Protein: 17.25 g

Sausage and Sauerkraut with Vegetable

Prep Time: 20 minutes, Cook Time: 8-9 hours, Serves: 10 to 12

INGREDIENTS:

- 2½ lbs. (1.1 kg) fresh Polish sausage, cut into 3-inch pieces
- 2 (14-oz. 397 g) cans sauerkraut, rinsed and drained
- 4 cups cubed carrots
- 4 cups cubed red potatoes
- 3 garlic cloves, minced
- 1 medium onion, thinly sliced
- 1½ cups dry white wine or chicken broth
- 1 tsp. caraway seeds
- ½ tsp. pepper

DIRECTIONS:

1. Layer the carrots, potatoes, and sauerkraut in the crock pot.
2. In a skillet, brown the sausage and transfer to the crock pot. Reserve 1 Tbsp. drippings in the skillet.
3. Add the garlic and onion to the skillet, sauté them in drippings until tender. Stir in the wine. Bring to boil. Stir to loosen brown bits. Add the caraway seeds and pepper, stir well. Pour over the sausage in the cooker.
4. Cover and cook on Low for 8 to 9 hours.

Nutrition Info per Serving:

Calories: 544, Fat: 29.85 g, Carbohydrates: 49.43 g, Protein: 20.45 g

Pepper and Sausage in Spaghetti Sauce

Prep Time: 15 minutes, Cook Time: 3-6 hours, Serves: 12 to 15

INGREDIENTS:

- 4 lbs. (1.8 kg) sausage of your choice
- 26-oz. (728 g) jar spaghetti sauce
- 1 large onion
- 1 red bell pepper
- 1 green bell pepper

DIRECTIONS:

1. Heat a nonstick skillet over medium-high heat. In batches, brown the sausage. As a batch is finished browning on all sides, cut into 1½-inch chunks. Then transfer into the crock pot.
2. Slice or chop the peppers and onion, add to the cooker on top of the sausage.
3. Pour over with the spaghetti sauce.
4. Cover the cooker and cook on Low for 6 hours, or on High for 3 hours.

Nutrition Info per Serving:

Calories: 427, Fat: 28.4 g, Carbohydrates: 21.36 g, Protein: 29.17 g

Ham and Cheese with Mashed Potatoes

Prep Time: 30-40 minutes, Cook Time: 3-4 hours, Serves: 12 to 16

INGREDIENTS:

- 4 tbsps. butter
- 4 cups cooked ham, cut into chunks
- 2 (10¾-oz. 304 g) cans cream of mushroom soup
- 2 cups Velveeta cheese, cubed
- 1 pint sour cream
- 4 quarts mashed potatoes
- ½ cup chopped onions
- 1 tbsp. Worcestershire sauce
- 1 cup milk
- browned and crumbled bacon

DIRECTIONS:

1. In a saucepan, combine the butter, onions, ham, and Worcestershire sauce. Cook until the onions are tender. Transfer into a large crock pot, or divide between 2 4-5-quart crock pots.
2. In a saucepan, heat together the milk, cheese and soup until the cheese melts. Pour into the cooker(s).
3. In a bowl, add the sour cream and potatoes, mix well and spread over the mixture in the crock pot(s).
4. Sprinkle with the bacon.
5. Cover and cook on Low for 3 to 4 hours, or until the cheese mixture comes to top when done.

Nutrition Info per Serving:

Calories: 488, Fat: 29.79 g, Carbohydrates: 45.14 g, Protein: 13.74 g

Slow Cooked BBQ Spareribs

Prep Time: 5 minutes, Cook Time: 6-8 hours, Serves: 4

INGREDIENTS:

- 4-lb. (1.8 kg) country-style spareribs, cut into serving-size pieces
- 10¾-oz. (304 g) can tomato soup
- ½ cup cider vinegar
- ½ cup brown sugar
- 1 tbsp. soy sauce
- 1 tsp. celery seed
- 1 tsp. chili powder
- dash cayenne pepper
- 1 tsp. salt

DIRECTIONS:

1. In a crock pot, add the ribs.
2. In a bowl, mix all of the remaining ingredients and pour over the ribs in the cooker.
3. Cover and cook on Low for 6 to 8 hours.
4. After cooking, skim the fat from the juices and serve.

Nutrition Info per Serving:

Calories: 2350, Fat: 98.45 g, Carbohydrates: 339.46 g, Protein: 30.66 g

Parmesan Pork and Potatoes

Prep Time: 20 minutes, Cook Time: 7-9 hours, Serves: 8

INGREDIENTS:

- 1 (3-pound, 1.4kg) boneless pork loin
- 2 pounds (907g) small creamer potatoes, rinsed
- 4 large carrots, cut into chunks
- ½ cup grated Parmesan cheese
- 1 cup chicken stock
- 1 onion, chopped
- 12 garlic cloves, divided
- 1 tsp. dried marjoram leaves

DIRECTIONS:

1. Mix potatoes, carrots, and onions in a 6-quart crock pot. Chop 6 garlic cloves and stir in the vegetables.
2. Cut the remaining garlic cloves into thin slices. Poke a few holes in the pork loin with a knife, and then stuff the garlic strips into each hole.
3. Put the prepared pork tenderloin on the vegetables in the crock pot. Pour in all the chicken broth and sprinkle with marjoram.
4. Cook on low heat for 7 to 9 hours, close the lid until the pork is tender.
5. Finally, top with Parmesan cheese and serve.

Nutrition Info per Serving:

Calories: 393, Fat: 11g, Saturated Fat: 4g, Protein: 45g, Carbohydrates: 27g, Sugar: 5g, Fiber: 3g, Sodium: 404mg

Apple and Pork Chops

Prep Time: 10 minutes, Cook Time: 6-8 hours, Serves: 1

INGREDIENTS:

- 1 sweet onion, cut into thick rings
- 1 apple, cored, peeled, and cut into 8 wedges
- ¼ tsp. ground cinnamon
- 1 tsp. fresh thyme
- ¼ cup apple cider
- ⅛ tsp. sea salt
- Freshly ground black pepper
- 2 bone-in pork chops

DIRECTIONS:

1. In the crock pot, add the onion, apple, cinnamon and thyme, and stir to combine. Pour in the apple cider.
2. Use the salt and a few grinds of the black pepper to season the pork chops. On top of the apple and onion mixture, add the chops.
3. Cover the cooker and cook on low for 6 to 8 hours, until the pork is cooked through and the apples and onion are very soft.

Nutrition Info per Serving:

Calories: 286, Saturated Fat: 5 g, Trans Fat: 0 g, Carbohydrates: 22 g, Protein: 21 g, Fiber: 4 g, Sodium: 521 mg

Pork Ribs and Peaches

Prep Time: 10 minutes, Cook Time: 8-10 hours, Serves: 4 to 6

INGREDIENTS:

- 4-lb. (1.8 kg) boneless pork spareribs
- 15-oz. (425 g) can spiced cling peaches, cubed, with juice
- 2 tbsps. soy sauce
- ¼ cup ketchup
- ¼ cup white vinegar
- ½ cup brown sugar
- 1 garlic clove, minced
- 1 tsp. salt
- 1 tsp. pepper

DIRECTIONS:

1. Cut the ribs in serving-size pieces, in a broiler or a saucepan, add the meat and brown in the oil. Drain well and transfer into the crock pot.
2. In a bowl, mix the remaining ingredients and pour over the ribs.
3. Cover the cooker and cook on Low for 8 to 10 hours.

Nutrition Info per Serving:

Calories: 519, Fat: 17.33 g, Carbohydrates: 41.44 g, Protein: 52.59 g

Creamy Potatoes and Sausage with Cheese

Prep Time: 15 minutes, Cook Time: 6-8 hours, Serves: 6

INGREDIENTS:

- 3 lbs. (1.4 kg) small potatoes, peeled and quartered
- 1 lb. (454 g) smoked sausage, cut into ¼-inch slices
- 10¾-oz. (304 g) can cream of celery soup
- 8-oz. (227 g) pkg. cream cheese, softened
- 1 envelope dry ranch salad dressing mix

DIRECTIONS:

1. In the crock pot, add the potatoes and sausage.
2. Combine the soup, cream cheese and salad dressing mix in a bowl, beat them together until smooth. Pour this mixture over the potatoes and sausage.
3. Cover and cook on Low for 6 to 8 hours, or until the potatoes are tender, stirring half-way through cooking time if you're home. Stir well before serving.

Nutrition Info per Serving:

Calories: 499, Fat: 29.45 g, Carbohydrates: 50.25 g, Protein: 21.66 g

Garlic Lemon Pork

Prep Time: 15 minutes, Cook Time: 7 to 8 hours on low, Serves: 6

INGREDIENTS:

- 3 tbsps. extra-virgin olive oil, divided
- 1 tbsp. butter
- 2 pounds (907 g) pork loin roast
- ½ cup heavy (whipping) cream
- ¼ cup chicken broth
- ¼ tsp. freshly ground black pepper
- ½ tsp. salt
- Juice and zest of 1 lemon
- 1 tbsp. minced garlic

DIRECTIONS:

1. Use 1 tablespoon of the olive oil to lightly grease the insert of the crock pot.
2. Heat the remaining 2 tablespoons of the olive oil and the butter in a large skillet over medium-high heat.
3. Use pepper and salt to lightly season the pork. Place the pork into the skillet and brown the roast on all sides for about 10 minutes. Transfer it to the insert.
4. Add the lemon juice and zest, broth and garlic to a small bowl, stir them together.
5. Transfer the broth mixture to the roast.
6. Cover the cooker, and cook on low for 7 to 8 hours.
7. After cooking, add the heavy cream, stir well and serve.

Nutrition Info per Serving:

Calories: 448, Total Fat: 31 g, Total Carbs: 1 g, Net Carbs: 1 g, Protein: 39 g, Fiber: 0 g

Sauerkraut and Trail Bologna with Brown Sugar

Prep Time: 5 minutes, Cook Time: 6-8 hours, Serves: 10

INGREDIENTS:

- 32-oz. (907 g) bag sauerkraut, rinsed
- ¼-½ cup brown sugar
- 1 ring Trail Bologna

DIRECTIONS:

1. In the crock pot, combine the brown sugar and sauerkraut.
2. Remove casing from the bologna and cut into ¼-inch slices. Stir into the sauerkraut.
3. Cover the cooker and cook on Low for 6 to 8 hours.

Nutrition Info per Serving:

Calories: 111, Fat: 1.35 g, Carbohydrates: 24.31 g, Protein: 2.32 g

Cheesy Chili Hot Dogs

Prep Time: 10 minutes, Cook Time: 3-3½ hours, Serves: 10

INGREDIENTS:

- 1 lb. (454 g) hot dogs
- 10¾-oz. (304 g) can condensed cheddar cheese soup
- 2 (15-oz. 425 g) cans chili, with or without beans
- 4-oz. (113 g) can chopped green chilies
- 10 hot dog buns
- 1-2 cups corn chips, coarsely crushed
- 1 medium onion, chopped
- 1 cup shredded cheddar cheese

DIRECTIONS:

1. In the crock pot, add the hot dogs.
2. In a bowl, combine the soup, green chilies and chili. Pour over the hot dogs.
3. Cover the cooker and cook on Low for 3 to 3½ hours.
4. Serve hot dogs in buns. Top with the chili mixture, corn chips, onion, and cheese.

Nutrition Info per Serving:

Calories: 666, Fat: 32.47 g, Carbohydrates: 82.25 g, Protein: 32.88 g

Potato and Wiener Bake

Prep Time: 8 minutes, Cook Time: 3 hours, Serves: 6

INGREDIENTS:

- 1 lb. (454 g) wieners, sliced
- 4 cups cooked potatoes, peeled and diced
- 10¾-oz. (304 g) can cream of mushroom soup
- 1 cup sauerkraut, drained
- 1 cup mayonnaise

DIRECTIONS:

1. In the crock pot, add the sliced wieners, soup, potatoes, sauerkraut and mayonnaise, mix well.
2. Cover the cooker and cook on Low for 3 hours.

Nutrition Info per Serving:

Calories: 483, Fat: 35.14 g, Carbohydrates: 25.35 g, Protein: 17.36 g

Herbed Bacon Wrapped Pork Shoulder

Prep Time: 15 minutes, Cook Time: 9 to 10 hours on low, Serves: 8

INGREDIENTS:

- 3 tbsps. extra-virgin olive oil, divided
- 1 tsp. onion powder
- 1 tsp. garlic powder
- 2 pounds (907 g) pork shoulder roast
- 8 bacon strips, uncooked
- 2 tsps. chopped thyme
- ¼ cup chicken broth
- 1 tsp. chopped oregano

DIRECTIONS:

1. Use 1 tablespoon of the olive oil to lightly grease the insert of the crock pot.
2. Combine the onion powder and garlic powder in a bowl, then use the mixture to rub all over of the pork.
3. Heat the remaining 2 tablespoons of the olive oil in a large skillet over medium-high heat. Place the pork in the skillet and brown on all sides for about 10 minutes. Allow it stand to cool for about 10 minutes.
4. Use the bacon slices to wrap the pork, place in the insert, and add the thyme, broth, and oregano.
5. Cover the cooker and cook on low for 9 to 10 hours.
6. Turn off the heat and serve warm.

Nutrition Info per Serving:

Calories: 493, Total Fat: 40 g, Total Carbs: 1 g, Net Carbs: 1 g, Protein: 31 g, Fiber: 0 g

Savory Lemon Pork Chop

Prep Time: 20 minutes, Cook Time: 7-8 hours, Serves: 8

INGREDIENTS:

- 8 (5-ounce, 142g) bone-in pork loin chops
- 2 red bell peppers, stemmed, seeded, and chopped
- 2 leeks, chopped
- 1 cup chicken stock
- ⅓ cup lemon juice
- 8 garlic cloves, sliced
- 1 tsp. dried thyme leaves
- ½ tsp. salt

DIRECTIONS:

1. Combine leeks, garlic, and red bell peppers in a 6-quart crock pot. Place the pig on the vegetables.
2. Pour lemon juice, chicken broth, thyme and salt in a small bowl and mix thoroughly. Pour on the pork.
3. Close the lid and cook on low heat for 7 to 8 hours until the ribs show at least 145°F on the food thermometer. Serve immediately!

Nutrition Info per Serving:

Calories: 269, Fat: 13g, Saturated Fat: 4g, Protein: 30g, Carbohydrates: 6g, Sugar: 2g, Fiber: 1g, Sodium: 249mg

Healthy Pork Loin with Fruits

Prep Time: 20 minutes, Cook Time: 7-9 hours, Serves: 8

INGREDIENTS:

- 1 (3-pound, 1.4kg) boneless pork loin
- 1 cup dried apricots
- 1 cup dried pears, sliced
- 1 cup apricot nectar
- 2 leeks, sliced
- ½ cup golden raisins
- ½ tsp. salt
- 1 tsp. dried thyme leaves

DIRECTIONS:

1. Place leeks, apricots, pears, and raisins in a 6-quart crock pot. Put the pork on top, sprinkle with salt and thyme.
2. Drizzle apricot nectar on the pork and pour it on the fruit.
3. Turn on a low heat and cook for 7 to 9 hours until the temperature of the pork on the food thermometer is at least 150°F. Serve immediately!

Nutrition Info per Serving:

Calories: 370, Fat: 7g, Saturated Fat: 2g, Protein: 40g, Carbohydrates: 38g, Sugar: 10g, Fiber: 4g, Sodium: 239mg

Crock Pot Satay Pork

Prep Time: 25 minutes, Cook Time: 8 hours, Serves: 6

INGREDIENTS:

- 1 boneless pork shoulder butt roast (3 to 4 pounds, 1.4 to 1.8 kg), cut into 1 ½ inch cubes
- 2 medium parsnips, peeled and sliced
- 1 small sweet red pepper, thinly sliced
- ¼ cup reduced-sodium teriyaki sauce
- 2 tbsps. rice vinegar
- 1 cup chicken broth
- ¼ cup creamy peanut butter
- 1 tbsp. honey
- 2 garlic cloves, minced
- 1 tbsp. minced fresh gingerroot
- ½ tsp. crushed red pepper flakes
- Hot cooked rice, optional
- 2 tbsps. chopped dry roasted peanuts
- 2 green onions, chopped

DIRECTIONS:

1. Add all of the ingredients except the peanut butter, rice, onions and roasted peanuts into a 3-qt. crock pot, combine them together.
2. Cover the cooker and cook on low for 8-10 hours or until pork is tender. Skim fat, add the peanut butter and stir well.
3. Top with peanuts and onions, and serve with rice if desired.

Chinese Spiced Pork Spare Ribs

Prep Time: 10 minutes, Cook Time: 9 to 10 hours on low, Serves: 4

INGREDIENTS:

- 1 tbsp. extra-virgin olive oil
- 2 pounds (907 g) pork spare ribs
- ½ cup chicken broth
- 1 tbsp. Chinese five-spice powder
- 3 tbsps. sesame oil
- 3 tbsps. coconut aminos
- 2 tbsps. apple cider vinegar
- 2 tsps. garlic powder
- 1 tbsp. granulated erythritol

DIRECTIONS:

1. Use the olive oil to lightly grease the insert of the crock pot.
2. Combine the garlic powder and five-spice powder in a bowl, use this mixture to season the ribs, and place upright on their ends in the insert.
3. In the bottom of the insert, add the sesame oil, coconut aminos, broth, apple cider vinegar, and erythritol, stirring to blend.
4. Cover the cooker, and cook on low for 9 to 10 hours.
5. Serve warm.

Nutrition Info per Serving:

Calories: 518, Total Fat: 37 g, Total Carbs: 4 g, Net Carbs: 4 g, Protein: 36 g, Fiber: 0 g

Cranberry Glazed Pork Tenderloin

Prep Time: 10 minutes, Cook Time: 8 hours, Serves: 1

INGREDIENTS:

- ⅛ tsp. sea salt
- 1 cup prepared cranberry sauce
- 16 ounces (454 g) pork tenderloin
- 2 Belgian endives, halved
- Freshly ground black pepper
- ½ cup low-sodium chicken broth
- 1 tsp. extra-virgin olive oil

DIRECTIONS:

1. Combine the salt and a few grinds of the black pepper in a bowl, then use this mixture to season the pork and place it in the crock pot. Pour over the top of the tenderloin with the chicken broth and cranberry sauce.
2. Place over the pork with the endive, cut side up, and drizzle it with the olive oil.
3. Cover the cooker and set on low, cook for 8 hours.

Nutrition Info per Serving:

Calories: 612, Saturated Fat: 3 g, Trans Fat: 0 g, Carbohydrates: 59 g, Protein: 63 g, Fiber: 10 g, Sodium: 340 mg

Pork Carnitas

INGREDIENTS:

- 3 tbsps. extra-virgin olive oil, divided
- 2 pounds (907 g) pork shoulder, cut into 2-inch cubes
- 2 cups chicken broth
- 2 cups diced tomatoes
- ½ sweet onion, chopped
- Juice of 1 lime
- 2 fresh chipotle peppers, chopped
- 1 tsp. ground coriander
- 1 tsp. ground cumin
- ½ tsp. salt
- 1 cup sour cream, for garnish
- 1 avocado, peeled, pitted, and diced, for garnish
- 2 tbsps. chopped cilantro, for garnish

DIRECTIONS:

1. Use 1 tablespoon of the olive oil to lightly grease the insert of the crock pot.
2. Heat the remaining 2 tablespoons of the olive oil in a large skillet over medium-high heat.
3. Place the pork in the skillet and brown on all sides for about 10 minutes.
4. In the insert, add the pork and stir in the broth, tomatoes, onion, lime juice, peppers, coriander, cumin, and salt.
5. Cover the cooker and cook on low for 9 to 10 hours.
6. Use a fork to shred the cooked pork and stir the meat into the sauce.
7. Top with the sour cream, avocado, and cilantro, serve.

Nutrition Info per Serving:

Calories: 508, Total Fat: 41 g, Total Carbs: 7 g, Net Carbs: 4 g, Protein: 29 g, Fiber: 3 g

Hot Wieners

INGREDIENTS:

- 12-oz. (340 g) jar hot pepper jelly
- 12-oz. (340 g) bottle chili sauce
- 1½ lbs. (680 g) little smokie wieners

DIRECTIONS:

1. In the crock pot, add the jelly and chili sauce, mix well. Then add the wieners.
2. Cover and cook on High for 1 to 2 hours, until the sauce thickens.
3. After cooking, serve in buns, or over cooked pasta or rice. Or serve on a buffet from the warm cooker, along with toothpicks to spear the wieners.

Nutrition Info per Serving:

Calories: 190, Fat: 5.94 g, Carbohydrates: 25.36 g, Protein: 8.44 g

Sweet and Sour Pork with Mushroom

INGREDIENTS:

- 1½ pounds (680 g) pork tenderloin, cut into 1-inch cubes
- 1 can (8 ounces, 227 g) unsweetened pineapple chunks, drained
- 1 can (4 ½ ounces, 128 g) sliced mushrooms, drained
- 1 can (15 ounces, 425 g) tomato sauce
- 1 medium green pepper, cut into strips
- 1 medium onion, halved and sliced
- 4½ tsps. white vinegar
- 2 tsps. steak sauce
- 3 tbsps. brown sugar
- 1 tsp. salt
- 1 tbsp. olive oil
- Hot cooked rice

DIRECTIONS:

1. Add all of the ingredients except the pork, olive oil, pineapple and rice into a large bowl, combine them together, set aside.
2. Place the oil and pork in a large skillet, brown the meat in batches. Then transfer to a 3- or 4-qt. crock pot. Pour over pork with the tomato sauce mixture. Cover the cooker and cook on low for 7-8 hours or until meat is tender.
3. Add the pineapple, cover the cooker and cook for another 30 minutes or until heated through. Serve with rice.

Ginger Citrus Ham

INGREDIENTS:

- 1 boneless fully cooked ham (3 to 4 pounds, 1.4 to 1.8 kg)
- 1 can (12 ounces, 340 g) lemon-lime soda, divided
- 1 medium lemon, thinly sliced
- 1 medium navel orange, thinly sliced
- 1 medium lime, thinly sliced
- ½ cup packed dark brown sugar
- 1 tbsp. chopped crystallized ginger

DIRECTIONS:

1. Cut ham in half, transfer into a 5-qt. crock pot. Add ¼ cup soda and brown sugar into a small bowl, combine them together, then rub over the ham. Place the lemon, orange, and lime slices on the top. Then add crystallized ginger and remaining soda to the crock pot.
2. Cover the cooker and cook on low for 4-5 hours or until a meat thermometer reads 140°F(60°C), basting occasionally with cooking juices. Allow it to stand for 10 minutes before slicing.

Spicy Curry Pork Chop and Peppers

Prep Time: 20 minutes, Cook Time: 7-8 hours, Serves: 8

INGREDIENTS:

- 8 (5.5-ounce, 156g) bone-in pork loin chops
- 2 onions, chopped
- 2 yellow bell peppers, stemmed, seeded, and chopped
- 2 red bell peppers, stemmed, seeded, and chopped
- 1 cup chicken stock
- 4 garlic cloves, minced
- 1 tbsp. curry powder
- 1 tbsp. grated fresh ginger root
- ½ tsp. salt

DIRECTIONS:

1. Mix the onion, garlic and bell pepper in a crock pot. Place the pig on the vegetables in the crock pot.
2. Combine salt, curry powder, ginger root and chicken broth in a small bowl, then pour into a crock pot.
3. Cook on low heat for 7 to 8 hours, close the lid, until the pork chops are very tender.

Nutrition Info per Serving:

Calorie: 306, Fat: 14g, Saturated Fat: 5g, Protein: 34g, Carbohydrates: 10g, Sugar: 3g, Fiber: 2g, Sodium: 268mg

Crock Pot Pork Chops with Sweet Potatoes

Prep Time: 10 minutes, Cook Time: 6-8 hours, Serves: 1

INGREDIENTS:

- Zest of 1 orange
- 2 bone-in pork chops, about 8 ounces (227 g) each
- 2 sweet potatoes, peeled and diced
- Pinch ground nutmeg
- ½ cup low-sodium chicken broth
- Freshly ground black pepper
- Sea salt

DIRECTIONS:

1. In the crock pot, add the orange zest, sweet potatoes, nutmeg, and broth. Gently stir together.
2. Use black pepper and salt to season the pork chops and place them over the sweet potatoes.
3. Cover the cooker and cook on low for 6 to 8 hours, until the sweet potatoes are completely soft and the pork is cooked through.
4. If there are still some large sweet potato chunks, use potato masher to mash them or use the back of a fork, and serve.

Nutrition Info per Serving:

Calories: 529, Saturated Fat: 7 g, Trans Fat: 0 g, Carbohydrates: 44 g, Protein: 36 g, Fiber: 7 g, Sodium: 163 mg

Garlic Dijon Pork Chops

Prep Time: 10 minutes, Cook Time: 8 hours on low, Serves: 4

INGREDIENTS:

- 1 tbsp. extra-virgin olive oil
- 4 (4-ounce, 113 g) boneless pork chops
- 1 cup heavy (whipping) cream
- 1 sweet onion, chopped
- ¼ cup Dijon mustard
- 1 tsp. maple extract
- 1 tsp. minced garlic
- 1 cup chicken broth
- 1 tsp. chopped fresh thyme, for garnish

DIRECTIONS:

1. Use the olive oil to lightly grease the insert of the crock pot.
2. Stir in the garlic, Dijon mustard, onion, broth, and maple extract, and mix well. Then add the pork chops to the insert.
3. Cover the cooker and set on low, cook for 8 hours.
4. Add the heavy cream and stir well
5. Top with the thyme and serve.

Nutrition Info per Serving:

Calories: 490, Total Fat: 42 g, Total Carbs: 6 g, Net Carbs: 5 g, Protein: 22 g, Fiber: 1 g

Tender Sweet and Sour Pork Chops

Prep Time: 10 minutes, Cook Time: 6 hours on low, Serves: 4

INGREDIENTS:

- 3 tbsps. extra-virgin olive oil, divided
- 1 pound (454 g) boneless pork chops
- ½ cup granulated erythritol
- ¼ cup chicken broth
- ¼ cup tomato paste
- 2 tbsps. coconut aminos
- 2 tsps. minced garlic
- 2 tbsps. red chili paste
- ¼ tsp. salt
- ¼ tsp. freshly ground black pepper

DIRECTIONS:

1. Use 1 tablespoon of the olive oil to lightly grease the insert of the crock pot.
2. Heat the remaining 2 tablespoons of the olive oil in a large skillet over medium-high heat. Stir in the pork chops, brown for about 5 minutes, and transfer to the insert.
3. Add the broth, erythritol, coconut aminos, tomato paste, garlic, chili paste, salt and pepper into a medium bowl, stir them together. Pour the sauce into the chops.
4. Cover and set on low, cook for 6 hours.

Nutrition Info per Serving:

Calories: 297, Total Fat: 20 g, Total Carbs: 8 g, Net Carbs: 6 g, Protein: 24 g, Fiber: 2 g

Chili Pork Shoulder

Prep Time: 10 minutes, Cook Time: 8 hours, Serves: 8

INGREDIENTS:

- 2 pounds (907 g) pork shoulder, trimmed of excess fat and cut into 1-inch cubes
- 3 (4-ounce, 113 g) cans diced jalapeño peppers, with their juice
- 2 onions, chopped
- 2 cups (480 ml) poultry broth
- 1 tsp. ground cumin
- 1 tsp. garlic powder
- ½ tsp. sea salt
- ¼ tsp. freshly ground black pepper
- Pinch cayenne pepper

DIRECTIONS:

1. Combine all the ingredients in your crock pot.
2. Cover and cook on low for 8 hours.
3. Skim any fat from the top and discard.

Nutrition Info per Serving:

Calories: 357, Total Fat: 25g, Saturated Fat: 9g, Carbohydrates: 5g, Protein: 28g, Cholesterol: 102mg, Fiber: 2g

Simple Pork Chops and Green Beans

Prep Time: 10 minutes, Cook Time: 8 hours, Serves: 1

INGREDIENTS:

- 1 tsp. extra-virgin olive oil
- 2 bone-in pork chops, about 8 ounces (227 g) each
- 3 cups whole green beans, stems removed
- ½ cup low-sodium chicken or vegetable broth
- ¼ cup low-sodium soy sauce
- Freshly ground black pepper
- 1 tsp. minced garlic
- 2 tsps. minced fresh ginger

DIRECTIONS:

1. Use the olive oil to grease the inside of the crock pot.
2. In the bottom of the crock, add the pork chops and use a few grinds of the black pepper to season them. On top of the pork, place with the green beans.
3. Add the garlic, ginger, broth and sou sauce into a small bowl, whisk them together. Pour this mixture over the green beans and pork.
4. Cover the cooker and cook on low for 8 hours, until the green beans are tender and the pork is cooked through.

Nutrition Info per Serving:

Calories: 333, Saturated Fat: 4 g, Trans Fat: 0 g, Carbohydrates: 17 g, Protein: 35 g, Fiber: 6 g, Sodium: 2498 mg

Glazed Pork Tenderloin

Prep Time: 10 minutes, Cook Time: 8 hours, Serves: 4

INGREDIENTS:

- 1 pound (454 g) pork tenderloin
- 1 cup (240 ml) dry white wine
- 1 cup (240 ml) poultry broth
- 1 tsp. dried rosemary
- 3 tbsps. Dijon mustard
- 1 tbsp. cornstarch
- 1 tsp. dried thyme
- 1 tsp. dried marjoram
- 1 tsp. garlic powder
- ¼ tsp. sea salt
- ¼ tsp. freshly ground black pepper

DIRECTIONS:

1. Put the tenderloin in your crock pot.
2. Whisk together all the remaining ingredients in a small bowl. Pour the mixture into the crock pot.
3. Cover and cook on low for 8 hours.
4. Slice the tenderloin and serve with the sauce on top.

Nutrition Info per Serving:

Calories: 233, Total Fat: 5g, Saturated Fat: 1g, Carbohydrates: 5g, Protein: 31g, Fiber: 1g

Savory Ginger Pork Chop

Prep Time: 20 minutes, Cook Time: 6 to 8 hours on low, Serves: 8

INGREDIENTS:

- 4 large carrots, peeled and cut into chunks
- 8 (5-ounce, 42g) pork chops
- 2 onions, chopped
- ½ cup chicken stock
- 3 garlic cloves, minced
- 3 tbsps. honey
- 3 tbsps. grated fresh ginger root
- ½ tsp. ground ginger
- ½ tsp. salt
- ⅛ tsp. freshly ground black pepper

DIRECTIONS:

1. Mix the onion, garlic, and carrot in a 6-quart crock pot and place the pig on top of the mixed vegetables.
2. Put ginger root, honey, stock, ginger, salt and pepper in a small bowl. Pour the liquid mixture into the crock pot and close the lid.
3. Cook on low heat for 6 to 8 hours, until the pork is tender.

Nutrition Info per Serving:

Calories: 241, Fat: 6g, Saturated Fat: 2g, Protein: 32g, Carbohydrates: 15g, Sugar: 11g, Fiber: 2g, Sodium: 267mg

Sausage and Pineapple Dish

Prep Time: 15 minutes, Cook Time: 3-6 hours,
Serves: 8 to 10

INGREDIENTS:

- 3 (16-oz. 454 g) pkgs. smoked sausage, cut into 1-inch chunks
- 2 (20-oz. 567 g) cans pineapple chunks, drained
- 2 large green peppers, sliced into bite-sized strips
- 18-oz. (504 g) bottle honey barbecue sauce

DIRECTIONS:

1. In the crock pot, add the sausage, pineapples and peppers, and mix well.
2. Pour the barbecue sauce over the sausage mixture and stir.
3. Cover and cook on High for 3 hours, or on Low for 6 hours, or until the dish is heated through.

Nutrition Info per Serving:

Calories: 602, Fat: 24.85 g, Carbohydrates: 72.42 g, Protein: 29.9 g

Rosemary Pork and Vegetables

Prep Time: 10 minutes, Cook Time: 7 to 8 hours on Low,
Serves: 8

INGREDIENTS:

- 1 (4-pound, 1.8 kg) boneless pork loin roast
- 4 large carrots, cut into 1-inch pieces
- 2 large beets (about 1 pound, 454 g), peeled and sliced
- 2 cups cubed peeled sweet potato
- 1 cup sliced parsnips
- 1 large Vidalia onion, sliced
- 8 sprigs fresh rosemary
- 1 cup (240 ml) low-sodium beef broth

DIRECTIONS:

1. Coat the inside of crock pot with cooking spray or insert a crock pot liner.
2. Line the bottom of the crock pot with half of the beets, parsnips, carrots, sweet potato, and onion. Put the pork on top of the vegetables. Lay the rosemary on top of the pork and cover with the remaining beets, sweet potato, carrots, parsnips, and onion. Pour the broth over them.
3. Cover and cook on LOW for 7 to 8 hours, or until the pork reaches an internal temperature of 160°F (71ºC).
4. Remove the pork from the crock pot and set aside for 3 minutes. Slice and serve with the root vegetables.

Nutrition Info per Serving:

Calories: 393, Total fat: 9 g, Saturated fat: 2 g, Total carbohydrates: 22 g, Protein: 53 g, Fiber: 5 g, Sugars: 9 g

Thai Pork and Mushroom with Peanut Sauce

Prep Time: 20 minutes, Cook Time: 7-9 hours, Serves: 8

INGREDIENTS:

- 1 (3-pound, 1.4kg) boneless pork loin roast
- 2 onions, chopped
- 2 cups chopped portabello mushrooms
- 1 cup chopped unsalted peanuts
- 1 cup chicken stock
- 1 cup peanut butter
- 4 garlic cloves, minced
- 1 small dried red chili pepper, sliced
- 2 tbsps. apple cider vinegar
- ¼ tsp. cayenne pepper

DIRECTIONS:

1. Combine onions, mushrooms, garlic, peppers, and peppers in a 6-quart crock pot.
2. In a medium-sized bowl, pour peanut butter, chicken broth and vinegar, and stir until well combined.
3. Put the roast pork on top of the vegetables in the crock pot. Then drizzle with peanut butter.
4. Cook on low heat for 7 to 9 hours, close the lid, until the pork is very tender.
5. Sprinkle with crushed peanuts and serve immediately.

Nutrition Info per Serving:

Calories: 664, Fat: 44g, Saturated Fat: 7g, Protein: 54g, Carbohydrates: 19g, Sugar: 6g, Fiber: 6g, Sodium: 232mg

Savory Roast Pork with Cabbage

Prep Time: 20 minutes, Cook Time: 7-9 hours, Serves: 8

INGREDIENTS:

- 1 (3-pound, 1.4kg) pork loin roast
- 1 large head red cabbage, chopped
- 2 medium pears, peeled and chopped
- 2 red onions, chopped
- 1 cup chicken stock
- ¼ cup apple cider vinegar
- 4 garlic cloves, minced
- 3 tbsps. honey
- 1 tsp. dried thyme leaves
- ½ tsp. salt

DIRECTIONS:

1. Combine cabbage, onion, pear, and garlic in a 6-quart crock pot.
2. Put the chicken broth, vinegar, honey, thyme and salt in a small bowl, mix and pour into a crock pot.
3. Put the pork into the crock pot.
4. Cook on low heat for 7 to 9 hours, close the lid until the pork is tender. Serve immediately!

Nutrition Info per Serving:

Calories: 365, Fat: 14g, Saturated Fat: 3g, Protein: 38g, Carbohydrates: 21g, Sugar: 14g, Fiber: 3g, Sodium: 263mg

Pork Tenderloin and Peach

Prep Time: 10 minutes, Cook Time: 6-8 hours, Serves: 1

INGREDIENTS:

- 16 ounces (454 g) pork tenderloin
- 2 peaches, peeled and cut into wedges
- ½ red onion, halved and sliced thin
- 1 sprig rosemary, needles only
- ⅛ tsp. sea salt
- Freshly ground black pepper

DIRECTIONS:

1. In the crock pot, add the onion, peaches, and rosemary needles and stir to combine.
2. Use the salt and a few grinds of the black pepper to season the pork tenderloin. Place the tenderloin over the onion and peach mixture.
3. Cover the cooker and cook on low for 6 to 8 hours, until the pork is tender and cooked through and the onion and fruit has softened.

Nutrition Info per Serving:

Calories: 374, Saturated Fat: 3 g, Trans Fat: 0 g, Carbohydrates: 12 g, Protein: 61 g, Fiber: 2 g, Sodium: 247 mg

Cranberry Pork Roast

Prep Time: 15 minutes, Cook Time: 7 to 8 hours on low, Serves: 6

INGREDIENTS:

- 3 tbsps. extra-virgin olive oil, divided
- 2 tbsps. butter
- 2 pounds (907 g) pork shoulder roast
- ½ cup chicken broth
- ½ cup cranberries
- ½ cup granulated erythritol
- ¼ tsp. allspice
- 1 tsp. ground cinnamon
- ⅛ tsp. freshly ground black pepper
- ¼ tsp. salt
- 2 tbsps. Dijon mustard
- Juice and zest of ½ orange
- 1 scallion, white and green parts, chopped, for garnish

DIRECTIONS:

1. Use 1 tablespoon of the olive oil to lightly grease the insert of the crock pot.
2. Heat the remaining 2 tablespoons of the olive oil and the butter in a large skillet over medium-high heat.
3. Use allspice, cinnamon, pepper and salt to lightly season the pork. Transfer the pork to the skillet and brown on all sides for about 10 minutes. Then place into the insert.
4. Add the broth, cranberries, mustard, erythritol and orange juice and zest into a small bowl, stir them together, and add the mixture to the pork.
5. Cover the cooker and cook on low for 7 to 8 hours.
6. Top with the scallion and serve.

Nutrition Info per Serving:

Calories: 492, Total Fat: 40 g, Total Carbs: 4 g, Net Carbs: 3 g, Protein: 26 g, Fiber: 1 g

Slow-Cooked Lime Pork

Prep Time: 20 minutes, Cook Time: 4 hours, Serves: 6

INGREDIENTS:

- 1 tbsp. canola oil
- 1 boneless pork shoulder butt roast (2 to 3 pounds, 907 g to 1.4 kg)
- 1 medium mango, peeled and chopped
- 2 cups broccoli coleslaw mix
- 1 large onion, chopped
- ½ cup water
- 3 garlic cloves, peeled
- and thinly sliced
- 2 chipotle peppers in adobo sauce, seeded and chopped
- ½ tsp. pepper, divided
- 1 tsp. salt, divided
- 2 tbsps. molasses
- 1½ tsps. grated lime peel
- 2 tbsps. lime juice
- 6 prepared corn muffins, halved

DIRECTIONS:

1. Over the roast, sprinkle with 1/4 teaspoon pepper and 3/4 teaspoon salt. Add the oil and pork into a large skillet, brown the meat on all sides. Then transfer the meat to a 3- or 4-qt. crock pot.
2. Add the onion into the same skillet, saute until tender. Stir in the garlic, cook for another 1 minute. Add chipotle peppers, water and molasses, stirring to loosen browned bits from pan. Pour the mixture over the pork. Cover the cooker and cook on high for 4-5 hours or until meat is tender.
3. After cooking, remove the roast, allow it to cool slightly. Skim fat from cooking juices. Use two forks to shred pork and place it back to the crock pot, heat through.
4. Combine the mango, coleslaw mix, lime peel, lime juice and remaining salt and pepper in a large bowl.
5. Place muffin halves on an ungreased baking sheet, cut side down. Broil 4 in. from the heat for 2-3 minutes or until lightly toasted. Serve pork with muffins, top with slaw.

Cocktail Sausages and Beef Hot Dogs

Prep Time: 5 minutes, Cook Time: 3-4 hours, Serves: 12

INGREDIENTS:

- 2 lbs. (907 g) cocktail sausages
- 1 lb. (454 g) all-beef hot dogs, sliced 1½-inches thick
- 1 cup ketchup
- 1 cup light brown sugar
- 12-oz. (340 g) can beer
- ½-1 cup barbecue sauce

DIRECTIONS:

1. In a bowl, combine the ketchup, brown sugar, beer, and barbecue sauce. Pour into the crock pot.
2. Add the sausages and hot dogs to the cooker and combine well.
3. Cover the cooker and cook on Low for 3 to 4 hours.

Nutrition Info per Serving:

Calories: 426, Fat: 19.64 g, Carbohydrates: 39.69 g, Protein: 26.79 g

Pork Tenderloin with Carrot

Prep Time: 10 minutes, Cook Time: 6-8 hours, Serves: 1

INGREDIENTS:

- 2 garlic cloves, minced
- 4 carrots, cut into 2-inch pieces
- ½ red onion, halved and sliced thin
- ⅛ tsp. sea salt
- Freshly ground black pepper
- 16 ounces (454 g) pork tenderloin
- ½ cup low-sodium chicken or vegetable broth
- ¼ cup balsamic vinegar

DIRECTIONS:

1. In the crock pot, add the garlic, carrots and onion, and stir to combine.
2. Use salt and a few grinds of the black pepper to season the pork tenderloin. Place the tenderloin over the vegetables. On top of the meat, add the broth and vinegar.
3. Cover the cooker and cook on low for 6 to 8 hours, until the meat is cooked through and the vegetables are tender.

Nutrition Info per Serving:

Calories: 400, Saturated Fat: 3 g, Trans Fat: 0 g, Carbohydrates: 16 g, Protein: 61 g, Fiber: 4 g, Sodium: 351 mg

BBQ Hot Dogs with Apricot

Prep Time: 5 minutes, Cook Time: 4½ hours, Serves: 8

INGREDIENTS:

- 1 tbsp. oil
- 2 lbs. (907 g) hot dogs, cut into 1-inch pieces
- 4 oz. (113 g) tomato sauce
- 1 cup apricot preserves
- 2 tbsps. soy sauce
- 2 tbsps. honey
- ⅓ cup vinegar
- 1 tsp. salt
- ¼ tsp. ground ginger

DIRECTIONS:

1. In the crock pot, add the oil, tomato sauce, apricot preserves, soy sauce, honey, vinegar, salt and ginger, mix together well.
2. Cover the cooker and cook on High for 30 minutes. Add the hot dog pieces. Cover and cook on Low for 4 hours.
3. After cooking, serve over the rice as a main dish, or as an appetizer.

Nutrition Info per Serving:

Calories: 131, Fat: 2.77 g, Carbohydrates: 26.78 g, Protein: 3.26 g

Mustard Spiced Ham and Chunky Potatoes

Prep Time: 5 minutes, Cook Time: 10 hours, Serves: 6 to 8

INGREDIENTS:

- 6-8 medium red or russet potatoes, cut into chunks
- 2-3-lb. (907 g to 1.4 kg) boneless ham
- ½ cup brown sugar
- 1 tsp. dry mustard

DIRECTIONS:

1. Use a fork to prick the potato pieces. Place in a crock pot.
2. Top the potatoes, add the ham. Then crumble the brown sugar over the ham. Sprinkle over with the dry mustard.
3. Cover the cooker and cook on Low for 10 or more hours, until the potatoes are tender.
4. After cooking, pour the juices over the potatoes and ham to serve.

Nutrition Info per Serving:

Calories: 387, Fat: 4.1 g, Carbohydrates: 64.63 g, Protein: 25.13 g

Slow-Cooked Thai Pork with Peanuts

Prep Time: 20 minutes, Cook Time: 8 hours, Serves: 8

INGREDIENTS:

- 2 medium sweet red peppers, julienned
- 1 boneless pork shoulder butt roast (3 pounds, 1.4 kg)
- 3 tbsps. rice vinegar
- ⅓ cup reduced-sodium teriyaki sauce
- 2 garlic cloves, minced
- ½ tsp. crushed red pepper flakes
- ¼ cup creamy peanut butter
- 4 green onions, sliced
- ½ cup chopped unsalted peanuts
- 4 cups hot cooked rice

DIRECTIONS:

1. In a 3-qt. crock pot, add the peppers. Halve the roast, and then place on top of peppers. In a bowl, add the vinegar, teriyaki sauce, and garlic, combine well and pour over the roast in the crock pot. Sprinkle with pepper flakes. Cover the cooker and cook on low for 8-9 hours or until meat is tender.
2. After cooking, take the meat out from the crock pot. Allow it to cool, and when the meat is cool enough to handle, use two forks to shred it. Reserve 2 cups cooking juices, skim fat. Add peanut butter into the reserved juices, and stir well.
3. Place the pork and cooking juices back into the crock pot, cook until them heated through. Sprinkle with onions and peanuts, and serve hot with rice.

CHAPTER 11

SOUP AND STEW

Healthy Chicken and Vegetables Soup

Prep Time: 15 minutes, Cook Time: 7 to 8 hours on low, Serves: 6

INGREDIENTS:

- 1 tbsp. extra-virgin olive oil
- 2 cups diced chicken breast
- 2 celery stalks, chopped
- 1 carrot, diced
- ½ sweet onion, chopped
- ½ cup chopped cauliflower
- 2 cups coconut milk
- 4 cups chicken broth
- 1 tsp. chopped thyme
- 2 tsps. minced garlic
- 1 tsp. chopped oregano
- ¼ tsp. freshly ground black pepper

DIRECTIONS:

1. Use olive oil to lightly grease the insert of the crock pot.
2. In the insert, add the chicken, coconut milk, broth, onion, carrot, celery, cauliflower, thyme, garlic, oregano, and pepper.
3. Cover the cooker and cook on low for 7 to 8 hours.
4. Serve warm.

Nutrition Info per Serving:

Calories: 299, Total Fat: 25 g, Total Carbs: 8 g, Net Carbs: 5 g, Protein: 14 g, Fiber: 3 g

Chicken and Bean Chili

Prep Time: 15 minutes, Cook Time: 8 hours, Serves: 4

INGREDIENTS:

- 1 pound (454 g) boneless, skinless chicken thighs, cut into 1-inch pieces
- 1 pound (454 g) dried white beans, soaked overnight and rinsed
- 3 cups (720 ml) poultry
- broth
- 1 tbsp. chili powder
- 2 onions, chopped
- 2 green bell peppers, seeded and chopped
- 2 tsps. garlic powder
- 1 tsp. ground cumin
- ¼ tsp. sea salt

DIRECTIONS:

1. Mix all the ingredients in your crock pot.
2. Cover and cook on low for 8 hours.

Nutrition Info per Serving:

Calories: 562, Total Fat: 5g, Saturated Fat: 3g, Carbohydrates: 80g, Protein: 52g, Cholesterol: 70mg, Fiber: 21g

Asian Beef and Carrot Stew

Prep Time: 15 minutes, Cook Time: 8 hours, Serves: 6

INGREDIENTS:

- 1 pound (454 g) stew beef, trimmed and cut into 1-inch cubes
- 3 carrots, peeled and chopped
- 1 (14-ounce, 397 g) can crushed tomatoes, with their juice
- 1 onion, sliced
- 2 cups (480 ml) beef
- broth
- 1 tbsp. cornstarch
- 1 tsp. Asian fish sauce
- 1 tbsp. five-spice powder
- 1 tbsp. honey
- 1 tsp. garlic powder
- ¼ tsp. freshly ground black pepper

DIRECTIONS:

1. Mix together the broth and cornstarch in a small bowl.
2. Add the mixture to your crock pot, along with other ingredients.
3. Cover and cook on low for 8 hours.

Nutrition Info per Serving:

Calories: 187, Total Fat: 5g, Saturated Fat: 0g, Carbohydrates: 15g, Protein: 20g, Cholesterol: 0mg, Fiber: 4g

Chayote and Black Bean Soup

Prep Time: 20 minutes, Cook Time: 6 hours (low), 3 hours (high), Serves: 6

INGREDIENTS:

- 4 garlic cloves, minced
- 1 cup fresh or frozen corn
- 2 cups cooked black beans
- 4 cups chicken stock or vegetable stock
- 1 medium onion, chopped
- ½ cup diced green bell pepper
- ¼ cup diced red bell pepper
- ¼ cup chopped fresh cilantro
- 1 small poblano chile (or ½ medium), seeded and chopped
- 2 chayotes, pitted, peeled, and diced
- 1 tsp. dried Mexican oregano
- ½ tsp. ground cumin

DIRECTIONS:

1. Add all of the ingredients to the crock pot, combine together.
2. Cover the cooker and cook on low for 6 hours or on high for 3 hours.
3. Well stirred the soup, and serve hot.

Bean Tomato and Beef Soup

Prep Time: 15 minutes, Cook Time: 8 hours (low), 4 hours (high), Serves: 8

INGREDIENTS:

- 1½ pounds (680 g) lean ground beef
- 2 (15-ounce, 425 g) cans ranch-style beans
- 2 (14.5-ounce, 411 g) cans diced tomatoes with chiles
- 2 cups fresh or frozen corn
- 1 medium onion, chopped
- 2 tbsps. Taco Seasoning Mix
- 1 cup beef stock
- FOR THE TOPPINGS:
- ½ cup grated Cheddar cheese
- Sour cream
- Diced avocado
- Salsa

DIRECTIONS:

1. Combine all of the ingredients except the toppings in the crock pot.
2. Cover the cooker and cook on low for 8 hours or on high for 4 hours.
3. Use a wooden spoon to stir the soup until well blended and ladle it into bowls. Sprinkle the grated cheese in the soup before serving, and pass the sour cream, avocado and salsa at the table.

Beef Cheeseburger Soup

Prep Time: 15 minutes, Cook Time: 6 hours on low, Serves: 8

INGREDIENTS:

- 3 tbsps. olive oil, divided
- 1 pound (454 g) ground beef
- 1 (28-ounce, 784 g) can diced tomatoes
- 2 celery stalks, chopped
- 1 carrot, chopped
- 1 sweet onion, chopped
- 2 cups shredded Cheddar Cheese
- 1 cup heavy (whipping) cream
- 6 cups beef broth
- 2 tsps. minced garlic
- ½ tsp. freshly ground black pepper
- 1 scallion, white and green parts, chopped, for garnish

DIRECTIONS:

1. Use 1 tablespoon of the olive oil to lightly grease the insert of the crock pot.
2. Heat the remaining 2 tablespoons of the olive oil in a large skillet over medium-high heat. Stir in the ground beef and sauté for 6 minutes, until it is cooked through.
3. Stir in the garlic and onion, sauté for another 3 minutes.
4. Place the beef mixture into the insert, and add the tomatoes, broth, carrot and celery, stir well.
5. Cover the cooker and cook on low for 6 hours.
6. Add the cheese, heavy cream, and pepper, mix well.
7. Top with the scallion and serve.

Nutrition Info per Serving:

Calories: 413, Total Fat: 32 g, Total Carbs: 8 g, Net Carbs: 6 g, Protein: 26 g, Fiber: 2 g

Bratwurst, Beans and Veggies Stew

Prep Time: 15 minutes, Cook Time: 3-4 hours, Serves: 8

INGREDIENTS:

- 5 fully cooked bratwurst links, cut into ½-inch slices
- 2 (1-lb. 454 g) cans Great Northern beans, drained
- 2 (10¾-oz. 304 g) cans fat-free chicken broth
- 3 cups chopped cabbage
- 2 ribs of celery, cut in chunks
- 4 medium carrots, sliced
- 1 medium onion, chopped
- 1 tsp. dried basil
- ½ tsp. garlic powder

DIRECTIONS:

1. In the crock pot, add all of the ingredients and mix well.
2. Cover and cook on High for 3 to 4 hours, or until the veggies are tender.

Nutrition Info per Serving:

Calories: 120, Total Fat: 3.5 g, Total Carbohydrate: 15 g, Protein: 7 g, Sugar: 4 g, Fiber: 5 g

Homemade Beef Meatball Soup

Prep Time: 20 minutes, Cook Time: 8 hours (low), 4 hours (high), Serves: 6

INGREDIENTS:

- FOR THE MEATBALLS:
- 1½ pounds (680 g) lean ground beef
- 3 eggs
- ¼ cup unseasoned breadcrumbs
- 1½ tbsps. minced onion
- 1½ tbsps. minced fresh cilantro
- 1½ tbsps. minced poblano chile
- 1 tsp. sea salt
- FOR THE SOUP:
- 4 garlic cloves, chopped
- 2 Roma tomatoes, diced
- 3 dried ancho chiles
- 3 dried guajillo chiles
- 8 cups Beef Stock
- 2 medium carrots, sliced
- 1 medium onion, chopped
- 1 tsp. ground cumin
- Sea salt, to taste

DIRECTIONS:

The Night Before:

1. Add all of the meatball ingredients to a large bowl, mix them together. Gently shape 24 meatballs, using about 1 tablespoon of the mixture for each meatball.
2. On a baking sheet in a single layer, place the meatballs, cover and chill overnight.

In the Morning:

1. Combine all the soup ingredients in the crock pot, add the meatballs.
2. Cover the cooker and and cook on low for 8 hours or on high for 4 hours. Take out and discard the chiles from the pot. Taste and adjust the seasonings as needed.
3. Ladle in large bowls and serve the soup hot.

Cheese Vegetable Soup

Prep Time: 15 minutes, Cook Time: 6 hours on low, Serves: 6

INGREDIENTS:

- 1 tbsp. butter
- 1 carrot, chopped
- 2 celery stalks, chopped
- ½ sweet onion, chopped
- 5 cups chicken broth
- 8 ounces (227 g) cream cheese, cubed
- 2 cups shredded Cheddar cheese
- 1 cup coconut milk
- Pinch cayenne pepper
- Salt, for seasoning
- freshly ground black pepper, for seasoning
- 1 tbsp. chopped fresh thyme, for garnish

DIRECTIONS:

1. Use butter to lightly grease the insert of the crock pot.
2. In the insert of the cooker, add the coconut milk, broth, carrot, celery, onion, and cayenne pepper.
3. Cover the cooker and place on low, cook for 6 hours.
4. Add the cream cheese and Cheddar, stir well and then season with salt and pepper.
5. Top with the thyme and serve.

Nutrition Info per Serving:

Calories: 406, Total Fat: 36 g, Total Carbs: 7 g, Net Carbs: 6 g, Protein: 15 g, Fiber: 1 g

Pork Stew with Fennel and Apple

Prep Time: 15 minutes, Cook Time: 8 hours, Serves: 6

INGREDIENTS:

- 1 pound (454 g) pork shoulder, trimmed of as much fat as possible and cut into 1-inch cubes
- ¼ cup (60 ml) apple cider vinegar
- 2 cups (480 ml) poultry broth
- 1 tsp. garlic powder
- 1 tsp. ground mustard
- 2 sweet-tart apples (such as Braeburn), peeled, cored, and sliced
- 1 fennel bulb, sliced
- 2 red onions, sliced
- ½ tsp. ground cinnamon
- ½ tsp. sea salt
- ⅛ tsp. freshly ground black pepper

DIRECTIONS:

1. Mix all the ingredients in your crock pot.
2. Cover and cook on low for 8 hours.

Nutrition Info per Serving:

Calories: 297, Total Fat: 11g, Saturated Fat: 4g, Carbohydrates: 15g, Protein: 21g, Fiber: 4g

Chicken and Carrots Soup

Prep Time: 10 minutes, Cook Time: 8 hours, Serves: 6

INGREDIENTS:

- 1 pound (454 g) boneless, skinless chicken thighs, cut into 1-inch pieces
- 3 carrots, peeled and sliced
- 2 celery stalks, sliced
- 1 onion, chopped
- 3 cups cooked brown rice
- 6 cups (1440 ml) poultry broth, or store bought
- ¼ tsp. sea salt
- ¼ tsp. freshly ground black pepper
- 1 tsp. garlic powder
- 1 tsp. dried rosemary

DIRECTIONS:

1. In your crock pot, combine the carrots, celery, chicken, onion, broth, salt, and pepper, garlic powder and rosemary.
2. Cover and cook on low for 8 hours.
3. Stir in the rice about 10 minutes before serving to warm it.

Nutrition Info per Serving:

Calories: 354, Total Fat: 7g, Saturated Fat: 2g, Carbohydrates: 43g, Protein: 28g, Fiber: 3g

Beef and Veggies Stew

Prep Time: 15 minutes, Cook Time: 8 hours, Serves: 6

INGREDIENTS:

- 1 pound (454 g) red potatoes, scrubbed and chopped
- 1 pound (454 g) fresh mushrooms, halved
- 1 pound (454 g) stew beef, trimmed and cut into 1-inch cubes
- 4 carrots, peeled and chopped
- 4 slices turkey bacon, browned and crumbled
- 2 cups (480 ml) beef broth
- ½ cup (120 ml) red wine
- 1 tbsp. cornstarch
- 1 tbsp. ground mustard
- 1 tsp. dried rosemary
- ¼ tsp. sea salt
- ¼ tsp. freshly ground black pepper

DIRECTIONS:

1. Mix together the broth and cornstarch in a small bowl.
2. Add the mixture to your crock pot, along with other ingredients.
3. Cover and cook on low for 8 hours.
4. Skim any excess fat from the surface and discard.

Nutrition Info per Serving:

Calories: 244, Total Fat: 6g, Saturated Fat: 0g, Carbohydrates: 21g, Protein: 24g, Fiber: 3g

Chickpea, Zucchini and Kale Soup

INGREDIENTS:

- 2 (14-ounce, 397 g) cans diced tomatoes, with their juice
- 2 cups chopped kale leaves
- 1 summer squash, quartered lengthwise and sliced crosswise
- 1 zucchini, quartered lengthwise and sliced crosswise
- 5 cups (1200 ml) vegetable broth, poultry broth, or store bought
- 2 cups cooked chickpeas, rinsed
- 1 cup uncooked quinoa
- 1 tsp. garlic powder
- 1 tsp. onion powder
- 1 tsp. dried thyme
- ½ tsp. sea salt

DIRECTIONS:

1. In your crock pot, mix the tomatoes (with their juice), broth, chickpeas, quinoa, garlic powder, onion powder, thyme, salt, summer squash and zucchini.
2. Cover and cook on low for 8 hours.
3. Stir in the kale. Cover and cook on low for 1 more hour.

Nutrition Info per Serving:

Calories: 221, Total Fat: 3g, Saturated Fat: 0g, Carbohydrates: 40g, Protein: 10g, Cholesterol: 0mg, Fiber: 7g

Creamy Garlic Poblano and Corn Chowder

INGREDIENTS:

- 4 poblano chiles, fire-roasted, peeled, and seeded
- 2 (14.5-ounce, 411 g) cans cream-style corn
- 2 cups fresh or frozen corn
- 3 garlic cloves, minced
- 2 medium onions, chopped
- ½ tsp. ground cumin
- 2 cups Chicken Stock
- 1 medium russet potato, peeled and diced
- 1 cup heavy cream or half-and-half
- ½ cup chopped fresh cilantro

DIRECTIONS:

1. Add all of the ingredients except the cilantro and cream into the crock pot.
2. Cover the cooker and cook on low for 8 hours or on high for 4 hours.
3. Add the cream, stir well. Taste and adjust the seasonings as needed. Top with the chopped cilantro and serve.

Beef Soup with Carrots and Mushroom

INGREDIENTS:

- 1 pound (454 g) extra-lean ground beef
- 1 pound (454 g) fresh mushrooms, quartered
- 6 cups (1440 ml) beef broth, or store bought
- 2 onions, chopped
- 3 carrots, peeled and sliced
- 1½ cups dried barley
- ¼ tsp. sea salt
- ⅛ tsp. freshly ground black pepper
- 1 tsp. ground mustard
- 1 tsp. dried thyme
- 1 tsp. garlic powder

DIRECTIONS:

1. Put the ground beef in your crock pot.
2. Add the remaining ingredients.
3. Cover and cook on low for 8 hours.

Nutrition Info per Serving:

Calories: 319, Total Fat: 5g, Saturated Fat: 2g, Carbohydrates: 44g, Protein: 28g, Cholesterol: 40mg, Fiber: 11g

Coconut Pumpkin and Carrot Soup

INGREDIENTS:

- 1 (29-ounce, 822 g) can pumpkin purée
- 2 carrots, peeled and chopped
- 1 onion, chopped
- 1 (14-ounce, 397 g) can light coconut milk
- 5 cups (1200 ml) vegetable broth, or store bought
- 1 tsp. garlic powder
- 1 tsp. onion powder
- 1 tsp. ground cumin
- ½ tsp. sea salt
- ¼ tsp. freshly ground black pepper
- 3 tbsps. toasted pumpkin seeds (optional)
- 1 tbsp. chopped fresh chives (optional)

DIRECTIONS:

1. In your crock pot, mix the pumpkin purée, carrots, coconut milk, garlic powder, onion powder, cumin, salt, pepper, onion and broth.
2. Cover and cook on low for 8 hours.
3. Purée with an immersion blender.
4. Sprinkle with pumpkin seeds and chives, if you like.

Nutrition Info per Serving:

Calories: 264, Total Fat: 18g, Saturated Fat: 14g, Carbohydrates: 24g, Protein: 4g, Fiber: 6g

Garlicky Red Chile and Pork Stew

Prep Time: 15 minutes, Cook Time: 8 hours (low), 5 hours (hour), Serves: 6

INGREDIENTS:

- 3 pounds (1.4 kg) lean, boneless pork roast
- 3 medium onions, cut into chunks
- 6 cups chicken stock, divided
- 1 cup New Mexico red chile powder
- 6 garlic cloves, chopped
- 2 tsps. dried Mexican oregano

DIRECTIONS:

1. Add the chile powder and 3 cups of the chicken stock into a blender, process them until smooth.
2. Transfer the mixture into the crock pot, whisk with the rest of the stock until the mixture is well blended. Add the garlic, onions and oregano.
3. Cover and cook on low for 8 hours or on high for 5 hours, until the pork is very tender.
4. Shred or chop the pork, and serve it with rice, and warm flour tortillas.

Hearty Pumpkin and Turkey Stew

Prep Time: 20 minutes, Cook Time: 7 to 8 hours on low, Serves: 6

INGREDIENTS:

- 3 tbsps. extra-virgin olive oil, divided
- 1 pound (454 g) boneless turkey breast, cut into 1-inch pieces
- 2 celery stalks, chopped
- 2 cups diced pumpkin
- 1 carrot, diced
- 1 leek, thoroughly cleaned and sliced
- 1 cup coconut milk
- 2 cups chicken broth
- 2 tsps. minced garlic
- 2 tsps. chopped thyme
- Salt, for seasoning
- Freshly ground black pepper, for seasoning
- 1 scallion, white and green parts, chopped, for garnish

DIRECTIONS:

1. Use 1 tablespoon of the olive oil to lightly grease the insert of the crock pot.
2. Heat the remaining 2 tablespoons of the olive oil in a large skillet over medium-high heat. Stir in the turkey and sauté for 5 minutes, until browned.
3. Stir in the garlic and leek, sauté for another 3 minutes.
4. In the insert of the crock pot, place the turkey mixture and stir in the coconut milk, broth, pumpkin, celery, carrot, and thyme.
5. Cover the cooker and cook on low for 7 to 8 hours.
6. Season with pepper and salt.
7. Top with the scallion and serve.

Nutrition Info per Serving:

Calories: 356, Total Fat: 27 g, Total Carbs: 11 g, Net Carbs: 7 g, Protein: 21 g, Fiber: 4 g

Creamy Potato and Celery Soup

Prep Time: 10 minutes, Cook Time: 8 hours, Serves: 1

INGREDIENTS:

- ½ cup minced onion
- 2 russet potatoes, peeled and diced
- ¼ cup minced celery
- 2 cups low-sodium chicken broth
- ¼ cup grated sharp Cheddar cheese, for garnish
- ¼ cup thinly sliced scallions, white and green parts, for garnish
- 1 tbsp. heavy cream
- ⅛ tsp. sea salt
- 2 tbsps. crumbled cooked bacon, for garnish

DIRECTIONS:

1. In the crock pot, add the onion, potatoes, celery, broth, and salt, stir them together.
2. Cover the cooker and set on low, cook for 8 hours.
3. Add the cream, stir well and use an immersion blender to purée the soup for a smooth soup. Or leave the soup chunky.
4. Top with the Cheddar cheese, scallions, and bacon, serve hot.

Nutrition Info per Serving:

Calories: 314, Saturated Fat: 6 g, Trans Fat: 0 g, Carbohydrates: 39 g, Protein: 13 g, Fiber: 6 g, Sodium: 523 mg

Crock Pot Chicken and Vegetable Soup with Chestnut

Prep Time: 10 minutes, Cook Time: 4 hours, Serves: 4

INGREDIENTS:

- 1 pound (450 g) boneless, skinless chicken breasts, chopped
- 3 celery stalks, chopped into 1-inch pieces
- 2 medium potatoes, peeled and chopped into 1-inch pieces
- 2 cups baby carrots, chopped
- 2 cups black beans, drained and rinsed
- 1 cup white onion, chopped
- 2 cups low-sodium chicken broth
- 3 tbsps. raw chestnut, shelled and diced
- 2 tbsps. Italian seasoning
- Freshly ground black pepper

DIRECTIONS:

1. Put the potatoes, celery, carrots, onion, black beans, broth, chestnut, Italian seasoning, and chicken into a crock pot and cook on high for 4 hours.
2. Season with freshly ground black pepper.

Nutrition Info per Serving:

Calories: 232, Total Fat: 3 g, Protein: 30 g, Carbohydrates: 25 g, Sugars: 7 g, Fiber: 6 g, Sodium: 180 mg

Garlicky Chipotle and Black Bean Soup

Prep Time: 10 minutes, plus soaking time, Cook Time: 10 hours (low), Serves: 8

INGREDIENTS:

- 1 pound (454 g) dried black beans
- 3 tbsps. chopped chipotles in adobo
- 1 tsp. ground cinnamon
- 6 Roma tomatoes, diced
- 2 garlic cloves, chopped
- Juice of 1 orange
- Juice of 1 lime
- 1 tbsp. ground cumin
- ½ cup chopped fresh cilantro
- 5 cups Vegetable Stock
- 2 limes, cut into wedges

DIRECTIONS:

The Night Before:

1. In a large bowl, add the beans and fill water to cover. Let them soak overnight at room temperature.

In the Morning:

1. Drain and rinse the beans.
2. Combine all the ingredients except the lime wedges and cilantro into the crock pot.
3. Cover the cooker and cook on low for 10 hours.
4. When the beans are very soft, use a handheld immersion blender to blend the soup until smooth, or use a regular blender to blend it in batches. Add the chopped cilantro and stir well.
5. Serve the soup hot with the lime wedges.

Chicken Stew with Vegetables

Prep Time: 15 minutes, Cook Time: 8 hours, Serves: 6

INGREDIENTS:

- 6 chicken hindquarters
- 4 cups (960 ml) vegetable broth
- 2 cups (480 ml) dry white wine
- 8 ounces (227 g) baby carrots
- 8 ounces (227 g) fresh or frozen pearl onions
- ½ tsp. salt
- ⅛ tsp. black pepper
- 2 cups peas (fresh or frozen)
- 1 bay leaf
- 1 tsp. dried tarragon
- ¼ cup chopped fresh parsley

DIRECTIONS:

1. Mix the chicken, onion, baby carrots, tarragon, salt, pepper, broth, wine, bay leaf in your crock pot.
2. Cover and cook on low for 7½ hours.
3. Put in the peas. Cover and cook for an additional 30 minutes.
4. Add the parsley just before serving.

Nutrition Info per Serving:

Calories: 307, Total Fat: 6g, Saturated Fat: 2g, Carbohydrates: 15g, Protein: 32g, Fiber 4g

Garlicky Herb Vegetable Broth

Prep Time: 15 minutes, Cook Time: 8 hours on low, Serves: 8

INGREDIENTS:

- 1 tbsp. extra-virgin olive oil
- 1 sweet onion, quartered
- 4 garlic cloves, crushed
- 1 carrot, roughly chopped
- 2 celery stalks with greens, roughly chopped
- 4 thyme sprigs
- ½ cup chopped parsley
- 2 bay leaves
- ½ tsp. black peppercorns
- ½ tsp. salt
- 8 cups water

DIRECTIONS:

1. Use the olive oil to grease the insert of the crock pot lightly.
2. In the insert of the crock pot, add the onion, garlic, carrot, celery, thyme, parsley, bay leaves, peppercorns, and salt. Pour in the water.
3. Cover the cooker and cook on low for about 8 hours.
4. Pour the broth through a fine-mesh cheesecloth, strain and throw away the solids.
5. Place the broth in sealed containers, and store in the refrigerator for up to 5 days or in the freezer for up to 1 month.

Nutrition Info per Serving:

Calories: 27, Total Fat: 2 g, Total Carbs: 2 g, Net Carbs: 2 g, Protein: 0 g, Fiber: 0 g

Jalapeño and Pork Pozole

Prep Time: 5 minutes, Cook Time: 10 hours (low), 5 hours (high), Serves: 8

INGREDIENTS:

- 2½ pounds (1.1 kg) lean, boneless pork, cut into bite-size pieces
- 2 (28-ounce, 784 g) cans tomatillos, drained
- 1 (28-ounce, 784 g) can white hominy, drained
- 3 medium onions, chopped
- 3 jalapeños, seeded and chopped
- 2 tsps. ground cumin
- 1 cup chicken stock
- 1 bunch fresh cilantro, chopped, plus more for garnish
- 1 tsp. sugar (optional)
- 2 limes, cut into wedges

DIRECTIONS:

1. Combine all the ingredients except the limes into the crock pot.
2. Cover the cooker and cook on low for 10 hours or on high for 5 hours.
3. Taste the broth and adjust with the sugar if necessary to balance the acidity of the tomatillos.
4. Garnish with more cilantro, and squeeze the limes wedges into the soup, and serve.

Bacon Cauliflower and Chicken Soup

Prep Time: 15 minutes, Cook Time: 6 hours on low, Serves: 6

INGREDIENTS:

- 1 tbsp. extra-virgin olive oil
- 2 cups chopped cooked chicken
- 2 cups coconut milk
- 4 cups chicken broth
- 1 cup chopped cooked bacon
- 1 sweet onion, chopped
- 2 cups chopped cauliflower
- 3 tsps. minced garlic
- ½ cup cream cheese, cubed
- 2 cups shredded cheddar Cheese

DIRECTIONS:

1. Use the olive oil to lightly grease the insert of the crock pot.
2. In the insert of the cooker, add the chicken, coconut milk, broth, bacon, onion, cauliflower, and garlic.
3. Cover and set on low, cook for 6 hours.
4. Add the cream cheese and Cheddar, stir well and serve.

Nutrition Info per Serving:

Calories: 540, Total Fat: 44 g, Total Carbs: 7 g, Net Carbs: 6 g, Protein: 35 g, Fiber: 1 g

Sausage Kale Soup

Prep Time: 15 minutes, Cook Time: 6 hours on low, Serves: 6

INGREDIENTS:

- 3 tbsps. olive oil, divided
- 1½ pounds (680 g) sausage, without casing
- 2 celery stalks, chopped
- 6 cups chicken broth
- 1 leek, thoroughly cleaned and chopped
- 1 carrot, diced
- 2 tsps. minced garlic
- 2 cups chopped kale
- 1 tbsp. chopped fresh parsley, for garnish

DIRECTIONS:

1. Use 1 tablespoon of the olive oil to lightly grease the insert of the crock pot.
2. Heat the remaining 2 tablespoons of the olive oil in a large skillet over medium-high heat. Stir in the sausage and sauté for 7 minutes, until it is cooked through.
3. Place the sausage into the insert, and add the celery, broth, leek, carrot, and garlic, stir well.
4. Cover the cooker and cook on low for 6 hours.
5. Add the kale and stir well.
6. Top with the parsley and serve.

Nutrition Info per Serving:

Calories: 383, Total Fat: 31 g, Total Carbs: 5 g, Net Carbs: 4 g, Protein: 21 g, Fiber: 1 g

Pork and Sweet Potato Chowder

Prep Time: 20 minutes, Cook Time: 6 hours 15 minutes to 8 hours 20 minutes, Serves: 8

INGREDIENTS:

- 1 (3-pound, 1.4kg) pork loin, cut into 1½-inch cubes
- 3 tbsps. grated fresh ginger root
- 4 large sweet potatoes, peeled and cubed
- 2 leeks, chopped
- 2 cups frozen corn
- 2 tbsps. cornstarch
- 8 cups roasted vegetable broth
- 4 garlic cloves, minced
- 1 tsp. ground ginger
- ⅔ cup 2% milk

DIRECTIONS:

1. Combine pork, leeks, sweet potatoes, corn, garlic, ginger root, minced ginger, and vegetable broth in a 6-quart crock pot. Place the pot on the stove and cook on low heat for 6 to 8 hours, and cover until the sweet potatoes are tender.
2. Mix the milk and cornstarch in a small bowl and mix well. Pour this mixed liquid into a crock pot.
3. Cook on low heat for 15 to 20 minutes, until the chowder thickens. Serve immediately!

Nutrition Info per Serving:

Calories: 382, Fat: 8g, Saturated Fat: 2g, Protein: 42g, Carbohydrates: 33g, Sugar: 11g, Fiber: 4g, Sodium: 414mg

Smoked Flavor Lentil Soup

Prep Time: 10 minutes, Cook Time: 8 hours, Serves: 6

INGREDIENTS:

- 1 pound (454 g) dried lentils, soaked overnight and rinsed
- 3 carrots, peeled and chopped
- 1 celery stalk, chopped
- 1 onion, chopped
- 6 cups (1440 ml) vegetable broth, poultry broth, beef broth, or store bought
- 1½ tsp. garlic powder
- ¼ tsp. liquid smoke
- ¼ tsp. sea salt
- ¼ tsp. freshly ground black pepper
- 1 tsp. ground cumin
- 1 tsp. smoked paprika
- 1 tsp. dried thyme

DIRECTIONS:

1. Mix the lentils with all the other ingredients in your crock pot.
2. Cover and cook on low for 8 hours. Stir and serve.

Nutrition Info per Serving:

Calories: 307, Total Fat: 1g, Saturated Fat: 0g, Carbohydrates: 56g, Protein: 20g, Fiber: 25g

Pearl Barley and Black Beans Stew

Prep Time: 10 minutes, Cook Time: 8 hours, Serves: 6

INGREDIENTS:

- 1 (14-ounce, 397 g) can diced tomatoes and green chiles, drained
- 1 cup uncooked pearl barley
- 2 cups dried black beans, soaked overnight and rinsed
- 1 avocado, peeled, seeded, and cubed
- 1 onion, chopped
- 8 cups (1920 ml) vegetable broth
- 1 tsp. garlic powder
- 1 tsp. ground cumin
- 1 tsp. chili powder
- ½ tsp. sea salt

DIRECTIONS:

1. Mix the barley, black beans, broth, garlic powder, cumin, chili powder, onion, tomatoes, and salt in your crock pot.
2. Cover and cook on low for 8 hours.
3. Garnish with the cubed avocado.

Nutrition Info per Serving:

Calories: 438, Total Fat: 8g, Saturated Fat: 2g, Carbohydrates: 81g, Protein: 19g, Cholesterol: 0mg, Fiber: 19g

Crock Pot Vegetable Broth

Prep Time: 15 minutes, Cook Time: 8 hours, Serves: 4

INGREDIENTS:

- 1½ tsps. olive oil
- 2 celery stalks, chopped
- 3 carrots, scrubbed and sliced
- 1 medium potato, peeled and cut into 1-inch chunks
- 1 large yellow onion, thinly sliced
- 4 whole garlic cloves, crushed
- ¼ cup chopped parsley leaves
- 1½ tbsps. soy sauce
- ½ tsp. peppercorns
- 7 cups water
- 1 tsp. salt

DIRECTIONS:

1. In the bottom of a crock pot, drizzle with the oil.
2. Place the onion, garlic, celery, carrots, potato, parsley leaves, soy sauce, peppercorns, water, and salt into the crock pot. Combine them together, and cook on low for 8 hours.
3. Allow the stock to sit and cool, then use a colander to strain it into a bowl. Extract all available juices by pressing the vegetables.
4. Keep the stock into the refrigerator for up to 5 days, or freeze for up to 3 months.

Nutrition Info per Serving:

Calories: 88, Total fat: 2 g, Protein: 2 g, Sodium: 977 mg, Fiber: 3 g

Sweet Potato and Lentils with Curry

Prep Time: 10 minutes, Cook Time: 8 hours, Serves: 4

INGREDIENTS:

- 4 sweet potatoes, peeled and cut into 1-inch cubes
- 1 (14-ounce, 397 g) can chopped tomatoes, with their juice
- 1 cup dried green lentils, soaked overnight and rinsed
- 1 onion, chopped
- 1 cup (240 ml) canned light coconut milk
- 1 cup (240 ml) vegetable broth, or store bought
- 1 tsp. garlic powder
- 1 tbsp. curry powder
- ½ tsp. sea salt
- 2 tbsps. chopped fresh cilantro

DIRECTIONS:

1. In your crock pot, mix the sweet potatoes, lentils, tomatoes (with their juice), onion, coconut milk, broth, garlic powder, curry powder and salt.
2. Cover and cook on low for 8 hours.
3. Add cilantro and serve.

Nutrition Info per Serving:

Calories: 525, Total Fat: 16g, Saturated Fat: 13g, Carbohydrates: 83g, Protein: 18g, Fiber: 25g

Chicken and Carrots Stew

Prep Time: 15 minutes, Cook Time: 8 hours, Serves: 6

INGREDIENTS:

- 3 cups (720 ml) poultry broth, or store bought
- 2 tbsps. cornstarch
- 1 pound (454 g) red potatoes, scrubbed and cut into 1-inch pieces
- 1 fennel bulb, chopped
- 3 garlic cloves, minced
- 1 pound boneless, skinless chicken thighs, cut into 1-inch pieces
- 4 carrots, peeled and cut into ½-inch pieces
- 2 red onions, chopped
- ½ cup (120 ml) dry white wine
- 1 tsp. dried thyme
- ½ tsp. sea salt
- ¼ tsp. freshly ground black pepper

DIRECTIONS:

1. Whisk together the broth and cornstarch in a small bowl.
2. Add the mixture to the crock pot with all the other ingredients.
3. Cover and cook on low for 8 hours.

Nutrition Info per Serving:

Calories: 277, Total Fat: 6g, Saturated Fat: 2g, Carbohydrates: 26g, Protein: 26g, Fiber: 4g

Chicken Bone Broth

Prep Time: 15 minutes, Cook Time: 24 hours on low, Serves: 8

INGREDIENTS:

- 1 tbsp. extra-virgin olive oil
- 2 garlic cloves, crushed
- 2 chicken carcasses, separated into pieces
- 1 carrot, chopped
- 1 celery stalk, chopped
- 2 tbsps. apple cider vinegar
- ½ sweet onion, cut into eighths
- 2 bay leaves
- ½ tsp. black peppercorns
- Water

DIRECTIONS:

1. Use the olive oil to grease the insert of the crock pot lightly.
2. In the insert, add the garlic, chicken bones, carrot, celery, apple cider vinegar, onion, bay leaves, and peppercorns. Fill in water until the liquid reaches about 1½ inches from the top of the insert.
3. Cover the cooker and cook on low for about 24 hours.
4. Pour the broth through a fine-mesh cheesecloth, strain and throw away the solids.
5. Place the broth in sealed containers, and store in the refrigerator for up to 5 days or in the freezer for up to 1 month.

Nutrition Info per Serving:

Calories: 99, Total Fat: 6 g, Total Carbs: 5 g, Net Carbs: 5 g, Protein: 6 g, Fiber: 0 g

Ginger Turkey Soup with Rice

Prep Time: 10 minutes, Cook Time: 8 hours, Serves: 6

INGREDIENTS:

- 1 pound (454 g) boneless, skinless turkey thighs, cut into 1-inch pieces
- 1 pound (454 g) fresh shiitake mushrooms, halved
- 3 carrots, peeled and sliced
- 2 cups frozen peas
- 6 cups (1440 ml) poultry broth, or store bought
- 1½ cups cooked brown rice
- 1 tbsp. grated fresh ginger
- 1 tbsp. low-sodium soy sauce
- 2 tsps. garlic powder
- 1 tsp. toasted sesame oil

DIRECTIONS:

1. In your crock pot, combine the turkey, mushrooms, ginger, broth, carrots, peas, soy sauce, garlic powder and sesame oil.
2. Cover and cook on low for 8 hours.
3. About half an hour before serving, stir in the rice to warm it through.

Nutrition Info per Serving:

Calories: 318, Total Fat: 7g, Saturated Fat: 0g, Carbohydrates: 42g, Protein: 24g, Fiber: 6g

Turkey Pot Pie Soup

Prep Time: 20 minutes, Cook Time: 7 to 8 hours on low, Serves: 8

INGREDIENTS:

- 1 tbsp. extra-virgin olive oil
- ½ pound (227 g) skinless turkey breast, cut into ½-inch chunks
- 4 cups chicken broth
- 1 carrot, diced
- 2 celery stalks, chopped
- 1 sweet onion, chopped
- 2 tsps. minced garlic
- 2 tsps. chopped fresh thyme
- 2 cups heavy (whipping) cream
- 1 cup cream cheese, diced
- 1 cup green beans, cut into 1-inch pieces
- Salt, for seasoning
- Freshly ground black pepper, for seasoning

DIRECTIONS:

1. Use the olive oil to lightly grease the insert of the crock pot.
2. In the insert of the cooker, add the turkey, broth, carrot, celery, onion, garlic, and thyme.
3. Cover the cooker and set on low, cook for 7 to 8 hours.
4. Add the heavy cream, cream cheese, and green beans, stir well.
5. Season with salt and pepper and serve.

Nutrition Info per Serving:

Calories: 415, Total Fat: 35 g, Total Carbs: 7 g, Net Carbs: 5 g, Protein: 20 g, Fiber: 2 g

Traditional Hungarian Goulash

Prep Time: 15 minutes, Cook Time: 8 hours, Serves: 6

INGREDIENTS:

- 1 pound (454 g) stew beef, trimmed and cut into 1-inch cubes
- 3 carrots, peeled and sliced
- 2 onions, sliced
- 3 cups cooked quinoa
- 2 cups (480 ml) beef broth
- 1 tbsp. cornstarch
- ¼ cup tomato paste
- 2 tbsps. smoked paprika
- 1 tsp. garlic powder
- ½ tsp. sea salt

DIRECTIONS:

1. Mix together the broth and cornstarch in a small bowl.
2. Add the mixture to your crock pot, along with the tomato paste, beef, onions, carrots, paprika, garlic powder, and salt. Stir to combine.
3. Cover and cook on low for 8 hours.
4. Skim any excess fat from the surface and discard.
5. Serve over the quinoa.

Nutrition Info per Serving:

Calories: 321, Total Fat: 8g, Saturated Fat: 0g, Carbohydrates: 39g, Protein: 25g, Fiber: 6g

Turkey Meatball and Kale Soup

INGREDIENTS:

- 1 pound (454 g) ground turkey breast
- 1 egg, beaten
- 1 tsp. garlic powder
- 1 tsp. sea salt, divided
- 1½ cups cooked brown rice
- 1 onion, grated
- ¼ cup chopped fresh parsley
- 6 cups (1440 ml) poultry broth, or store bought
- ⅛ tsp. freshly ground black pepper
- Pinch red pepper flakes
- 1 pound (454 g) kale, tough stems removed, leaves chopped

DIRECTIONS:

1. In a small bowl, combine the turkey breast, egg, garlic powder, ½ teaspoon of sea salt, rice, onion and parsley.
2. Roll the mixture into ½-inch meatballs and put them in the crock pot.
3. Add the broth, red pepper flakes, black pepper, and the remaining ½ teaspoon of sea salt.
4. Cover and cook on low for 7 to 8 hours.
5. Stir in the kale an hour before serving. Cover and cook until the kale wilts.

Nutrition Info per Serving:

Calories: 302, Total Fat: 7g, Saturated Fat: 2g, Carbohydrates: 29g, Protein: 29g, Fiber: 3g

Spicy Italian Sausage and Fennel Soup

INGREDIENTS:

- 1 pound (454 g) Italian chicken or turkey sausage, cut into ½-inch slices
- 6 cups (1440 ml) poultry broth, or store bought
- ¼ cup (60 ml) dry sherry
- 2 onions, chopped
- 1 fennel bulb, chopped
- 1½ tsp. garlic powder
- 1 tsp. dried thyme
- Pinch red pepper flakes
- ½ tsp. sea salt
- ¼ tsp. freshly ground black pepper

DIRECTIONS:

1. Mix all the ingredients in your crock pot.
2. Cover and cook on low for 8 hours.

Nutrition Info per Serving:

Calories: 311, Total Fat: 22g, Saturated Fat: 7g, Carbohydrates: 8g, Protein: 18g, Fiber: 2g

Manhattan-Style Clam and Potato Chowder

INGREDIENTS:

- 1 pound (454 g) baby red potatoes, quartered
- 1 (10-ounce, 283 g) can chopped clams, with their juice
- 3 carrots, peeled and chopped
- 4 cups (960 ml) poultry broth, or store bought
- 1 red onion, chopped
- 1 fennel bulb and fronds, chopped
- 2 cups (480 ml) skim milk
- ¼ pound (113 g) turkey bacon, browned and crumbled, for garnish
- ½ tsp. sea salt
- ⅛ tsp. freshly ground black pepper

DIRECTIONS:

1. In your crock pot, mix the clams (with their juice), onion, carrots, broth, fennel bulb and fronds, potatoes, salt, and pepper.
2. Cover and cook on low for 8 hours.
3. Stir in the milk. Serve with the crumbled bacon.

Nutrition Info per Serving:

Calories: 172, Total Fat: 1g, Saturated Fat: 0g, Carbohydrates: 29g, Protein: 10g, Fiber: 4g

Spicy Butternut Squash and Apple Soup

INGREDIENTS:

- 1 butternut squash, peeled, seeded, and diced
- 3 cups (720 ml) vegetable broth, or store bought
- 1 sweet-tart apple (such as Braeburn), peeled, cored, and chopped
- 1 onion, chopped
- ½ cup (120 ml) fat-free half-and-half
- 1 tsp. garlic powder
- ½ tsp. ground sage
- ¼ tsp. sea salt
- ¼ tsp. freshly ground black pepper
- Pinch cayenne pepper
- Pinch nutmeg

DIRECTIONS:

1. In your crock pot, mix the squash, broth, garlic powder, sage, salt, black pepper, onion, apple, cayenne, and nutmeg.
2. Cover and cook on low for 8 hours.
3. Using an immersion blender or food processor, purée the soup, adding the half-and-half. Stir to combine, and serve.

Nutrition Info per Serving:

Calories: 106, Total Fat: 0g, Saturated Fat: 0g, Carbohydrates: 26g, Protein: 3g, Fiber: 4g

Spicy Chicken Stew

Prep Time: 10 minutes, Cook Time: 8 hours, Serves: 6

INGREDIENTS:

- 1 pound (454 g) boneless, skinless chicken thighs, cut into 1-inch pieces
- 2 (4-ounce, 113 g) cans chopped jalapeño peppers, with their juice
- 3 carrots, peeled and sliced
- 2 red bell peppers, seeded and chopped
- 2 cups fresh or frozen corn
- 2 onions, chopped
- 2 cups (480 ml) poultry broth
- 1 tbsp. cornstarch
- ¼ tsp. sea salt
- ¼ cup chopped fresh cilantro

DIRECTIONS:

1. Mix together the poultry broth and cornstarch in a small bowl.
2. Add the mixture to the crock pot, along with the chicken, jalapeños (and their juice), red bell peppers, corn, onions, carrots and salt.
3. Cover and cook on low for 8 hours.
4. Add the cilantro before serving.

Nutrition Info per Serving:

Calories: 179, Total Fat: 5g, Saturated Fat: 3g, Carbohydrates: 20g, Protein: 20g, Cholesterol: 47mg, Fiber: 4g

Savory Ratatouille Soup

Prep Time: 20 minutes, Cook Time: 7-9 hours, Serves: 8

INGREDIENTS:

- 2 tbsps. olive oil
- 6 large tomatoes, seeded and chopped
- 2 medium eggplants, peeled and chopped
- 2 red bell peppers, stemmed, seeded, and chopped
- 2 onions, chopped
- 6 cups roasted vegetable broth
- 1½ cups shredded Swiss cheese
- 2 tsps. herbes de Provence
- 4 garlic cloves, minced
- 2 tbsps. cornstarch

DIRECTIONS:

1. Combine olive oil, onions, garlic, eggplants, bell peppers, tomatoes, vegetable broth and Provencal herbs in a 6-quart crock pot. Put the lid on and cook on low heat for 7 to 9 hours until the vegetables are soft.
2. Put the cheese and cornstarch in a small bowl and stir together. Pour the cheese mixture into the crock pot. Let stand for 10 minutes, stir the soup gently and serve.

Nutrition Info per Serving:

Calories: 215, Fat: 10g, Saturated Fat: 4g, Protein: 9g, Carbohydrates: 23g, Sugar: 11g, Fiber: 8g, Sodium: 144mg

Vegetable Salmon Chowder

Prep Time: 20 minutes, Cook Time: 6½ to 8½ hours, Serves: 8

INGREDIENTS:

- 6 medium Yukon Gold potatoes, cut into 2-inch pieces
- 2 cups sliced cremini mushrooms
- 2 pounds (907g) skinless salmon fillets
- 4 large carrots, sliced
- 8 cups roasted vegetable broth or fish stock
- 3 garlic cloves, minced
- 2 tsps. dried dill weed
- 4 shallots, minced
- 1 cup whole milk
- 1½ cups shredded Swiss cheese

DIRECTIONS:

1. Place potatoes, carrots, mushrooms, shallots, garlic, vegetable broth, and dill grass in a 6-quart crock pot and stir to combine. Cover the lid and simmer for 6 to 8 hours until the vegetables are soft.
2. Put the salmon fillets in the crock pot. Continue to cook for 20 to 30 minutes until the salmon fillets are cooked through.
3. Stir the chowder gently with a fork to break up the salmon.
4. Pour the milk and Swiss cheese, and let the mixture sit for 10 minutes to melt the cheese. Stir the chowder and serve immediately.

Nutrition Info per Serving:

Calories: 453, Fat: 20g, Saturated Fat: 7g, Protein: 34g, Carbohydrates: 31g, Sugar: 6g, Fiber: 3g, Sodium: 252mg

Spicy Turkey Soup

Prep Time: 15 minutes, Cook Time: 8 hours, Serves: 6

INGREDIENTS:

- 1 pound (454 g) ground turkey breast
- 6 cups (1440 ml) poultry broth, or store bought
- 1 onion, chopped
- 1 (14-ounce, 397 g) can tomatoes and green chiles, with their juice
- ½ tsp. sea salt
- 1 tsp. chili powder
- 1 tsp. ground cumin
- ¼ cup chopped fresh cilantro
- Juice of 1 lime
- ½ cup grated low-fat Cheddar cheese

DIRECTIONS:

1. Put the turkey into the crock pot.
2. Add the broth, onion, tomatoes and green chiles (with their juice), salt, chili power and cumin.
3. Cover and cook on low for 8 hours.
4. Add the cilantro and lime juice.
5. Serve garnished with Cheddar cheese.

Nutrition Info per Serving:

Calories: 281, Total Fat: 10g, Saturated Fat: 4g, Carbohydrates: 20g, Protein: 30g, Fiber: 5g

Vegetable and Chicken Stew

Prep Time: 20 minutes, Cook Time: 6 hours on low, Serves: 6

INGREDIENTS:

- 3 tbsps. extra-virgin olive oil, divided
- 1 pound (454 g) chicken thighs, diced into 1½-inch pieces
- 1 carrot, diced
- 1 cup coconut cream
- 1 cup shredded kale
- 2 celery stalks, diced
- 2 cups chicken broth
- ½ sweet onion, chopped
- 2 tsps. minced garlic
- 1 tsp. dried thyme
- Salt, for seasoning
- Freshly ground black pepper, for seasoning

DIRECTIONS:

1. Use 1 tablespoon of the olive oil to lightly grease the insert of the crock pot.
2. Heat the remaining 2 tablespoons of the olive oil in a large skillet over medium-high heat. Stir in the chicken and sauté for 7 minutes, until it is just cooked through.
3. Stir in the garlic and onion, sauté for another 3 minutes.
4. In the insert of the crock pot, place the chicken mixture and stir in the celery, broth, carrot, and thyme.
5. Cover the cooker and cook on low for 6 hours.
6. Add the coconut cream and kale, stir well.
7. Season with pepper and salt, and serve warm.

Nutrition Info per Serving:

Calories: 276, Total Fat: 22 g, Total Carbs: 6 g, Net Carbs: 4 g, Protein: 17 g, Fiber: 2 g

Crock Pot Split Pea and Sweet Potato Soup

Prep Time: 10 minutes, Cook Time: 4 to 8 hours, Serves: 8

INGREDIENTS:

- 2½ cups green or yellow split peas, rinsed well
- 2 small sweet potatoes, cut into ½-inch dice
- 6½ cups water
- 1 tbsp. dried thyme
- 1½ tsps. salt, plus additional as needed

DIRECTIONS:

1. Add the water, split peas, sweet potatoes, thyme, and salt to a crock pot, combine together.
2. Cover the cooker and cook on low for 8 hours, or on high for 4 hours.
3. Working in batches as needed, add half or all of the soup in an immersion blender or in a regular blender, blend until smooth, taking care with the hot liquid.
4. Taste the soup and adjust the seasoning is needed.

Nutrition Info per Serving:

Calories: 51, Total Fat: 0 g, Total Carbohydrates: 12 g, Sugar: 0 g, Fiber: 2 g, Protein: 1 g, Sodium: 448 mg

Chicken Veggie Jambalaya Soup

Prep Time: 15 minutes, Cook Time: 6 to 7 hours on low, Serves: 8

INGREDIENTS:

- 1 tbsp. extra-virgin olive oil
- 1 cup chopped cooked chicken
- 1 pound (454 g) organic sausage, sliced
- ½ pound (227 g) medium shrimp, peeled, deveined, and chopped
- 1 (28-ounce, 784 g) can diced tomatoes
- 6 cups chicken broth
- ½ sweet onion, chopped
- 1 red bell pepper, chopped
- 1 jalapeño pepper, chopped
- 2 tsps. minced garlic
- 3 tbsps. cajun seasoning
- 1 avocado, diced, for garnish
- ½ cup sour cream, for garnish
- 2 tsps. chopped cilantro, for garnish

DIRECTIONS:

1. Use the olive oil to lightly grease the insert of the crock pot.
2. Stir in the chicken, sausage, tomatoes, broth, onion, red bell pepper, jalapeño pepper, garlic, and Cajun seasoning.
3. Cover the cooker and cook on low for 6 to 7 hours.
4. Add the shrimp to the cooker and cook on low until the shrimp are cooked through, about 30 minutes.
5. Top with the avocado, sour cream, and cilantro, and serve.

Nutrition Info per Serving:

Calories: 400, Total Fat: 31 g, Total Carbs: 9 g, Net Carbs: 5 g, Protein: 24 g, Fiber: 4 g

Crock Pot Cabbage and Noodles Soup

Prep Time: 15 minutes, Cook Time: 7-8 hours, Serves: 4

INGREDIENTS:

- 2 carrots, scrubbed and sliced
- ½ head napa cabbage, chopped
- 1 celery stalk, diced
- 6 cups vegetable broth or store bought
- 1 (½-inch) piece fresh ginger, peeled and minced
- 1 tsp. minced garlic (2 cloves)
- 1 tbsp. white miso paste
- ¼ tsp. red pepper flakes (optional)
- ½ package rice noodles (about 4 ounces, optional, 113 g)

DIRECTIONS:

1. In a crock pot, add the vegetable broth, miso paste, cabbage, carrots, celery, garlic, ginger, and red pepper flakes (if using). Stir them to combine well.
2. Cover the cooker and cook for 7 to 8 hours on low or 3 to 4 hours on high.
3. Add the rice noodles to the crock pot 20 minutes before serving is using.

Nutrition Info per Serving:

Calories: 126, Total fat: 3 g, Protein: 9 g, Sodium: 1,342 mg, Fiber: 2 g

Loaded Chicken Nacho Soup

INGREDIENTS:

- 3 tbsps. extra-virgin olive oil, divided
- 1 pound (454 g) ground chicken
- 2 tsps. minced garlic
- 1 sweet onion, diced
- 1 red bell pepper, chopped
- 2 tbsps. taco seasoning
- 2 cups coconut milk
- 1 tomato, diced
- 4 cups chicken broth
- 1 jalapeño pepper, chopped
- 2 cups shredded Cheddar Cheese
- 1 scallion, white and green parts, chopped, for garnish
- ½ cup sour cream, for garnish

DIRECTIONS:

1. Use 1 tablespoon of the olive oil to lightly grease the insert of the crock pot.
2. Heat the remaining 2 tablespoons of the olive oil in a large skillet over medium-high heat. Stir in the chicken and sauté for 6 minutes, until it is cooked through.
3. Stir in the garlic, onion, red bell pepper and taco seasoning, and sauté for another 3 minutes.
4. Place the chicken mixture into the insert, and add the coconut milk, tomato, broth and jalapeño pepper.
5. Cover the cooker and set on low, cook for 6 hours.
6. Add the cheese and stir well.
7. Top with the scallion and sour cream, serve.

Nutrition Info per Serving:

Calories: 434, Total Fat: 35 g, Total Carbs: 9 g, Net Carbs: 7 g, Protein: 22 g, Fiber: 2 g

CHAPTER 12

APPETIZER AND SNACK

Crock Pot Spinach with Artichoke

Prep Time: 20 minutes, Cook Time: 4 to 5 hours on low, Serves: 10

INGREDIENTS:
- 2 tbsps. olive oil
- 3 garlic cloves, minced
- 1 (15-ounce, 425g) BPA-free can no-salt-added cannellini beans, drained and rinsed
- 1 red onion, chopped
- 2 (14-ounce, 397g) BPA-free cans no-salt-added artichoke hearts, drained and quartered
- 1 (10-ounce, 283g) bag chopped frozen spinach, thawed and drained
- 1 cup shredded Swiss cheese
- ½ cup sour cream
- 2 tbsps. freshly squeezed lemon juice

DIRECTIONS:
1. Pour the beans into a potato masher and mash them, then remove them and place them in a 6-quart crock pot.
2. Pour the onion, garlic and artichoke hearts into the crock pot.
3. Then add spinach, sour cream, lemon juice, olive oil and Swiss cheese.
4. Turn on a low heat, close the lid, and cook on low heat for 4 to 5 hours, until the sauce is hot and bubbling. Serve immediately!

Nutrition Info per Serving:

Calories: 145, Fat: 9g, Saturated Fat: 4g, Protein: 6g, Carbohydrates: 10g, Sugar: 1g, Fiber: 4g

Cheesy Mushrooms Meatballs

Prep Time: 10 minutes, Cook Time: 6-8 hours, Serves: 12 to 15

INGREDIENTS:
- 3-4-lb. (1.4 kg-1.8 kg) bag prepared meatballs
- 1 medium onion, diced
- 3 (304 g) cans cream of mushroom
- 16-oz. (454 g) jar Cheese Whiz
- 4-oz. (113 g) can button mushrooms

DIRECTIONS:
1. Mix all ingredients in the crock pot.
2. Cover and cook on Low for 6-8 hours.
3. Serve as an appetizer, or as a main dish over noodles or rice.

Nutrition Info per Serving:

Calories: 774, Carbohydrates: 84.43 g, Protein: 29.54 g, Fat: 35.57 g

Cheese Stuffed Jalapeño Peppers

Prep Time: 15 minutes, Cook Time: 4 hours (low), 2 hours (high), Serves: 24 poppers

INGREDIENTS:
- 24 slices bacon
- 12 jalapeños, washed, seeded, and halved lengthwise
- 8 ounces cream cheese, at room temperature
- ¼ cup sour cream
- ¼ cup grated Cheddar cheese
- ⅓ cup chicken stock or water

DIRECTIONS:
1. Add the sour cream, cream cheese and grated Cheddar cheese into a medium bowl, mix them together until well blended.
2. Evenly divide the cheese mixture among the jalapeño halves, and use a slice of bacon to wrap each stuffed jalapeño half, then with a toothpick to secure the bacon.
3. Pour the chicken stock in the crock pot, and add the stuffed jalapeños.
4. Cover the cooker and cook on low for 4 hours or on high for 2 hours.
5. Remove the stuffed jalapeños from the crock pot with a slotted spoon and serve hot or at room temperature.

Creamy Spinach and Artichoke

Prep Time: 10 minutes, Cook Time: 4 hours, Serves: 1½ cups

INGREDIENTS:
- 2 (14-ounce, 397 g) cans artichoke hearts, drained and chopped
- 8 ounces (227 g) fat-free cream cheese
- 2 cups (480 ml) fat-free sour cream
- 2 cups baby spinach, stemmed
- ½ red onion, minced
- 3 garlic cloves, minced
- Zest of 1 lemon
- ¼ tsp. sea salt
- ¼ tsp. freshly ground black pepper
- Pinch cayenne pepper

DIRECTIONS:
1. Combine all the ingredients in your crock pot.
2. Cover and cook on low for 4 hours.

Nutrition Info per Serving:

Calories: 283, Total Fat: 13g, Saturated Fat: 8g, Carbohydrates: 30g, Protein: 10g, Fiber: 7g

Garlic Onion and Potatoes

Prep Time: 10 minutes, Cook Time: 5-6 hours, Serves: 6

INGREDIENTS:

- 2 tbsps. olive oil
- 6 garlic cloves, minced
- 6 potatoes, peeled and cubed
- ¼ cup dried onion, or 1 medium onion, chopped

DIRECTIONS:

1. In a crock pot, add the garlic, potatoes, onion and olive oil.
2. Cover the cooker and cook on Low for 5-6 hours, or until potatoes are soft but not turning brown.

Nutrition Info per Serving:

Calories: 220, Fat: 4.5 g, Carbohydrate: 40 g, Protein: 5 g, Fiber: 5 g, Sugar: 3 g, Sodium: 15 mg

Kielbasa and Onion in Applesauce

Prep Time: 20 minutes, Cook Time: 4-8 hours, Serves: 6

INGREDIENTS:

- 2 lbs. (907 g) smoked kielbasa
- 3 medium onions, sliced
- 3 cups unsweetened applesauce
- ½ cup brown sugar

DIRECTIONS:

1. Slice kielbasa into ¼-inch slices, add to a skillet, brown the slices and drain.
2. In a bowl, combine the brown sugar and applesauce.
3. In the crock pot, layer with the browned kielbasa slices, onions, and applesauce mixture.
4. Cover the cooker and cook on Low for 4 to 8 hours.

Nutrition Info per Serving:

Calories: 464, Fat: 26.74 g, Carbohydrates: 38.05 g, Protein: 20.09 g

Ginger Glazed Kielbasa

Prep Time: 5 minutes, Cook Time: 4 hours, Serves: 12

INGREDIENTS:

- 3 pounds (1.4 kg) smoked kielbasa or Polish sausage, cut into 1-inch chunks
- 1½ cups ginger ale
- ½ cup packed brown sugar

DIRECTIONS:

1. In a 3-qt. crock pot, add the sausage, sprinkle with brown sugar. Over the sausage and sugar, pour in the ginger ale.
2. Cover the cooker and set on low, cook for 4-5 hours, or until heated through.
3. Use a slotted spoon to serve.

Rosemary New Potatoes

Prep Time: 15 minutes, Cook Time: 2-6 hours, Serves: 4 to 6

INGREDIENTS:

- 1½ lbs. (680 g) new red potatoes, unpeeled
- 1 tbsp. olive oil
- 1 tbsp. fresh chopped rosemary, or 1 tsp. dried rosemary
- 1 tsp. garlic and pepper seasoning, or 1 large minced clove garlic, ½ tsp. salt and ¼ tsp. pepper

DIRECTIONS:

1. Cut the potatoes in half or in quarters, if they are larger than golf balls.
2. Toss potatoes with olive oil in a bowl or plastic bag, coating well.
3. Add the garlic and pepper seasoning and rosemary (or the minced garlic, salt, and pepper). Toss again until the potatoes are well coated.
4. In the crock pot, add the potatoes. Cook on High for 2 to 3 hours, or on Low for 5 to 6 hours, or until the potatoes are tender but not mushy or dry.

Nutrition Info per Serving:

Calories: 102, Fat: 2.43 g, Carbohydrates: 18.76 g, Protein: 2.3 g

Crock Pot Honey Buffalo Meatballs

Prep Time: 10 minutes, Cook Time: 2 hours, Serves: 6

INGREDIENTS:

- ¼ cup honey
- ¼ cup Louisiana-style hot sauce
- ¼ cup packed brown sugar
- 2 tbsps. cornstarch
- ¼ cup apricot preserves
- 2 tbsps. reduced-sodium soy sauce
- 1 pkg. (24 oz., 672 g) frozen fully cooked Italian turkey meatballs, thawed
- Additional hot sauce, optional
- Bibb lettuce leaves
- 12 mini buns
- Crumbled blue cheese, optional
- Ranch salad dressing, optional

DIRECTIONS:

1. Add the honey, hot sauce, brown sugar, cornstarch, apricot and soy sauce into a 3- or 4-qt. crock pot, mix them together until smooth. Add the meatballs and stir until coated. Cover and cook on low for 2 to 3 hours, until meatballs are heated through.
2. Stir in additional hot sauce, if desired. Serve meatballs on lettuce-lined buns, top with cheese and dressing if desired.

Nutrition Info per Serving:

Calories: 524, Fat: 21 g, Carbohydrates: 61 g, Protein: 110 mg, Sugar: 29 g, Fiber: 1 g

Honey-Soy Chicken Wings

Prep Time: 5 minutes, Cook Time: 8 hours, Serves: 6

INGREDIENTS:

- 2 pounds (907 g) chicken wings
- ¼ cup (60 ml) honey
- ¼ cup low-sodium soy sauce
- 3 scallions, thinly sliced
- 1 tbsp. grated fresh ginger
- 1 tsp. garlic powder
- Juice of 1 orange
- 1 tsp. sesame seeds

DIRECTIONS:

1. Whisk together the honey, soy sauce, orange juice, ginger, and garlic powder in a small bowl.
2. Put the chicken wings in your crock pot. Pour the sauce over the wings and stir to coat.
3. Cover and cook on low for 8 hours.
4. Serve sprinkled with the sesame seeds and scallions.

Nutrition Info per Serving:

Calories: 344, Total Fat: 12g, Saturated Fat: 3g, Carbohydrates: 14g, Protein: 45g, Fiber: 0g

Pork Carnitas with Avocado

Prep Time: 10 minutes, Cook Time: 8 hours, Serves: 1

INGREDIENTS:

- 1 tsp. extra-virgin olive oil
- 10 ounces (283 g) boneless pork shoulder roast
- 1 cup low-sodium chicken broth or water
- 1 tsp. garlic powder
- 1 tsp. ground cumin
- ½ tsp. ground coriander
- ⅛ tsp. sea salt
- Freshly ground black pepper
- 1 tbsp. lime juice
- 4 corn tortillas
- ½ avocado, thinly sliced, for garnish
- ¼ cup diced red onions, for garnish
- 2 tbsps. crumbled queso fresco, for garnish
- ¼ cup roughly chopped fresh cilantro, for garnish

DIRECTIONS:

1. Use the oil to grease the inside of the crock pot crock.
2. In a small bowl, add the garlic powder, pepper, cumin, coriander and salt. Use this mixture to season the pork and then transfer the meat into the crock pot. Pour the broth around the meat, but not over it or the seasoning will wash off.
3. Cover the cooker and cook on low for 8 hours, until the meat is easily shredded with a fork in the crock pot. After the pork is shredded, add the lime juice and stir well.
4. Divide the meat between the tortillas and garnish each with the avocado, onions, queso fresco, and cilantro, and serve.

Nutrition Info per Serving:

Calories: 581, Saturated Fat: 11 g, Trans Fat: 0 g, Carbohydrates: 32 g, Protein: 33 g, Fiber: 8 g, Sodium: 340 mg

Best Cuban Pulled Pork Tacos

Prep Time: 10 minutes, Cook Time: 8 hours, Serves: 1

INGREDIENTS:

- 1 tsp. extra-virgin olive oil
- 16 ounces (454 g) pork tenderloin
- 2 garlic cloves, minced
- Zest of 1 lime
- Juice of 1 lime
- Zest of 1 orange
- Juice of 1 orange
- 1 tsp. ground cumin
- ⅛ tsp. sea salt
- 1 tsp. ground coriander
- Freshly ground black pepper
- 1 red bell pepper, cored and sliced thin
- 1 green bell pepper, cored and sliced thin
- 1 red onion, halved and sliced thin
- 4 corn tortillas
- ¼ cup fresh cilantro, for garnish

DIRECTIONS:

1. Use olive oil to grease the inside of the crock pot.
2. In the crock pot, add the pork tenderloin.
3. Add the garlic, lime zest, lime juice, orange zest, orange juice, cumin, salt, coriander and a few grinds of the black pepper into a small measuring cup, whisk them together. Pour over the pork with this mixture.
4. In the crock, add the red bell pepper, green bell pepper and onion. Let them around and on top of the pork.
5. Cover the cooker and cook on low for 8 hours.
6. Remove the pork from the crock pot and let the meat rest for 10 minutes, then use a fork to shred it. Place the shredded meat back to the crock pot and toss it with the vegetables and juices.
7. Serve the pork in warm corn tortillas, and garnish with the cilantro.

Nutrition Info per Serving:

Calories: 510, Saturated Fat: 3 g, Trans Fat: 0 g, Carbohydrates: 34 g, Protein: 64 g, Fiber: 7 g, Sodium: 308 mg

Five-Spice Apples

Prep Time: 15 minutes, Cook Time: 8 hours, Serves: 4

INGREDIENTS:

- ¼ cup (60 ml) honey
- Zest and juice of 1 orange
- 1½ tsp. Chinese five-spice powder
- 3 tbsps. chopped pecans
- 4 sweet-tart apples, cored, bottoms intact

DIRECTIONS:

1. Whisk together the honey, five-spice powder and orange zest (reserve the juice) in a small bowl. Add the pecans and stir to coat.
2. Spoon the mixture evenly into the apples.
3. Put the apples in your crock pot.
4. Pour the reserved orange juice over the top of the apples.
5. Cover and cook on low for 8 hours.

Nutrition Info per Serving:

Calories: 232, Total Fat: 8g, Saturated Fat: 1g, Carbohydrates: 44g, Protein: 2g, Fiber: 6g

Mustard Glazed Ham Loaf or Balls

Prep Time: 30 minutes, Cook Time: 4-6 hours, Serves: 8 to 10

INGREDIENTS:

- FOR THE HAM LOAF OR BALLS:
- 2 eggs, slightly beaten
- 1 lb. (454 g) ground ham
- 1 lb. (454 g) ground pork or ground beef 1 cup soft bread crumbs
- 2 tbsps. minced onions
- 1 cup milk
- 1¼ tsp. salt
- ⅛ tsp. pepper
- FOR THE GLAZE:
- ¾ cup brown sugar
- ¼ cup vinegar
- ½ cup water
- 1 tbsp. cornstarch
- 1 tsp. dry mustard

DIRECTIONS:

1. In a large bowl, combine all of the ham loaf or balls ingredients. Shape into loaf or balls and place in the crock pot.
2. In a separate bowl, combine the cornstarch, brown sugar and dry mustard. Mix in the vinegar and water until smooth. Pour into a saucepan. Cook until slightly thickened, then pour over the meat in the crock pot.
3. Cover and cook on High for 4 to 6 hours.

Nutrition Info per Serving:

Calories: 313, Fat: 8.28 g, Carbohydrates: 43.52 g, Protein: 15.97 g

Spicy Peanuts

Prep Time: 10 minutes, Cook Time: 1 hour 15 minutes, Serves: 6

INGREDIENTS:

- 2 tsps. extra virgin olive oil
- 3 cups peanuts
- ½ tsp. powdered garlic
- ½ tsp. smoked paprika
- ½ tsp. cayenne powder
- ½ tsp. ground cumin
- ½ tsp. salt

DIRECTIONS:

1. In a crock pot, add the peanuts and the oil, stir to make a little bit of oil on all the peanuts. It will be enough.
2. Place the spices in the cooker and stir.
3. Set on low and cook for 1 hour.
4. Uncover and then cook for another 15 minutes.

Honey Apple Crumble with Peach

Prep Time: 20 minutes, Cook Time: 4 to 5 hours, Serves: 8

INGREDIENTS:

- 2 tbsps. lemon juice
- 6 large Granny Smith apples, peeled and cut into chunks
- 3 tbsps. honey
- 4 large peaches, peeled and sliced
- 3 cups quick-cooking oatmeal
- 1 cup almond flour
- 1 tsp. ground cinnamon
- ⅓ cup coconut sugar
- ½ cup coconut oil, melted
- ½ cup slivered almonds

DIRECTIONS:

1. Combine apples, peaches, honey, and lemon juice in a 6-quart crock pot.
2. Pour the almond flour, cinnamon, oatmeal, coconut sugar, and almonds into a large bowl until completely combined. Drizzle with melted coconut oil and stir until loose.
3. Drizzle the almond mixture on the mixed fruit.
4. Boil on low heat for 4 to 5 hours, and cover until the fruit is soft and frothy with crumbs on the edges.

Nutrition Info per Serving:

Calories: 547, Fat: 26g, Saturated Fat: 14g, Protein: 10g, Carbohydrates: 75g, Sugar: 42g, Fiber: 11g

Slow Cooked Onion Dip

Prep Time: 10 minutes, Cook Time: 10 hours, Serves: 2 cups

INGREDIENTS:

- 3 onions, thinly sliced
- 3 tbsps. olive oil
- ¾ cup fat-free sour cream
- ¾ cup fat-free cream cheese, softened
- Pinch cayenne pepper
- 1 tsp. dried thyme
- ½ tsp. sea salt
- ⅛ tsp. freshly ground black pepper

DIRECTIONS:

1. Toss the onions with the olive oil, thyme, salt, and pepper in your crock pot.
2. Cover and cook on low for 8 hours.
3. Remove the lid. Turn the crock pot to high. Continue cooking for 1 to 2 hours, stirring occasionally, until the liquid nearly evaporates. Allow the onions to cool for 1 hour.
4. Beat together the sour cream, cream cheese, and cayenne in a small bowl.
5. Stir in the onions and serve.

Nutrition Info per Serving:

Calories: 160, Total Fat: 13g, Saturated Fat: 6g, Carbohydrates: 8g, Protein: 3g, Fiber: 1g

Vegan Crock Pot Chana Masala

Prep Time: 15 minutes, Cook Time: 6 to 8 hours, Serves: 4

INGREDIENTS:

- 4½ cups cooked chickpeas (or 3 cans, drained and rinsed)
- 1 medium yellow onion, finely diced
- 1 (14.5-ounce, 411 g) can diced tomatoes, with juice
- 1 (1-inch) piece fresh ginger, peeled and minced
- 1 serrano or jalapeño chile, seeded and minced
- 1½ tsps. minced garlic (3 cloves)
- 2 tsps. garam masala
- 2 tsps. smoked paprika
- 2 tsps. ground coriander
- 1 tsp. ground cumin
- ¼ tsp. ground turmeric
- ½ tsp. salt
- ½ tsp. freshly ground black pepper
- ¼ cup water
- Handful spinach, chopped (optional)

DIRECTIONS:

1. In the crock pot, add the chickpeas, onion, diced tomatoes, ginger, jalapeño, garlic, garam masala, paprika, coriander, cumin, turmeric, salt, pepper, water, and spinach (if using), combine them together.
2. Cook the mixture on low for 6 to 8 hours.
3. Mash one-third of the chickpeas in the crock pot with a potato masher before serving.

Nutrition Info per Serving:

Calories: 406, Total fat: 7 g, Protein: 21 g, Sodium: 331 mg, Fiber: 20 g

Savory Root Vegetables

Prep Time: 20 minutes, Cook Time: 6 to 8 hours, Serves: 8

INGREDIENTS:

- 3 tbsps. olive oil
- 6 carrots, cut into 1-inch chunks
- 6 Yukon Gold potatoes, cut into chunks
- 4 parsnips, peeled and cut into chunks
- 2 sweet potatoes, peeled and cut into chunks
- 2 yellow onions, each cut into 8 wedges
- 8 whole garlic cloves, peeled
- 1 tsp. dried thyme leaves
- ½ tsp. salt
- ⅛ tsp. freshly ground black pepper

DIRECTIONS:

1. Put all the ingredients together in a 6-quart crock pot and close the lid. Turn on a low heat and cook for 6 to 8 hours, until the vegetables are tender. Serve immediately.
2. If you can't finish it, you can put it in the refrigerator and keep it for up to a week.

Nutrition Info per Serving:

Calories: 214, Fat: 5g, Saturated Fat: 1g, Protein: 4g, Carbohydrates: 40g, Sugar: 7g, Fiber: 6g

Asian Turkey Meatballs

Prep Time: 15 minutes, Cook Time: 8 hours, Serves: 6

INGREDIENTS:

- 1 pound (454 g) ground turkey
- ½ tsp. sesame-chili oil
- 1 tbsp. grated fresh ginger
- ¼ cup chopped fresh cilantro
- 6 garlic cloves, minced
- 6 scallions, minced
- 1 egg, beaten
- 2 tbsps. low-sodium soy sauce
- ¼ cup (60 ml) poultry broth

DIRECTIONS:

1. Combine the ground turkey, scallions, ginger, garlic, cilantro, egg, soy sauce, and sesame-chili oil in a medium bowl until well mixed.
2. Form the mixture into balls with a small scoop. Put the meatballs in the crock pot. Add the broth.
3. Cover and cook on low for 8 hours.

Nutrition Info per Serving:

Calories: 176, Total Fat: 10g, Saturated Fat: 2g, Carbohydrates: 3g, Protein: 23g, Fiber: 1g

Black Bean Chicken Nachos

Prep Time: 15 minutes, Cook Time: 8 hours (low), 4 hours (high), Serves: 8

INGREDIENTS:

- 2 large tomatoes, diced
- 2 pounds (907 g) boneless, skinless chicken breast
- 3 medium jalapeños, seeded and chopped
- 8 ounces (227 g) grated Colby or Cheddar cheese
- 8 ounces (227 g) grated pepper Jack cheese
- 1 medium onion, chopped
- 1 cup cooked black beans, drained and rinsed
- ½ cup chicken stock
- ½ tsp. garlic powder
- ½ tsp. freshly ground black pepper
- 1 tbsp. chili power
- ½ tsp. sea salt
- 1 tbsp. packed brown sugar
- Tortilla chips
- Sliced jalapeños, olives, and other favorite nacho toppings

DIRECTIONS:

1. Add the tomatoes, chicken, jalapeños and onion to the crock pot, combine them together. Spoon over the vegetables and chicken with the black beans.
2. Add the garlic powder, black pepper, chili powder, salt, brown sugar and chicken sugar into a medium bowl, mix them together. Pour over the chicken, vegetables, and beans with the mixture.
3. Sprinkle over the top with the cheeses.
4. Cover the cooker and cook on low for 8 hours or on high for 4 hours.
5. Remove the lid and shred the chicken, then return it in with the other ingredients. Serve hot with tortilla chips and your choice toppings.

Hot Chicken Wings with Blue Cheese

Prep Time: 10 minutes, Cook Time: 8 hours, Serves: 6

INGREDIENTS:

- 1 cup (240 ml) Louisiana hot sauce
- 2 tbsps. olive oil
- ½ tsp. cayenne pepper
- 1 tbsp. Dijon mustard
- 1 tsp. low-sodium Worcestershire sauce
- 3 celery stalks, cut into sticks
- 2 pounds (907 g) chicken wings
- ¼ cup fat-free sour cream
- ¼ cup fat-free mayonnaise
- ¼ cup blue cheese crumbles

DIRECTIONS:

1. Whisk together the hot sauce, olive oil, and cayenne in a small bowl. Pour the mixture into the crock pot.
2. Add the chicken wings and toss to coat.
3. Cover and cook on low for 8 hours.
4. Whisk together the sour cream, mayonnaise, blue cheese crumbles, Dijon mustard, and Worcestershire sauce in a small bowl.
5. Serve the wings and celery sticks with the blue cheese mixture on the side for dipping.

Nutrition Info per Serving:

Calories: 401, Total Fat: 21g, Saturated Fat: 5g, Carbohydrates: 6g, Protein: 45g, Fiber: 0g

Honey Cranberry Stuffed Acorn Squash

Prep Time: 10 minutes, Cook Time: 5-6 hours, Serves: 4 as a side dish

INGREDIENTS:

- 1 acorn squash
- 1 tbsp. olive oil (not extra-virgin)
- 1 tbsp. honey
- ¼ cup chopped pecan or walnuts
- ¼ cup chopped dried cranberries

DIRECTIONS:

1. Halve the squash. Remove the seeds and pulp from the middle. Cut the halves in half again so you have quarters.
2. In the crock pot, add the squash quarters, cut-side up.
3. In a small bowl, combine the olive oil, honey, pecans, and cranberries.
4. Spoon the pecan mixture into the center of each squash quarter. Season with salt. Cover and cook on low for 5 to 6 hours, or until the squash is tender. Serve hot.

Walnut and Apple Herb Stuffing

Prep Time: 20 minutes, Cook Time: 4-5 hours, Serves: 4 to 5

INGREDIENTS:

- 14-oz. (397 g) pkg. dry herb-seasoned stuffing mix 1½ cups applesauce
- 2 onions, chopped
- 1 stick (½ cup) butter, divided
- 1 cup chopped walnuts
- water

DIRECTIONS:

1. Melt 2 tbsps. of butter in a nonstick skillet. Add walnuts, sauté over medium heat for about 5 minutes, stir frequently. Then remove from skillet and set aside.
2. Melt the remaining butter, add onions and cook until almost tender. Set aside.
3. Place dry stuffing mix in crock pot sprayed with nonstick cooking spray.
4. Add onion-butter mixture and applesauce. Stir.
5. Cover. Heat on Low 4-5 hours. If it's sticking to the cooker, drying out, or becoming too brown on the edges, add ½-1 cup water. Stir and continue cooking.
6. Top with walnuts before serving.

Nutrition Info per Serving:

Calories: 318, Protein: 3.25 g, Fat: 28.29 g, Carbohydrates: 15.26 g

Spiced Pecans

Prep Time: 5 minutes, Cook Time: 4 hours, Serves: 6

INGREDIENTS:

- 1 tbsp. olive oil
- 1 cup unsalted raw pecans (or other raw nuts of your choice)
- 2 tbsps. honey
- 1 tsp. ground cinnamon
- ½ tsp. ground ginger
- ¼ tsp. ground nutmeg
- Nonstick cooking spray
- ½ tsp. sea salt
- ⅛ tsp. cayenne pepper
- Zest of 1 orange

DIRECTIONS:

1. Spray the jar of your crock pot with nonstick cooking spray.
2. Whisk together the honey, olive oil, cinnamon, orange zest, ginger, nutmeg, sea salt, and cayenne in a small bowl.
3. Add the nuts to the crock pot. Pour the spice mixture over the top.
4. Cover and cook on low for 4 hours.
5. Turn off the crock pot. Uncover and cool down the nuts for 2 hours, stirring occasionally to keep the nuts coated.

Nutrition Info per Serving:

Calories: 125, Total Fat: 11g, Saturated Fat: 1g, Carbohydrates: 8g, Protein: 1g, Fiber: 2g

Mustard Spiced Hot Dogs

Prep Time: 5 minutes, Cook Time: 2 hours, Serves: 3 to 4

INGREDIENTS:

- 1 lb. (454 g) hot dogs, cut in pieces
- ½ cup chopped onions
- 3 tbsps. vinegar
- 2 tbsps. brown sugar
- ½ cup ketchup
- ½ cup water
- 2 tsps. prepared mustard

DIRECTIONS:

1. In the crock pot, add the hot dogs.
2. In a saucepan, add the onions, vinegar, brown sugar, ketchup, water and mustard, stir well. Simmer. Pour over the hot dogs.
3. Cover the cooker and cook on Low for 2 hours.

Nutrition Info per Serving:

Calories: 101, Fat: 0.35 g, Carbohydrates: 24.35 g, Protein: 2.83 g

Salty Tomato Juice

Prep Time: 20 minutes, Cook Time: 4-6 hours, Serves: 4 cups

INGREDIENTS:

- 10-12 large ripe tomatoes
- 1 tbsp. sugar
- 1 tsp. seasoned salt
- 1 tsp. salt
- ¼ tsp. pepper

DIRECTIONS:

1. Wash tomatoes and cut away the core and blossom ends.
2. Add tomatoes into the crock pot.
3. Heat on Low for 4-6 hours, until tomatoes are very soft.
4. Press them through a food mill.
5. Add sugar, salt and pepper. Chill.

Nutrition Info per Serving:

Calories: 91, Protein: 4.06 g, Fat: 0.92 g, Carbohydrates: 19.96 g

Mustard and Orange Glazed Ham

Prep Time: 7 minutes, Cook Time: 6-8 hours, Serves: 12

INGREDIENTS:

- 5 lbs. (2.3 kg) cooked ham
- 3 tbsps. orange juice
- 1 tbsp. Dijon mustard

DIRECTIONS:

1. Rinse meat and add in a cooking bag.
2. Combine the mustard and orange juice in a bowl. Spread over the ham.
3. Use a twist tie to seal the bag. Poke 4 holes in the top of the bag. Place in the crock pot.
4. Cover the cooker and cook on Low for 6 to 8 hours.
5. After cooking, remove the ham from the bag, reserving juices. Slice ham, spoon over juices to serve.

Nutrition Info per Serving:

Calories: 782, Fat: 25.9 g, Carbohydrates: 9.43 g, Protein: 128.06 g

Baked Oatmeal with Pumpkin

Prep Time: 15 minutes, Cook Time: 6 to 8 hours, Serves: 10

INGREDIENTS:

- 1 (16-ounce, 454g) can solid pack pumpkin
- 3 cups steel-cut oats
- 2 cups canned coconut milk
- 4 cups water
- 1 tsp. ground cinnamon
- 2 tsps. vanilla extract
- 1 cup granola
- ¼ tsp. salt
- ¼ cup honey
- ½ tsp. ground ginger

DIRECTIONS:

1. Dip a brush with ordinary vegetable oil and spread it evenly on the inside of the 6-quart crock pot. Add oats.
2. Use a wire whisk to mix canned pumpkin and coconut milk in a medium bowl. Pour in water, honey, vanilla, salt, cinnamon and ginger and mix thoroughly. Pour into the crock pot, mix with the oats and stir. Finally put in the granola and close the lid.
3. Cook on low heat for 6 to 8 hours, until the oatmeal is soft and the edges begin to turn yellow. Serve immediately!

Nutrition Info per Serving:

Calories: 278, Fat: 5g, Saturated Fat: 2g, Protein: 7g, Carbohydrates: 51g, Sugar: 13g, Fiber: 7g

Slow-Cooked Italian Sausages

Prep Time: 5 minutes, Cook Time: 6-8 hours, Serves: 6 to 8

INGREDIENTS:

- 2 lbs. (907 g) sweet Italian sausage, cut into 5-inch lengths
- 6-oz. (170 g) can tomato paste
- 48-oz. (1.4 kg) jar spaghetti sauce
- 1 large onion, thinly sliced
- 1 large green pepper, thinly sliced
- 1 tsp. dried parsley, or 1 tbsp. chopped fresh parsley
- 1 tbsp. grated Parmesan cheese
- 1 cup water

DIRECTIONS:

1. In a skillet, add the sausage. Fill in the water to cover and simmer for 10 minutes. Drain well.
2. In the crock pot, add the tomato paste, spaghetti sauce, onion, green pepper, parsley, cheese and water, mix well. Stir in the cooked sausage.
3. Cover the cooker and cook on Low for 6 hours.
4. After cooking, serve in buns, or cut sausage into bite-sized pieces and serve over cooked spaghetti. Sprinkle with more Parmesan cheese, if desired.

Nutrition Info per Serving:

Calories: 282, Fat: 12.37 g, Carbohydrates: 21.59 g, Protein: 22.11 g

CHAPTER 13

DESSERT

Missouri Haystack Cookies

Prep Time: 15 minutes, Cook Time: 1 ½ hours on high, Serves: 24 small cookies

INGREDIENTS:

- ½ cup coconut oil
- 1 overripe banana, mashed well
- 3 cups rolled oats
- ½ cup unsweetened almond milk
- ½ cup almond butter
- ¼ cup cacao powder
- ½ cup coconut sugar
- 1 tsp. vanilla extract
- ¼ tsp. sea salt

DIRECTIONS:

1. Add the coconut oil, banana, almond milk, cacao powder, coconut sugar, vanilla and salt into a medium bowl, stir them together. Pour the mixture into the crock pot.
2. Over the mixture, cover with the oats without stirring.
3. Then place the almond butter on top of the oats without stirring.
4. Cover the cooker and cook on high for 1½ hours.
5. Stir well of the mixture. While it cools, scoop tablespoon-size balls out and press onto a baking sheet to continue to cool. Serve when hardened.
6. Place leftovers in an airtight container, and store in the refrigerator for up to 1 week.

Nutrition Info per Serving:

Calories: 140, Total Fat: 9g, Saturated Fat: 1g, Protein: 2g, Total Carbs: 14g, Fiber: 2g, Sugars: 5g

Bourbon- Maple Peaches

Prep Time: 10 minutes, Cook Time: 8 hours, Serves: 6

INGREDIENTS:

- 6 peaches, peeled, pitted, and cut into quarters
- ¼ cup chopped walnuts
- ¼ cup (60 ml) bourbon
- ¼ cup (60 ml) pure maple syrup
- ½ tsp. ground cinnamon

DIRECTIONS:

1. Combine all the ingredients in your crock pot.
2. Cover and cook on low for 8 hours.

Nutrition Info per Serving:

Calories: 127, Total Fat: 3g, Saturated Fat: 0g, Carbohydrates: 19g, Protein: 2g, Fiber: 2g

Apple Cider Bacon Jam

Prep Time: 10 minutes, Cook Time: 3 to 4 hours on low, Serves: 3

INGREDIENTS:

- 3 tbsps. bacon fat, melted and divided
- 1 pound (454 g) cooked bacon, chopped into ½-inch pieces
- 1 sweet onion, diced
- 1 cup brewed decaffeinated coffee
- ½ cup apple cider vinegar
- ¼ cup granulated erythritol
- 1 tbsp. minced garlic

DIRECTIONS:

1. Use 1 tablespoon of the bacon fat to grease the insert of the crock pot lightly.
2. In the insert of the crock pot, add the remaining 2 tablespoons of the bacon fat, onion, bacon, erythritol, apple cider vinegar, garlic, and coffee. Stir to combine.
3. Uncovered and cook on high until the liquid has thickened and reduced, about 3 to 4 hours.
4. After cooking, allow to cool completely.
5. Place the bacon jam in a sealed container, and store in the refrigerator for up to 3 weeks.

Nutrition Info per Serving:

Calories: 52, Total Fat: 5 g, Total Carbs: 1 g, Net Carbs: 1 g, Protein: 1 g, Fiber: 0 g

Spiced Apples

Prep Time: 5 minutes, Cook Time: 4-5 hours, Serves: 10 to 12

INGREDIENTS:

- 16 cups sliced apples, peeled or unpeeled, divided
- ½ cup brown sugar, divided
- 3 tbsps. minute tapioca, divided
- 1 tsp. ground cinnamon, divided

DIRECTIONS:

1. In a crock pot, combine half of the sliced apples, sugar, tapioca, and cinnamon.
2. Add the remaining ingredients to the cooker.
3. Cover and cook on High for 4 hours.
4. Stir and serve warm.

Nutrition Info per Serving:

Calories: 130, Protein: 0 g, Fat: 0 g, Carbohydrates: 24 g, Fiber: 3 g, Sodium: 33 mg

Coconut Milk Vanilla Yogurt

Prep Time: 15 minutes, Cook Time: 1 to 2 hours on high, plus overnight to ferment, Serves: 3½ cups

INGREDIENTS:

- 1 tsp. raw honey
- 3 (13.5-ounce) cans full-fat coconut milk
- ½ tsp. vanilla extract
- 5 probiotic capsules (not pills)

DIRECTIONS:

1. In the crock pot, add the coconut milk.
2. Cover the cooker and cook on high for 1 to 2 hours, until the temperature of the milk reaches 180ºF(82ºC) when use a candy thermometer to measure.
3. Turn off the crock pot and let the temperature of the milk come down close to 100ºF(38ºC).
4. Open the probiotic capsules and add the contents, then stir in the vanilla and honey. Stir to well combined.
5. Re-cover the crock pot, turn it off and unplug it, and use an insulating towel to wrap it to keep warm overnight as it ferments.
6. Transfer the yogurt into sterilized jars and refrigerate. The yogurt should thicken slightly in the refrigerator, and it will keep for up to 1 week.

Nutrition Info per Serving:

Calories: 305, Total Fat: 30g, Saturated Fat: 3g, Protein: 2g, Total Carbs: 7g, Fiber: 0g, Sugars: 3g

Classic Maple-Banana Sundae

Prep Time: 10 minutes, Cook Time: 2 hours, Serves: 6

INGREDIENTS:

- Nonstick cooking spray
- 4 bananas, peeled, halved crosswise, and then halved lengthwise
- ½ cup (120 ml) pure maple syrup
- 6 scoops low-fat vanilla ice cream or frozen yogurt
- 2 tbsps. chopped unsalted pecans
- Zest and juice of 1 orange
- 1 tbsp. unsalted butter, melted
- 1 tsp. rum extract
- Pinch sea salt

DIRECTIONS:

1. Spray the jar of your crock pot with nonstick cooking spray.
2. Put the bananas and unsalted pecans in the bottom of the jar.
3. Whisk together the maple syrup, butter, orange zest and juice, rum extract and salt in a small bowl. Pour the syrup mixture over the pecans and bananas.
4. Cover and cook on low for 2 hours.
5. Spoon the bananas, pecans, and syrup over the ice cream. Serve.

Nutrition Info per Serving:

Calories: 368, Total Fat: 15g, Saturated Fat: 8g, Carbohydrates: 59g, Protein: 5g, Fiber: 3g

Vanilla Chocolate Brownies

Prep Time: 15 minutes, Cook Time: 2½ to 3 hours on low, Serves: 4 to 6

INGREDIENTS:

- 3 tbsps. coconut oil, divided
- 2 ripe bananas
- 2 large eggs
- 1 cup almond butter
- 1 cup unsweetened cacao powder
- ½ cup coconut sugar
- 2 tsps. vanilla extract
- 1 tsp. baking soda
- ½ tsp. sea salt

DIRECTIONS:

1. Use 1 tablespoon of coconut oil to coat the bottom of the crock pot.
2. Add the eggs, bananas, almond butter, coconut sugar, cacao powder, baking soda, vanilla and salt into a medium bowl, mash the bananas and stir well until a batter forms. Transfer the batter into the crock pot.
3. Cover the cooker and cook on low for 2½ to 3 hours, until firm to a light touch but still gooey in the middle, and serve.

Nutrition Info per Serving:

Calories: 779, Total Fat: 51 g, Total Carbs: 68 g, Sugar: 35 g, Fiber: 15 g, Protein: 18 g, Sodium: 665 mg

Coconut and Pumpkin Pudding

Prep Time: 5 minutes, Cook Time: 3 to 4 hours on low, Serves: 8

INGREDIENTS:

- 1 tbsp. coconut oil
- 2 eggs
- 2 cups pumpkin purée
- 1½ cups coconut milk
- 1 cup whipped coconut cream
- ½ cup almond flour
- 1 ounce (28 g) protein powder
- 1 tbsp. grated fresh ginger
- ¾ tsp. liquid stevia
- Pinch ground cloves

DIRECTIONS:

1. Use the coconut oil to grease the insert of the crock pot lightly.
2. Add all of the ingredients except the coconut cream to a large bowl, stir them together.
3. Place the mixture into the insert of the crock pot.
4. Cover the cooker and cook on low 3 to 4 hours
5. Top with whipped coconut cream and serve warm.

Nutrition Info per Serving:

Per Serving: Calories: 217, Total Fat: 19 g, Total Carbs: 7 g, Net Carbs: 3 g, Protein: 8 g, Fiber: 4 g

Blueberry Peach Cobbler

INGREDIENTS:

- 5 tbsps. coconut oil, divided
- 3 large peaches, peeled and sliced
- 2 cups frozen blueberries
- 1 cup rolled oats
- 1 cup almond flour
- 1 tbsp. maple syrup
- 1 tbsp. coconut sugar
- 1 tsp. ground cinnamon
- ½ tsp. vanilla extract
- Pinch ground nutmeg

DIRECTIONS:

1. Use 1 tablespoon of coconut oil to coat the bottom of the crock pot.
2. In the bottom of the crock pot, arrange with the blueberries and peaches.
3. Add the remaining 4 tablespoons of coconut oil, oats, almond flour, coconut sugar, maple syrup, vanilla, cinnamon and nutmeg into a small bowl, stir them together until a coarse mixture forms. Gently crumble the topping over the fruit in the crock pot.
4. Cover the cooker and cook on high for 2 hours and serve.

Nutrition Info per Serving:

Calories: 516, Total Fat: 34g, Saturated Fat: 4g, Protein: 10g, Total Carbs: 66g, Fiber: 10g, Sugars: 17g

Sweet Banana Oatmeal

INGREDIENTS:

- 4 cups coconut milk
- 4 cups water
- 3 ripe bananas, peeled and mashed
- 2 cups steel cut oats
- 2 tsps. ground cinnamon
- ⅓ cup coconut sugar
- 2 tsps. vanilla extract
- 1 cup chopped pecans
- ½ tsp. ground nutmeg

DIRECTIONS:

1. Pour coconut milk and water into a 6-quart crock pot. Then put steel-cut oats, bananas, coconut sugar, cinnamon, nutmeg, vanilla and pecans in the pot, mix and cover.
2. Turn on a low heat and cook for 7 to 8 hours until the oats are soft. Enjoy!

Nutrition Info per Serving:

Calories: 545, Fat: 35g, Saturated Fat: 24g, Protein: 9g, Carbohydrates: 50g, Sugar: 17g, Fiber: 7g, Sodium: 21mg

Chunky Applesauce with Cranberry

INGREDIENTS:

- 6 Winesap apples, peeled, cut into 1-inch cubes
- ½ cup apple juice
- ½ cup fresh or frozen cranberries
- ¼ cup sugar
- ¼ tsp. ground cinnamon

DIRECTIONS:

1. Put all ingredients in a crock pot. Mix well.
2. Cover. Heat on Low until apples are as soft as you like them.
3. Serve warm from the cooker.

Nutrition Info per Serving:

Calories: 169, Protein: 0.51 g, Fat: 0.34 g, Carbohydrates: 44.14 g

Roasted Apples with Walnuts

INGREDIENTS:

- 2 tbsps. freshly squeezed lemon juice
- 8 large apples
- 1½ cups buckwheat flakes
- 1 cup chopped walnuts
- ⅓ cup coconut sugar
- ½ cup apple juice
- 1 tsp. ground cinnamon
- 6 tbsps unsalted butter, cut into pieces

¼ tsp. salt

DIRECTIONS:

1. Deal with apples. Peel a bark on top of each apple to prevent cracking. Carefully remove the apple core, making sure not to cut all the way to the bottom. Dip a brush with lemon juice and apply it evenly on the surface of the apple and set it aside.
2. Combine buckwheat flakes, walnuts, coconut sugar, cinnamon and salt in a medium bowl.
3. Drizzle the melted butter on the buckwheat mixture, stirring constantly. Fill the apples with the butter mixture and round the filling on the top of each apple.
4. Place the stuffed apples in a 6-quart crock pot and pour the apple juice around the apples.
5. Simmer on low heat for 4 to 6 hours, close the lid until the apples are soft. Serve immediately!

Nutrition Info per Serving:

Calories: 369, Fat: 17g, Saturated Fat: 6g, Protein: 4g, Carbohydrates: 53g, Sugar: 36g, Fiber: 6g

Cheesy Pumpkin and Carrot Pudding

Prep Time: 15 minutes, Cook Time: 6 hours on low, Serves: 6

INGREDIENTS:

*   1 tbsp. extra-virgin olive oil or ghee
*   2 cups puréed pumpkin
*   2 cups finely shredded carrots
*   2 eggs
*   1 cup heavy (whipping) cream
*   ½ cup cream cheese, softened
*   ½ sweet onion, finely chopped
*   1 tbsp. granulated erythritol
*   1 tsp. ground nutmeg
*   ½ tsp. salt
*   ¼ cup pumpkin seeds, for garnish

DIRECTIONS:

1. Use the olive oil or ghee to lightly grease the insert of the crock pot.
2. Add all of the remaining ingredients except for the pumpkin seeds to a large bowl, whisk them together.
3. Cover the cooker and cook on low for 6 hours.
4. Garnish with the pumpkin seeds and serve warm.

Nutrition Info per Serving:

Calories: 239, Total Fat: 19 g, Total Carbs: 11 g, Net Carbs: 7 g, Protein: 6 g, Fiber: 4 g

Homemade Caramel Apples

Prep Time: 10 minutes, Cook Time: 1-1½ hours, Serves: 8 to 10

INGREDIENTS:

*   2 (14-oz. 397 g) bags of caramels
*   8-10 medium apples
*   granulated sugar
*   ¼ cup water
*   waxed paper
*   sticks

DIRECTIONS:

1. Put caramels and water into a crock pot, mix well.
2. Cover the crock pot and heat on High for 1-1½ hours, stirring every 5 minutes.
3. Wash the apples and insert a stick into the stem end of each apple. Turn cooker to Low. Dip the apple in the hot caramel and coat the entire surface.
4. Scrape off the excess caramel at the bottom of the apple.
5. Dip the bottom of the caramel-coated apple in granulated sugar to prevent it from sticking. Place apple on greased waxed paper to cool.

Nutrition Info per Serving:

Calories: 481, Protein: 6.28 g, Fat: 20.69 g, Carbohydrates: 71.05 g

Cinnamon Sugar Pecans

Prep Time: 15 minutes, Cook Time: 3 to 4 hours on low, Serves: 3½ cups

INGREDIENTS:

*   1 tbsp. coconut oil
*   3 cups pecan halves
*   1 large egg white
*   2 tsps. vanilla extract
*   2 tbsps. ground cinnamon
*   2 tbsps. coconut sugar
*   ¼ cup maple syrup
*   ¼ tsp. sea salt

DIRECTIONS:

1. Use coconut oil to coat the crock pot.
2. Add the egg white into a medium bowl, whisk well.
3. Then whisk in the vanilla, cinnamon, coconut sugar, maple syrup, and salt. Combine well.
4. Mix in the pecans and stir to coat. Pour the pecans into the crock pot.
5. Cover the cooker and cook on low for 3 to 4 hours.
6. Take the pecans out from the crock pot and spread them on a baking sheet or other cooling surface. Allow to cool for 5 to 10 minutes before serving.
7. Place in an airtight container and store at room temperature for up to 2 weeks.

Nutrition Info per Serving:

Calories: 195, Total Fat: 18 g, Total Carbs: 9 g, Sugar: 6 g, Fiber: 3 g, Protein: 2 g, Sodium: 46 mg

Cinnamon Apple Oatmeal

Prep Time: 15 to 20 minutes, Cook Time: 2-2½ hours, Serves: about 7 cups

INGREDIENTS:

*   3 tbsps. flour
*   5 large baking apples, pared, cored, and diced into ¾-inch pieces
*   ¾ cup sugar
*   half a stick (¼ cup) butter, melted
*   ½ cup rolled oats
*   1½ tsp. cinnamon
*   3 tbsps. water

DIRECTIONS:

1. Spray the inside of the crock pot with nonstick spray.
2. Combine sugar, flour, cinnamon and rolled oats in a large bowl. Set aside.
3. Add apples, butter and water into a crock pot. Stir the flour mixture gently until the apples are coated.
4. Heat on High for 1½ hours, and then on Low for 30-60 minutes,
5. Pour milk over top. Serve hot.

Nutrition Info per Serving:

Calories: 229, Protein: 0.74 g, Fat: 6.78 g, Carbohydrates: 43.97 g

Baked Apples with Walnuts

Prep Time: 15 to 30 minutes, Cook Time: 2½-5 hours, Serves: 6 to 8

INGREDIENTS:

- 6-8 medium baking apples, cored but left whole and unpeeled
- ¼ cup brown sugar
- 2 tbsps. chopped walnuts
- ½ cup water
- 1 tsp. ground cinnamon
- frozen yogurt

DIRECTIONS:

1. Take a small bowl, add chopped walnuts and sugar into it. Mix well.
2. Place the apples on the bottom of the crock pot. Use a spoon to pour the mixture into the center of the apple and divide it evenly among apples.
3. Sprinkle cinnamon on the apple filling.
4. Add ½ cup of water along the edge of the cookware.
5. Cover lid and heat on Low for 3-5 hours.
6. Serve with frozen yogurt.

Nutrition Info per Serving:

Calories: 214, Protein: 0.49 g, Fat: 4.21 g, Carbohydrates: 47.03 g

Spiced Carmeled Pears with Wine

Prep Time: 10 minutes, Cook Time: 4-6 hours, Serves: 6

INGREDIENTS:

- 6 medium fresh pears with stems
- 2 apple cinnamon sticks, each about 2½-3-inch long
- 1 cup white wine
- 3 tbsps. lemon juice
- 3 whole dried cloves
- ¼ tsp. ground nutmeg
- ½ cup sugar
- ½ cup water
- 6 tbsps. fat-free caramel apple dip

DIRECTIONS:

1. Peel the pears and leave the stems intact.
2. Put it upright in the crock pot.
3. Take a big bowl, add wine, sugar, water, lemon juice, cinnamon, cloves, and nutmeg into it and mix well. Pour over pears.
4. Cover lid and cook on low for 4-6 hours.
5. Cool pears and transfer to individual serving dishes.
7. Heat caramel soak in the microwave for 20 seconds. Stir.
8. Drizzle caramel over pears. Serve.

Nutrition Info per Serving:

Calories: 290, Protein: 2 g, Fat: 2.5 g, Carbohydrates: 62 g, Fiber: 4 g, Sodium: 140 mg

Turmeric Ginger Golden Milk

Prep Time: 15 minutes, Cook Time: 3 to 4 hours on low, Serves: 4 to 6

INGREDIENTS:

- 2 tbsps. coconut oil
- 4 cups unsweetened almond milk
- 1 (2-inch) piece fresh ginger, roughly chopped
- 1 (4-inch) piece turmeric root, roughly chopped
- 4 cinnamon sticks
- 1 tsp. raw honey, plus more to taste

DIRECTIONS:

1. Add the coconut oil, ginger, almond milk, cinnamon sticks and turmeric into the crock pot, combine them together.
2. Cover the cooker and cook on low for 3 to 4 hours.
3. Set a fine-mesh sieve over a clean container, pour in the contents of the cooker, discard the solids.
4. Add raw honey to taste, start with 1 teaspoon.

Nutrition Info per Serving:

Calories: 133, Total Fat: 11g, Saturated Fat: 2g, Protein: 1g, Total Carbs: 10g, Fiber: 1g, Sugars: 7g

Creamy Berry and Pumpkin Compote

Prep Time: 10 minutes, Cook Time: 3 to 4 hours on low, Serves: 10

INGREDIENTS:

- 1 tbsp. coconut oil
- 2 cups diced pumpkin
- 1 cup cranberries
- 1 cup blueberries
- 1 cup whipped cream
- ½ cup coconut milk
- ½ cup granulated erythritol
- Juice and zest of 1 orange
- ½ tsp. ground allspice
- ¼ tsp. ground nutmeg
- 1 tsp. ground cinnamon

DIRECTIONS:

1. Use the coconut oil to grease the insert of the crock pot lightly.
2. In the insert of the crock pot, add all of the ingredients except the whipped cream.
3. Cover the cooker and set on low, cook for 3 to 4 hours.
4. After cooking, allow the compote to cool for 1 hour and top with a generous scoop of whipped cream, serve warm.

Nutrition Info per Serving:

Calories: 113, Total Fat: 9 g, Total Carbs: 7 g, Net Carbs: 4 g, Protein: 4 g, Fiber: 3 g

Homemade Apple Schnitz Pie

Prep Time: 5 minutes, Cook Time: 2½ hours, Serves: 8

INGREDIENTS:

- 1 quart dried apples
- 1 cup sugar
- 3 cups water
- 1 tsp. ground cinnamon
- 1 tsp. salt

DIRECTIONS:

1. Place apples, sugar, cinnamon, water, and salt in a crock pot.
2. Cover lid and heat on High for 2½ hours.
3. For the pie filling, remove apples from the crock pot. Use the potato masher to mash apples until smooth. Cool.

Nutrition Info per Serving:

Calories: 61, Protein: 0.07 g, Fat: 0.04 g, Carbohydrates: 15.87 g

Mixed Honey Granola with Berry

Prep Time: 15 minutes, Cook Time: 3½ to 5 hours, Serves: 20

INGREDIENTS:

- 10 cups rolled oats
- 2 cups macadamia nuts
- 2 cups whole almonds
- 2 cups whole walnuts
- 2 cups dried blueberries
- 2 cups dried cherries
- ½ cup honey
- ¼ tsp. ground cardamom
- 1 tbsp. vanilla extract
- 2 tsps. ground cinnamon

DIRECTIONS:

1. Put the oatmeal, almonds, walnuts, and macadamia nuts in a 6-quart crock pot and stir to combine.
2. Mix honey, cinnamon, cardamom and vanilla in a small bowl. Drizzle it evenly over the oatmeal mixture in the crock pot.
3. Partially cover the crock pot with a lid. Cook on low heat for 3.5 to 5 hours, stirring twice in the process, until the oatmeal and nuts are cooked.
4. Remove the mixture from the crock pot and spread on two large baking sheets. Sprinkle with dried blueberries and cherries and stir gently.
5. Store granola in an airtight container for up to a week at room temperature.

Nutrition Info per Serving:

Calories: 255, Fat: 12g, Saturated Fat: 2g, Protein: 6g, Carbohydrates: 33g, Sugar: 16g, Fiber: 4g

Savory Berries Crisp

Prep Time: 20 minutes, Cook Time: 5-6 hours, Serves: 12

INGREDIENTS:

- ⅓ cup coconut oil, melted
- 3 cups frozen organic strawberries
- 3 cups frozen organic blueberries
- 3 cups frozen organic raspberries
- 1 cup whole-wheat flour
- ⅓ cup maple sugar
- 2½ cups rolled oats
- 2 tbsps. lemon juice
- 1 tsp. ground cinnamon

DIRECTIONS:

1. Place frozen berries directly in a 6-quart crock pot without defrosting berries. Drizzle with lemon juice.
2. Combine the oats, flour, maple syrup and cinnamon in a large bowl. Add melted coconut oil and stir until crumbly.
3. Drizzle the oatmeal mixture on the fruit in the crock pot.
4. Boil on low heat, cover with lid, about 5 to 6 hours, until the fruit is bubbling and the top is browned. Serve immediately!

Nutrition Info per Serving:

Calories: 219, Fat: 8g, Saturated Fat: 5g, Protein: 5g, Carbohydrates: 37g, Sugar: 12g, Fiber: 7g

Delicious Blueberry and Yogurt Parfait

Prep Time: 5 minutes, Cook Time: 10 hours, Serves: 1

INGREDIENTS:

- 4 cups 2% milk
- 2 cups blueberries
- ¼ cup plain yogurt with live cultures
- 1 cup low-fat, low-sugar granola

DIRECTIONS:

1. In the crock pot, add the milk. Cover and set on low, cook for 2 hours.
2. Unplug the crock pot, add the yogurt and stir well. Put the lid on and use a bath towel to wrap the crock pot to help insulate it. Let the yogurt rest for 8 hours or overnight.
3. For a thick yogurt, set a few layers of cheesecloth over a medium bowl, pour in the mixture and strain for 10 to 15 minutes. Discard the whey remaining in the cheesecloth or save it for making smoothies.
4. Layer the berries and the granola over the strained yogurt and serve.

Nutrition Info per Serving:

Calories: 266, Saturated Fat: 4 g, Trans Fat: 0 g, Carbohydrates: 44 g, Protein: 11 g, Fiber: 4 g, Sodium: 183 mg

Simple Stewed Fruit

Prep Time: 15 minutes, Cook Time: 6 to 8 hours, Serves: 12

INGREDIENTS:

- 2 cups prunes
- 2 cups dried unsulfured pears
- 2 cups dried apples
- 2 cups dried apricots
- 1 cup dried cranberries
- 6 cups water
- ¼ cup honey
- 1 tsp. dried basil leaves
- 1 tsp. dried thyme leaves

DIRECTIONS:

1. Combine all ingredients in a 6-quart crock pot and cover. Place the pot on the stove and cook on low heat for 6 to 8 hours until the fruit has absorbed the liquid and becomes soft.
2. If you can't finish it, you can keep it in the refrigerator for up to 1 week. Or you can divide the fruits into small bowls and store them frozen to extend the storage time.

Nutrition Info per Serving:

Calories: 242, Fat: 0g, Saturated Fat: 0g, Protein: 2g, Carbohydrates: 61g, Sugar: 43g, Fiber: 9g, Sodium: 11mg

Vanilla Chocolate Pot De Crème

Prep Time: 10 minutes, Cook Time: 3 hours on low, Serves: 6

INGREDIENTS:

- 2 cups heavy (whipping) cream
- 6 egg yolks
- ⅓ cup cocoa powder
- 1 tbsp. pure vanilla extract
- ½ tsp. liquid stevia
- Whipped coconut cream, for garnish (optional)
- Shaved dark chocolate, for garnish (optional)

DIRECTIONS:

1. Add the heavy cream, cocoa powder, yolks, vanilla and stevia to a medium bowl, whisk them together.
2. In a 1½-quart baking dish, add the mixture and put the dish in the insert of the crock pot.
3. Fill enough water to reach halfway up the sides of the baking dish.
4. Cover the cooker and set on low, cook for 3 hours.
5. Take the baking dish out from the insert, and transfer to a wire rack and allow it to cool to room temperature.
6. Transfer the dessert into the refrigerator and chill before serving, top with the whipped coconut cream and shaved dark chocolate (if desired).

Nutrition Info per Serving:

Calories: 198, Total Fat: 18 g, Total Carbs: 4 g, Net Carbs: 3 g, Protein: 5 g, Fiber: 1 g

Crock Pot Chai Spice Apples

Prep Time: 15 minutes, Cook Time: 2 to 3 hours on high, Serves: 5 apples

INGREDIENTS:

- ¼ cup melted coconut oil
- 5 apples
- ½ cup water
- ½ cup crushed pecans (optional)
- ½ tsp. ground ginger
- 1 tsp. ground cinnamon
- ¼ tsp. ground cardamom
- ¼ tsp. ground cloves

DIRECTIONS:

1. Core each apple, and from the top of each, peel off a thin strip.
2. In the crock pot, fill with the water. Place each apple gently upright along the bottom.
3. Add the coconut oil, ginger, cinnamon, cardamom, cloves and pecans (if using) into a small bowl, stir them together. Drizzle over the tops of the apples with the mixture.
4. Cover the cooker and cook on high for 2 to 3 hours, until the apples soften, and serve.

Nutrition Info per Serving:

Calories: 217, Total Fat: 12g, Saturated Fat: 1g, Protein: 0g, Total Carbs: 30g, Fiber: 6g, Sugars: 22g

Tasty Poblano Corn Pudding

Prep Time: 15 minutes, Cook Time: 3¼ hours (low), Serves: 8

INGREDIENTS:

- Cooking spray
- 2 cups fresh or frozen corn
- 6 poblano chiles, fire-roasted peeled, and seeded
- 1 (8.25-ounce, 234 g) can cream-style corn
- 2 eggs, lightly beaten
- ½ cup whole milk
- ¼ cup yellow cornmeal
- 2 tbsps. sugar
- ¼ cup all-purpose flour
- 1 tsp. baking powder
- 3 tbsps. unsalted butter, melted
- ½ cup grated pepper Jack cheese

DIRECTIONS:

1. Use cooking spray to spray the crock pot.
2. Add the cornmeal, milk, sugar, flour, eggs and baking powder into a large bowl, whisk them together until smooth. Then add the butter, poblano chiles, corn, and cheese, stir well. Spoon the batter into the crock pot.
3. Cover the cooker and cook on low for 3 hours, or until the pudding is set. Remove the lid and cook uncovered for another 15 minutes.
4. After cooking, turn off the heat and serve hot.

Apple-Oat Crisp

Prep Time: 10-15 minutes, Cook Time: 5-6 hours, Serves: 6

INGREDIENTS:

- 4 cups cooking apples, peeled and sliced
- 3½-oz. (99 g) cook-n-serve butterscotch pudding mix
- ½ cup quick-cooking oats
- ½ cup flour
- ¼ cup brown sugar
- 1 tsp. ground cinnamon
- ½ cup cold butter

DIRECTIONS:

1. Place apples in a crock pot.
2. Take a bowl, add the remaining ingredients into it, mix well. Add butter until the mixture resembles coarse crumbs. Sprinkle the mixture over apples.
3. Cover lid and heat on Low for 5-6 hours.
4. Serve with ice cream.

Nutrition Info per Serving:

Calories: 358, Protein: 2.39 g, Fat: 16.21 g, Carbohydrates: 53.75 g

Simple Mixed Dried Fruit

Prep Time: 5 minutes, Cook Time: 4-8 hours, Serves: 3 to 4

INGREDIENTS:

- ¼ cup water
- 2 cups mixed dried fruit

DIRECTIONS:

1. Combine dried fruit and water in a crock pot.
2. Cover lid and cook on Low for 4-8 hours.
3. Add a spoonful of sour cream and a dash of ground nutmeg on each individual serving before serving.
4. Serve warm.

Nutrition Info per Serving:

Calories: 91, Protein: 0.48 g, Fat: 0.09 g, Carbohydrates: 23.45 g

Crock Pot Spiced Apple

Prep Time: 10 minutes, Cook Time: 4-5 hours, Serves: 6

INGREDIENTS:

- 6 baking apples, peeled, cored, and quartered
- ¼ cup apple juice
- 2 tbsps. sugar
- ¾ tsp. Asian five-spice powder
- ¼ tsp. nutmeg

DIRECTIONS:

1. Place apples in a crock pot.
2. Combine all remaining ingredients in a small mixing bowl.
3. Pour the mixture into a crock pot, stir gently to coat apples.
4. Cover lid and cook on Low for 4-5 hours.
5. Mash apples and serve warm.

Nutrition Info per Serving:

Calories: 112, Protein: 0.51 g, Fat: 0.37 g, Carbohydrates: 29.39 g

Spiced Carrot and Pecan Pudding

Prep Time: 20 minutes, Cook Time: 5-7 hours, Serves: 12

INGREDIENTS:

- 1 cup almond flour
- 3 cups finely grated carrots
- 2 eggs, beaten
- 2 cups canned coconut milk
- 1½ cups chopped pecans
- 1 cup coconut flour
- 1 cup golden raisins
- ½ cup coconut sugar
- 1 tsp. baking powder
- 1½ tsps ground cinnamon

DIRECTIONS:

1. Combine all ingredients in a 6-quart crock pot. Turn on a low heat, close the lid, and cook for 5 to 7 hours until the pudding is set. Serve immediately!

Nutrition Info per Serving:

Calories: 359, Fat: 24g, Saturated Fat: 10g, Protein: 7g, Carbohydrates: 31g, Sugar: 22g, Fiber: 7g, Sodium: 70mg

Blueberry Pecan Crisp

Prep Time: 10 minutes, Cook Time: 3 to 4 hours on low, Serves: 8

INGREDIENTS:

- 5 tbsps. coconut oil, melted, divided
- ¾ cup plus 2 tbsps. granulated erythritol
- 4 cups blueberries
- 1 cup ground pecans
- 1 egg
- 1 tsp. baking soda
- ½ tsp. ground cinnamon
- 2 tbsps. coconut milk

DIRECTIONS:

1. Use 1 tablespoon of the coconut oil to grease a 4-quart crock pot lightly.
2. In the insert of the crock pot, add 2 tablespoons of erythritol and the blueberries.
3. Add the remaining ¾ cup of the erythritol, baking soda, ground pecans and cinnamon to a large bowl, stir them together until well mixed.
4. Stir in the egg, coconut milk, and remaining coconut oil, and stir until coarse crumbs form.
5. Place the pecan mixture in the insert, and top with the egg mixture.
6. Cover the cooker and cook on low for 3 to 4 hours.
7. After cooking, turn off the heat and serve warm.

Nutrition Info per Serving:

Calories: 222, Total Fat: 19 g, Total Carbs: 9 g, Net Carbs: 5 g, Protein: 9 g, Fiber: 4 g

Cardamom Yogurt with Mangoes

Prep Time: 5 minutes, Cook Time: 10 hours, Serves: 1

INGREDIENTS:

- 1 tbsp. honey
- 4 cups 2% milk
- 2 mangoes, cut into chunks
- ¼ cup plain yogurt with live cultures
- ¼ tsp. ground cardamom

DIRECTIONS:

1. In the crock pot, add the milk. Cover and set on low, cook for 2 hours.
2. Unplug the crock pot and add the yogurt, stir well. Use the lid to cover and with a bath towel to wrap the outside of the crock pot housing to help insulate it. Let it rest for 8 hours or overnight.
3. For a thick yogurt, set a few layers of cheesecloth over a medium bowl, pour in the mixture and strain for 10 to 15 minutes. Discard the whey remaining in the cheesecloth or save it for making smoothies.
4. Add the honey, mango chunks, and cardamom, stir well and serve. Refrigerate leftovers.

Nutrition Info per Serving:

Calories: 206, Saturated Fat: 3 g, Trans Fat: 0 g, Carbohydrates: 31 g, Protein: 9 g, Fiber: 2 g, Sodium: 128 mg

Sweet Peach Brown Betty

Prep Time: 20 minutes, Cook Time: 5-6 hours, Serves: 10

INGREDIENTS:

- 1 cup dried cranberries
- 8 ripe peaches, peeled and cut into chunks
- 3 tbsps. honey
- 2 tbsps. freshly squeezed lemon juice
- 1½ cups whole-wheat bread crumbs
- ¼ tsp. ground cardamom
- ⅓ cup coconut sugar
- 3 cups cubed whole-wheat bread
- ⅓ cup melted coconut oil

DIRECTIONS:

1. Combine the peaches, dried cranberries, lemon juice, and honey in a 6-quart crock pot.
2. Combine the bread cubes, bread crumbs, coconut sugar and cardamom in a large bowl. Sprinkle the melted coconut oil on everything and stir well.
3. Sprinkle the bread mixture on the fruit in the crock pot.
4. Cook on low heat for 5 to 6 hours, close the lid, until the fruit is bubbling and the top is browned. Serve warm!

Nutrition Info per Serving:

Calories: 322, Fat: 9g, Saturated Fat: 7g, Protein: 6g, Carbohydrates: 57g, Sugar: 31g, Fiber: 6g, Sodium: 69mg

Vanilla Lemon Custard

Prep Time: 10 minutes, Cook Time: 3 hours on low, Serves: 4

INGREDIENTS:

- ¼ cup freshly squeezed lemon juice
- 5 egg yolks
- 2 cups heavy (whipping) cream
- 1 cup whipped coconut cream
- 1 tbsp. lemon zest
- ⅓ tsp. liquid stevia
- 1 tsp. pure vanilla extract

DIRECTIONS:

1. Add the lemon juice and zest, yolks, liquid stevia and vanilla to a medium bowl, whisk them together.
2. Add the heavy cream and whisk well, divide the mixture between 4 (4-ounce, 113 g) ramekins.
3. At the bottom of the insert of the crock pot, put a rack, and place the ramekins on it.
4. Pour in enough water to reach halfway up the sides of the ramekins.
5. Cover and cook on low for 3 hours.
6. Remove the ramekins from the insert and cool to room temperature.
7. Chill the ramekins completely in the refrigerator and serve topped with whipped coconut cream.

Nutrition Info per Serving:

Calories: 319, Total Fat: 30 g, Total Carbs: 3 g, Net Carbs: 3 g, Protein: 7 g, Fiber: 0 g

Honey Pears with Hazelnut

Prep Time: 10 minutes, Cook Time: 8 hours, Serves: 6

INGREDIENTS:

- 6 pears, peeled, halved, and cored
- ¼ cup (60 ml) honey
- ¼ cup chopped hazelnuts
- Juice and zest of 1 orange
- 1½ tsp. ground fennel seed
- ½ tsp. ground cinnamon
- Pinch ground nutmeg
- Pinch sea salt

DIRECTIONS:

1. Arrange the pears cut-side up in your crock pot.
2. Whisk together the nutmeg, orange juice and zest, fennel seed, honey, cinnamon, and salt in a small bowl. Pour the mixture evenly over the pears.
3. Cover and cook on low for 8 hours.
4. Cook the hazelnuts on medium-heat in a small sauté pan for 3 to 5 minutes, stirring constantly, until fragrant.
5. Serve with sprinkled hazelnuts over the pears.

Nutrition Info per Serving:

Calories: 186, Total Fat: 2g, Saturated Fat: 0g, Carbohydrates: 44g, Protein: 1g, Fiber: 7g

Vanilla Spiced Pear Butter

Prep Time: 15 minutes, Cook Time: 6 to 8 hours on low, Serves: 3 cups

INGREDIENTS:

- 1 tbsp. freshly squeezed lemon juice
- 3 pounds (1.4 kg) unpeeled pears, cored and cut into chunks
- ½ cup water
- 2 tsps. ground cinnamon
- 1 tsp. vanilla extract
- ½ tsp. ground ginger
- 1½ tsps. coconut sugar (optional)

DIRECTIONS:

1. Add the lemon juice, pears, cinnamon, vanilla, ginger ans water into the crock pot, combine them together.
2. Cover the cooker and cook for 6 to 8 hours on low. After cooking, transfer to a blender or food processor and purée until smooth.
3. Taste and adjust with coconut sugar if needed. Place in an airtight container and store in the refrigerator.

Nutrition Info per Serving:

Calories: 230, Total Fat: 1 g, Total Carbs: 60 g, Sugar: 45 g, Fiber: 12 g, Protein: 1 g, Sodium: 0 mg

Warm Curried Fruit

Prep Time: 10 minutes, Cook Time: 8-10 hours, Serves: 8 to 10

INGREDIENTS:

- 1 large can pineapple chunks, undrained
- 1 can black cherries, undrained
- 1 can pears, undrained
- 1 can apricots, undrained
- 1 can peaches, undrained
- ½ cup brown sugar
- 3-4 tbsps. quick-cooking tapioca
- 1 tsp. curry powder

DIRECTIONS:

1. Combine fruit in a big mixing bowl. Let stand for at least 2 hours. Remove the mixture to a crock pot.
2. Add remaining ingredients into the cooker. Mix well.
3. Cover lid and cook on Low for 8-10 hours.
4. Serve warm.

Nutrition Info per Serving:

Calories: 85, Protein: 0.39 g, Fat: 0.16 g, Carbohydrates: 21.93 g

Orange-Cranberry Compote with Fennel

Prep Time: 10 minutes, Cook Time: 8 hours, Serves: 6

INGREDIENTS:

- 12 ounces (340 g) fresh or frozen cranberries
- Zest of 1 orange
- Juice of 2 oranges
- 1 fennel bulb, chopped
- ¼ cup (60 ml) honey
- 1 tsp. ground ginger
- ½ tsp. cinnamon
- ¼ cup chopped pecans
- Pinch sea salt

DIRECTIONS:

1. Combine the cranberries, fennel, orange juice, orange zest, ginger, honey, cinnamon, and salt in your crock pot.
2. Cover and cook on low for 8 hours.
3. Heat the pecans on medium for 3 to 5 minutes in a small sauté pan, stirring constantly, until fragrant.
4. Stir the pecans into the cranberry compote.

Nutrition Info per Serving:

Calories: 122, Total Fat: 4g, Saturated Fat: 0g, Carbohydrates: 21g, Protein: 1g, Cholesterol: 0mg, Fiber: 4g

Walnut Stuffed Apples

Prep Time: 25 minutes, Cook Time: 1½-3 hours, Serves: 4

INGREDIENTS:

- 4 large firm baking apples
- ⅓ cup chopped walnuts
- ⅓ cup chopped dried apricots
- ½ cup water
- 4 pecan halves
- 1 tbsp. lemon juice
- 3 tbsps. packed brown sugar
- 2 tbsps. butter, melted
- ½ tsp. cinnamon

DIRECTIONS:

1. Scoop out the center of the apple to form a cavity 1½ inches wide and stop at ½ inch from the bottom of each. Cut away the top of each apple about 1 inch. Brush the edges with lemon juice.
2. Take a bowl, add nuts, apricots, brown sugar, cinnamon and butter into it and mix well. Spoon the mixture evenly into the apples.
3. Put ½ cup of water into the bottom of the crock pot. Place 2 apples on the bottom and 2 apples on the top. Cover the cooker and heat on Low for 1½-3 hours.
4. Top each apple with a pecan half before serving.

Nutrition Info per Serving:

Calories: 959, Protein: 11.16 g, Fat: 81.79 g, Carbohydrates: 62.1 g

Cinnamon Gingerbread

INGREDIENTS:

- 1 tbsp. coconut oil
- 4 eggs
- ¾ cup granulated erythritol
- 2 cups almond flour
- ½ cup butter, melted
- ¾ cup heavy (whipping) cream
- 2 tbsps. coconut flour
- 2 tsps. baking powder
- 2 tbsps. ground ginger
- ½ tsp. ground nutmeg
- 2 tsps. ground cinnamon
- ¼ tsp. ground cloves
- Pinch salt
- 1 tsp. pure vanilla extract

DIRECTIONS:

1. Use coconut oil to grease the insert of the crock pot lightly.
2. Add the erythritol, almond flour, coconut flour, baking powder, ginger, nutmeg, cinnamon, cloves and salt to a large bowl, stir them together.
3. Add the butter, heavy cream, eggs and vanilla to a medium bowl, whisk
well.
4. Combine the wet ingredients with the dry ingredients.
5. Spoon the batter into the insert.
6. Cover the cooker and set on low, cook for 3 hours, or until a toothpick inserted in the center comes out clean.
7. After cooking, turn off the heat and serve warm.

Nutrition Info per Serving:

Calories: 259, Total Fat: 23 g, Total Carbs: 6 g, Net Carbs: 3 g, Protein: 7 g, Fiber: 3 g

CHAPTER 14

SAUCE AND DRESSING

Creamy Alfredo Sauce

Prep Time: 5 minutes, Cook Time: 6 hours on low, Serves: 6

INGREDIENTS:

- 1 tbsp. extra-virgin olive oil
- 2 cups heavy (whipping) cream
- 1 cup grated Parmesan cheese
- 4 cups chicken broth
- ½ cup butter
- 3 tsps. minced garlic
- 2 tbsps. chopped fresh parsley
- Freshly ground black pepper, for seasoning

DIRECTIONS:

1. Use the olive oil to grease the insert of the crock pot lightly.
2. Add the heavy cream, broth and garlic, and stir until combined.
3. Cover the cooker and set on low, cook for 6 hours.
4. Add the Parmesan cheese, butter, and parsley, stir well.
5. Use pepper to season and serve.

Nutrition Info per Serving:

Calories: 280, Total Fat: 27 g, Total Carbs: 4 g, Net Carbs: 4 g, Protein: 7 g, Fiber: 0 g, Cholesterol: 84 mg

Cheesy Chicken Nacho Dip

Prep Time: 5 minutes, Cook Time: 4 hours (low), Serves: 16

INGREDIENTS:

- 1½ cups shredded cooked chicken
- 1 (12-ounce, 340 g) can evaporated milk
- 3 medium jalapeños, seeded and chopped
- 1 large tomato, diced
- 1 cup cooked black beans, drained and rinsed
- 4 ounces (113 g) grated pepper Jack cheese
- 4 ounces (113 g) grated Cheddar cheese
- ⅓ cup sour cream
- ¼ cup diced scallions
- ½ cup fresh or frozen corn
- 1 tbsp. cornstarch
- 1 tbsp. Taco Seasoning Mix

DIRECTIONS:

1. Add all of the ingredients into the crock pot, use a wooden spoon to stir until combined.
2. Cover the cooker and cook on low for 4 hours.
3. Quickly stir the dip. If the dip is not thick enough, remove the lid and cook for another 30 minutes.
4. Stir well and serve hot.

Ketchup Meatball Sauce

Prep Time: 10 minutes, Cook Time: 3-8 hours, Serves: 10

INGREDIENTS:

- 3 lbs. (1.4 kg) fully cooked meatballs
- 32-oz. (907 g) bottle of ketchup
- 16 oz. (454 g) ginger ale
- 3 tbsps. vinegar
- 3 tbsps. brown sugar
- 3 tbsps. Worcestershire sauce, optional

DIRECTIONS:

1. Mix sauce ingredients in crock pot.
2. Cover, turn to High, and simmer. Gently spoon in meatballs.
3. Cover and simmer 3-4 hours on Low if the meatballs are thawed, 6-8 hours if they're frozen when you put them in.

Nutrition Info per Serving:

Calories: 299, Carbohydrates: 18.59 g, Protein: 28.85 g, Fat: 12.25 g

Cornbread Dressing

Prep Time: 10 minutes, Cook Time: 2-4 hours, Serves: 16

INGREDIENTS:

- 4 eggs
- 2 boxes Jiffy Cornbread mix
- 8 slices day-old bread
- 2 (10¾-oz. 304 g) cans cream of chicken soup
- 2 (14½-oz. 411 g) cans chicken broth
- 1 onion, chopped
- ½ cup chopped celery
- ½-¾ cup butter
- 1½ tbsps. sage or poultry seasoning
- ½ tsp. pepper
- 1 tsp. salt

DIRECTIONS:

1. Prepare cornbread in an 8-inch-square baking pan
2. Crush cornbread and bread together.
3. Mix all ingredients in a large bowl, apart from butter. Add 6-quart greased to crock pot, dot top with butter.
4. Cover lid and heat on High for 2-4 hours.
5. Serve warm.

Nutrition Info per Serving:

Calories: 335, Protein: 15.56 g, Fat: 23.27 g, Carbohydrates: 20.83 g

Homemade Ghee

Prep Time: 2 minutes, Cook Time: 6 hours on low, Serves: 2

INGREDIENTS:

- 1 pound (454 g) unsalted butter, diced

DIRECTIONS:

1. In the insert of the crock pot, add the butter.
2. Cook on low for 6 hours, with the lid set slightly open.
3. Set a fine-mesh cheesecloth over a bowl, pour in the melted butter.
4. Allow the ghee to cool for 30 minutes and transfer into a jar.
5. Keep the ghee in the refrigerator for up to 2 weeks.

Nutrition Info per Serving:

Calories: 100, Total Fat: 11 g, Total Carbs: 0 g, Net Carbs: 0 g, Protein: 0 g, Fiber: 0 g, Cholesterol: 30 mg

Pumpkin Pie Spice Applesauce

Prep Time: 15 minutes, Cook Time: 6 to 8 hours on low, Serves: 4 to 6

INGREDIENTS:

- 3 pounds (1.4 kg) apples of choice, peeled, cored, and roughly chopped
- ½ cup water
- 1 tsp. freshly squeezed lemon juice
- ½ tsp. pumpkin pie spice

DIRECTIONS:

1. Add the lemon juice, apples, pumpkin pie spice and water into the crock pot, combine them together.
2. Cover the cooker and cook for 6 to 8 hours on low. Blend with an immersion blender after the applesauce cools if you prefer a smoother applesauce. Place in an airtight container and store in the refrigerator.

Nutrition Info per Serving:

Calories: 181, Total Fat: 1g, Saturated Fat: 0g, Protein: 1g, Total Carbs: 48g, Fiber: 8g, Sugars: 12g

Sweet Rhubarb Sauce

Prep Time: 10 minutes, Cook Time: 4-5 hours, Serves: 6

INGREDIENTS:

- 1½ lbs. rhubarb
- ½ cup water
- ½ cup sugar
- pinch of baking soda
- ⅛ tsp. salt

DIRECTIONS:

1. Cut rhubarb into ½-inch thick slices.
2. Put all ingredients into a crock pot, apart from baking soda.
3. Cover lid and cook on Low for 4-5 hours.
4. Add baking soda, stir well. Serve chilled.

Nutrition Info per Serving:

Calories: 90, Protein: 1 g, Fat: 0 g, Carbohydrates: 22 g, Fiber: 2 g, Sodium: 55 mg

Spiced Cheese and Corn Dip

Prep Time: 5 minutes, Cook Time: 4 hours (low), Serves: 16

INGREDIENTS:

- ½ cup sour cream
- 1 cup grated pepper Jack cheese
- 4½ cups fresh or frozen corn
- 8 ounces (227 g) cream cheese, cut into 1-inch cubes
- 2 jalapeños, seeded and diced
- ½ small poblano chile, seeded and diced (about ¼ cup)
- 1 tbsp. Taco Seasoning Mix
- ½ tsp. ground cumin
- 1 cup chopped fresh cilantro
- Juice of 1 lime

DIRECTIONS:

1. Combine all of the ingredients except the cilantro and lime juice in the crock pot.
2. Cover the cooker and set on low, cook for 4 hours.
3. Remove the lid, use a wooden spoon to stir, and add the cilantro. Squeeze over the top with the lime juice and serve hot.

Homemade Fire Roasted Red Enchilada Sauce

Prep Time: 5 minutes, Cook Time: 8 hours (low), 4 hours (high), Serves: 5 cups

INGREDIENTS:

- 1 (7-ounce, 198 g) can chipotles in adobo, seeded
- 5 garlic cloves, minced
- 1 (32-ounce, 896 g) can fire-roasted tomatoes
- 4 medium onions, chopped
- 1 medium bell pepper (any color), seeded and diced (about 1 cup)
- 2 cups chicken stock
- 1½ tsps. chili powder
- 1 tbsp. ground cumin
- 1 tsp. sugar

DIRECTIONS:

1. Measure out 3 tablespoons of adobo sauce and set it aside. In a nonreactive bowl, place the remaining adobo sauce and store it in the refrigerator for another use.
2. Combine all the remaining ingredients in the crock pot, and cook on low for 8 hours or on high for 4 hours.
3. In a blender, pour the sauce and blend until smooth, 2 cups at a time. Plan to use about 1 to 1½ cups of sauce for every 8 to 10 enchiladas you make.
4. In 1-cup portions to freeze unused sauce, make sure to leave some room in your resealable freezer bags for some expansion. Then place the portion in the refrigerator to thaw the night before you plan to use it on the next batch of enchiladas.

Garlic Marinara Sauce

Prep Time: 15 minutes, Cook Time: 5 hours, Serves: 4

INGREDIENTS:

- 1 (28-ounce, 784 g) can diced tomatoes, with juice
- 1 (28-ounce, 784 g) can crushed tomatoes
- 1 (6-ounce, 170 g) can tomato paste
- 1 medium onion, diced
- 2 bay leaves
- 2½ tsps. minced garlic (5 cloves)
- 1 tbsp. brown sugar
- 1 tbsp. dried basil
- 1 tbsp. balsamic vinegar
- 1½ tsps. dried oregano
- ½ tsp. red pepper flakes
- 1 tsp. salt
- ½ tsp. freshly ground black pepper

DIRECTIONS:

1. In the crock pot, add the crushed tomatoes, diced tomatoes, tomato paste, onion, garlic, bay leaves, basil, brown sugar, balsamic vinegar, oregano, red pepper flakes, salt, and pepper, stir them thoroughly.
2. Cover the cooker and cook on low for 5 hours.

Nutrition Info per Serving:

Calories: 178, Total fat: <1 g, Protein: 9 g, Sodium: 1,016 mg, Fiber: 12 g

Easy Marinara Sauce

Prep Time: 10 minutes, Cook Time: 7 to 8 hours on low, Serves: 12

INGREDIENTS:

- 3 tbsps. extra-virgin olive oil, divided
- 2 (28-ounce, 784 g) cans crushed tomatoes
- ½ sweet onion, finely chopped
- 1 tbsp. chopped fresh oregano
- 1 tbsp. chopped fresh basil
- ½ tsp. salt
- 2 tsps. minced garlic

DIRECTIONS:

1. Use 1 tablespoon of the olive oil to grease the insert of the crock pot lightly.
2. In the insert, add the remaining 2 tablespoons of the olive oil, onion, tomatoes, salt and garlic, stirring to combine.
3. Cover the cooker and set on low, cook for 7 to 8 hours.
4. Remove the cover and add the oregano and basil, stir well.
5. Place the cooled sauce in a sealed container, and store in the refrigerator for up to 1 week.

Nutrition Info per Serving:

Calories: 66, Total Fat: 5 g, Total Carbs: 7 g, Net Carbs: 5 g, Protein: 1 g, Fiber: 2 g

Double-Chile Cheese Dip

Prep Time: 20 minutes, Cook Time: 2 hours (low), Serves: 16

INGREDIENTS:

- Cooking spray
- 1 large tomato, seeded and chopped
- 1 medium onion, chopped
- 1 garlic clove, minced
- 3 medium jalapeños, seeded and chopped
- 1 medium poblano chile, seeded and chopped
- 1 cup whole milk
- 8 ounces (227 g) grated American cheese, white or yellow
- 8 ounces (227 g) queso quesadilla or cream cheese, cut into 1-inch cubes

DIRECTIONS:

1. Use cooking spray to spray the inside of the crock pot, then place the tomato, onion, garlic, jalapeños, poblano chile, milk, and cheeses into the crock pot. Use a wooden spoon to quickly stir everything.
2. Cover the cooker and set on low, cook for 2 hours. When the cooking finishes, stir the dip and serve hot.

Garlicky Ketchup

Prep Time: 10 minutes, Cook Time: 6 to 7 hours on low, Serves: 2

INGREDIENTS:

- 1 tbsp. extra-virgin olive oil
- 1 (28-ounce, 784 g) can crushed tomatoes
- 1 sweet onion, finely chopped
- ½ cup apple cider vinegar
- ¼ cup granulated erythritol
- 2 bay leaves
- 2 tsps. minced garlic
- ¼ tsp. allspice
- ⅛ tsp. celery salt
- ⅛ tsp. ground colves

DIRECTIONS:

1. Use the olive oil to grease the insert of the crock pot lightly.
2. In the insert of the crock pot, add the garlic, tomatoes, onion, apple cider vinegar, erythritol, allspice, celery salt, cloves, and bay leaves.
3. Uncovered and cook on low for 6 to 7 hours, until thick.
4. Take the bay leaves out.
5. Purée the mixture with an immersion blender or a regular blender.
6. Allow the ketchup to cool and place into jars, seal, and refrigerate.
7. Keep the ketchup in the refrigerator for up to 1 week or in the freezer for up to 2 months.

Nutrition Info per Serving:

Calories: 17, Total Fat: 1 g, Total Carbs: 2 g, Net Carbs: 1 g, Protein: 0 g, Fiber: 1 g

Buffalo Cauliflower Dip

Prep Time: 15 minutes, plus 8 hours to soak, Cook Time: 5-6 hours, Serves: 4 to 6

INGREDIENTS:

- 1¼ cups raw cashews, soaked in water overnight, drained
- 1 pound (454 g) cauliflower, chopped
- ¾ cup hot sauce
- ½ cup water
- 1 tsp. garlic powder
- ½ tsp. paprika
- 1 tbsp. freshly squeezed lemon juice
- Sea salt
- Freshly ground black pepper
- Chopped veggies, for serving (optional)

DIRECTIONS:

1. Add the cashews, cauliflower, lemon juice, hot sauce, garlic powder, paprika and water into your crock pot, combine them together. Season with salt and pepper.
2. Cover the cooker and cook for 5 to 6 hours on low.
3. In a blender or food processor, add the mixture and pulse until your desired consistency. Serve with chopped veggies (if using).

Nutrition Info per Serving:

Calories: 302, Total Fat: 18 g, Total Carbs: 26 g, Sugar: 14 g, Fiber: 6 g, Protein: 9 g, Sodium: 574 mg

Apple Cider Sauce

Prep Time: 15 minutes, Cook Time: 3 to 4 hours on low, Serves: 2 cups

INGREDIENTS:

- 1¼ cups all-natural ketchup (choose the one with the lowest amount of sugar)
- ¼ cup molasses
- ¼ cup coconut sugar
- 3 tbsps. apple cider vinegar
- 1½ tsps. garlic powder
- 1 tsp. Dijon mustard
- 1 tbsp. Worcestershire sauce
- ½ tsp. sea salt
- ½ tsp. onion powder
- Pinch cayenne pepper

DIRECTIONS:

1. Add all of the ingredients into your crock pot, combine them together.
2. Cover the cooker and cook for 3 to 4 hours on low.
3. After cooking, allow it to cool and refrigerate in an airtight container.

Nutrition Info per Serving:

Calories: 416, Total Fat: 0g, Saturated Fat: 0g, Protein: 0g, Total Carbs: 105g, Fiber: 0g, Sugars: 9g

Classic Bolognese Sauce

Prep Time: 15 minutes, Cook Time: 7 to 8 hours on low, Serves: 10

INGREDIENTS:

- 3 tbsps. extra-virgin olive oil, divided
- 1 pound (454 g) ground pork
- ½ pound (227 g) bacon, chopped
- ½ pound (227 g) ground beef
- 2 (28-ounce, 784 g) cans diced tomatoes
- 2 celery stalks, chopped
- 1 carrot, chopped
- 1 sweet onion, chopped
- ½ cup coconut milk
- ¼ cup apple cider vinegar
- 1 tbsp. minced garlic

DIRECTIONS:

1. Use 1 tablespoon of the olive oil to grease the insert of the crock pot lightly.
2. Heat the remaining 2 tablespoons of the olive oil in a large skillet over medium-high heat. Add the beef, pork, and bacon, and sauté for 7 minutes, until cooked through.
3. Add the garlic and onion, stir well and sauté for another 2 minutes.
4. In the insert, add the meat mixture and add the remaining ingredients.
5. Cover the cooker and set on low, cook for 7 to 8 hours.
6. Serve, or allow it to cool completely, and place in a sealed container, and store in the refrigerator for up to 4 days or in the freezer for 1 month.

Nutrition Info per Serving:

Calories: 333, Total Fat: 23 g, Total Carbs: 9 g, Net Carbs: 6 g, Protein: 25 g, Fiber: 3 g

Classic Queso Cheese Sauce

Prep Time: 10 minutes, Cook Time: 3 to 4 hours on low, Serves: 4

INGREDIENTS:

- 1 tbsp. extra-virgin olive oil
- 2 cups salsa verde
- 12 ounces (340 g) cream cheese
- 1 cup Monterey Jack cheese, shredded
- 1 cup sour cream

DIRECTIONS:

1. Use the olive oil to grease the insert of the crock pot lightly.
2. Add the sour cream, cream cheese, Monterey Jack cheese and salsa verde to a large bowl, stir them together until blended.
3. Place the mixture into the insert.
4. Cover the cooker and cook on low for 3 to 4 hours.
5. After cooking, turn off the heat and serve warm.

Nutrition Info per Serving:

Calories: 278, Total Fat: 25 g, Total Carbs: 4 g, Net Carbs: 4 g, Protein: 9 g, Fiber: 0 g

Barbecue Sauce

Prep Time: 10 minutes, Cook Time: 3 hours on low, Serves: 2

INGREDIENTS:

- 3 tbsps. extra-virgin olive oil, divided
- 2 (6-ounce, 170 g) cans tomato paste
- ½ cup water
- ½ cup apple cider vinegar
- ¼ cup granulated erythritol
- 1 tbsp. smoked paprika
- 1 tsp. garlic powder
- 1 tsp. onion powder
- ½ tsp. chili powder
- ¼ tsp. salt

DIRECTIONS:

1. Use 1 tablespoon olive oil to grease the insert of the crock pot.
2. Add the remaining olive oil and the rest ingredients to a large bowl, whisk them together until blended.
3. In the insert of the crock pot, add the mixture.
4. Cover the cooker and cook on low for 3 hours.
5. After cooking, allow the sauce to cool, then place in a container, and store in the refrigerator for up to 2 weeks.

Nutrition Info per Serving:

Calories: 21, Total Fat: 1 g, Total Carbs: 2 g, Net Carbs: 1 g, Protein: 0 g, Fiber: 1 g, Cholesterol: 0 mg

Simple Tomato Sauce

Prep Time: 15 minutes, Cook Time: 7-8 hours, Serves: 6 cups

INGREDIENTS:

- 2 (28-ounce, 784 g) cans diced tomatoes
- 1 carrot, minced
- 1 yellow onion, diced
- 1 celery stalk, minced
- 2 bay leaves
- 3 tbsps. tomato paste
- 1 tbsp. dried basil leaves
- 2 tsps. dried oregano
- 1½ tsps. garlic powder
- 1 tsp. sea salt
- Pinch red pepper flakes
- Freshly ground black pepper

DIRECTIONS:

1. Add all of the ingredients except the black pepper into the crock pot, combine them together, and season with black pepper.
2. Cover the cooker and cook on low for 7 to 8 hours.
3. Remove and discard the bay leaves. Blend the sauce to your desired consistency, or leave it naturally chunky with an immersion blender.

Nutrition Info per Serving:

Calories: 71, Total Fat: 0 g, Total Carbs: 17 g, Sugar: 11 g, Fiber: 3 g, Protein: 3 g

Red Salsa with Lime Juice

Prep Time: 5 minutes, Cook Time: 6 hours (low), 3 hours (high), Serves: 3 cups

INGREDIENTS:

- 2 pounds (907 g) Roma tomatoes
- 2 garlic cloves
- 1 onion, cut into quarters
- 3 jalapeños, stems removed
- 1 bunch fresh cilantro, stems removed
- Juice of 1 lime
- Sea salt

DIRECTIONS:

1. Add the garlic, onion, tomatoes and jalapeños into the crock pot, combine them together, and cook on low for 6 hours or on high for 3 hours.
2. In a food processor or blender, add 2 cups of the salsa, one-third of the cilantro, and pulse the mixture a few times to combine. Transfer the salsa to a large bowl and repeat until all the tomato mixture and all the cilantro has been used.
3. Squeeze over the salsa with the lime juice, and use a wooden spoon to stir gently to blend. Season with salt to taste.
4. Place the salsa in a tightly sealed, nonreactive container, and store in the refrigerator for up to 1 week, or freeze it for up to 3 months.

Mustard Turmeric Dressing

Prep Time: 15 minutes, Cook Time: 0, Serves: 4 to 6

INGREDIENTS:

- ¼ cup extra-virgin olive oil
- 1½ tbsps. raw honey
- 1 tbsp. apple cider vinegar
- 1 tsp. ground turmeric
- 1 tsp. Dijon mustard
- ½ tsp. ground ginger
- 2 tbsps. water
- 2 tbsps. freshly squeezed lemon juice
- ¼ tsp. sea salt
- Pinch freshly ground black pepper

DIRECTIONS:

1. Add all of the ingredients into a small bowl, whisk well to combine.
2. Place in an airtight container and keep in the refrigerator.

Nutrition Info per Serving:

Calories: 151, Total Fat: 14g, Saturated Fat: 2g, Protein: 0g, Total Carbs: 8g, Fiber: 0g, Sugars: 7g

Cranberry Jalapeño jelly

Prep Time: 5 minutes, Cook Time: 2-3 hours, Serves: 8

INGREDIENTS:

- 16-oz. (454 g) can whole berry cranberry sauce
- 10½-oz. (297g) jar jalapeño jelly
- 2 tbsps. chopped fresh cilantro

DIRECTIONS:

1. Combine jar jalapeño jelly, berry cranberry sauce and cilantro in a crock pot.
2. Cover lid and cook on Low for 2-3 hours. Cool.
3. Serve these spicy cranberries as a side dish.

Nutrition Info per Serving:

Calories: 185, Protein: 0.17 g, Fat: 0.09 g, Carbohydrates: 48.1 g

Maple Applesauce

Prep Time: 15 minutes, Cook Time: 8 hours, Serves: 6

INGREDIENTS:

- 3 tart green apples, peeled, cored, and sliced
- 3 sweet-tart red apples, peeled, cored, and sliced
- ½ cup (120 ml) pure maple syrup
- ¼ cup (60 ml) water
- Juice of ½ lemon
- 1 tbsp. grated fresh ginger
- 1 tsp. ground cinnamon
- Pinch sea salt

DIRECTIONS:

1. Combine all the ingredients in your crock pot.
2. Cover and cook on low for 8 hours.
3. Strain through a sieve for a smoother applesauce, or process in the food processor or blender.

Nutrition Info per Serving:

Calories: 167, Total Fat: 0g, Saturated Fat: 0g, Carbohydrates: 44g, Protein: 1g, Cholesterol: 0mg, Fiber: 5g

Avocado Dill Dressing

Prep Time: 15 minutes, Cook Time: 0, Serves: 1 cup

INGREDIENTS:

- 1 large, ripe avocado, peeled and pitted
- 2 tsps. freshly squeezed lemon juice
- 2 tsps. fresh dill
- ½ tsp. sea salt
- Dash red pepper flakes
- Chopped veggies, for serving (if desired)

DIRECTIONS:

1. Add all of the ingredients except the veggies into a blender, pulse until smooth.
2. Add water to thin as needed if the mixture is too thick.
3. Serve with chopped veggies (if using).

Nutrition Info per Serving:

Calories: 301, Total Fat: 27g, Saturated Fat: 3g, Protein: 4g, Total Carbs: 19g, Fiber: 6g, Sugars: 2g

Hot Chocolate Dip

Prep Time: 5 minutes, Cook Time: 4 hours, Serves: 6

INGREDIENTS:

- 6 ounces (170 g) bittersweet chocolate, chopped
- 3 cups (720 ml) skim milk
- ¼ cup (60 ml) pure maple syrup
- ½ tsp. pure vanilla extract
- ¼ tsp. ground cinnamon
- Pinch sea salt
- Pinch cayenne pepper

DIRECTIONS:

1. Combine all the ingredients in your crock pot.
2. Cover and cook on low for 4 hours, whisking occasionally as the chocolate melts. Serve immediately or keep warm to serve throughout the day.

Nutrition Info per Serving:

Calories: 232, Total Fat: 8g, Saturated Fat: 6g, Carbohydrates: 32g, Protein: 6g, Fiber: 1g

Homemade Enchilada Sauce

Prep Time: 10 minutes, Cook Time: 7 to 8 hours on low, Serves: 4

INGREDIENTS:

- ¼ cup extra-virgin olive oil, divided
- 2 cups puréed tomatoes
- 1 sweet onion, chopped
- 2 jalapeño peppers, chopped
- 1 cup water
- 2 tbsps. chili powder
- 2 tsps. minced garlic
- 1 tsp. ground coriander

DIRECTIONS:

1. Use 1 tablespoon of the olive oil to grease the insert of the crock pot lightly.
2. In the insert of the crock pot, add the remaining 3 tablespoons of the olive oil, onion, tomatoes, water, jalapeño peppers, chili powder, garlic, and coriander.
3. Cover the cooker and cook on low for 7 to 8 hours.
4. Serve over meat or poultry. After cooling, place the sauce in a sealed container and store in the refrigerator for up to 1 week.

Nutrition Info per Serving:

Calories: 92, Total Fat: 8 g, Total Carbs: 4 g, Net Carbs: 2 g, Protein: 2 g, Fiber: 2 g

Easy Chimichurri Sauce

Prep Time: 15 minutes, Cook Time: 0, Serves: 1 cup

INGREDIENTS:

- ½ cup extra-virgin olive oil
- 1 cup fresh flat-leaf Italian parsley
- ¼ cup white wine vinegar
- ½ cup fresh cilantro
- 3 garlic cloves, roughly chopped
- ½ tsp. dried oregano
- ½ tsp. sea salt
- ¼ tsp. ground cumin
- Dash red pepper flakes
- Freshly ground black pepper

DIRECTIONS:

1. Add all of the ingredients except the black pepper into a blender, food processor, or large bowl, blend until smooth and season with black pepper.
2. Serve at room temperature over red meat dishes or others.
3. Place any leftovers in an airtight container and store in the refrigerator for up to 1 week.

Nutrition Info per Serving:

Calories: 220, Total Fat: 12g, Saturated Fat: 2g, Protein: 4g, Total Carbs: 14g, Fiber: 5g, Sugars: 1g

APPENDIX 1: BASIC KITCHEN CONVERSIONS & EQUIVALENTS

DRY MEASUREMENTS CONVERSION CHART

3 tsps. = 1 tbsp. = 1/16 cup

6 tsps. = 2 tbsps. = 1/8 cup

12 tsps. = 4 tbsps. = ¼ cup

24 tsps. = 8 tbsps. = ½ cup

36 tsps. = 12 tbsps. = ¾ cup

48 tsps. = 16 tbsps. = 1 cup

METRIC TO US COOKING CONVERSIONS

OVEN TEMPERATURES

120 °C = 250 °F

160 °C = 320 °F

180 °C = 350 °F

205 °C = 400 °F

220 °C = 425 °F

LIQUID MEASUREMENTS

CONVERSION CHART

8 fluid ounces = 1 cup = ½ pint = ¼ quart

16 fluid ounces = 2 cups = 1 pint = ½ quart

32 fluid ounces = 4 cups = 2 pints = 1 quart = ¼ gallon

128 fluid ounces = 16 cups = 8 pints = 4 quarts = 1 gallon

BAKING IN GRAMS

1 cup flour = 140 grams

1 cup sugar = 150 grams

1 cup powdered sugar = 160 grams

1 cup heavy cream = 235 grams

VOLUME

1 milliliter = 1/5 teaspoon

5 ml = 1 teaspoon

15 ml = 1 tablespoon

240 ml = 1 cup or 8 fluid ounces

1 liter = 34 fluid ounces

WEIGHT

1 gram = .035 ounces

100 grams = 3.5 ounces

500 grams = 1.1 pounds

1 kilogram = 35 ounces

US TO METRIC COOKING CONVERSIONS

1/5 tsp = 1 ml

1 tsp = 5 ml

1 tbsp = 15 ml

1 fluid ounces = 30 ml

1 cup = 237 ml

1 pint (2 cups) = 473 ml

1 quart (4 cups) = .95 liter

1 gallon (16 cups) = 3.8 liters

1 oz = 28 grams

1 pound = 454 grams

BUTTER

1 cup butter = 2 sticks = 8 ounces = 230 grams = 16 tablespoons

WHAT DOES 1 CUP EQUAL

1 cup = 8 fluid ounces

1 cup = 16 tablespoons

1 cup = 48 teaspoons

1 cup = ½ pint

1 cup = ¼ quart

1 cup = 1/16 gallon

1 cup = 240 ml

BAKING PAN CONVERSIONS

9-inch round cake pan = 12 cups

10-inch tube pan =16 cups

10-inch bundt pan = 12 cups

9-inch springform pan = 10 cups

9 x 5 inch loaf pan = 8 cups

9-inch square pan = 8 cups

BAKING PAN CONVERSIONS

1 cup all-purpose flour = 4.5 oz

1 cup rolled oats = 3 oz

1 large egg = 1.7 oz

1 cup butter = 8 oz

1 cup milk = 8 oz

1 cup heavy cream = 8.4 oz

1 cup granulated sugar = 7.1 oz

1 cup packed brown sugar = 7.75 oz

1 cup vegetable oil = 7.7 oz

1 cup unsifted powdered sugar = 4.4 oz

APPENDIX 2: RECIPES INDEX

Made in the USA
Las Vegas, NV
28 February 2024

86327552R00079